WILLIAM OF GERMANY:

A Succinct Biography

OF

*WILLIAM I., GERMAN EMPEROR AND
KING OF PRUSSIA*

BY

ARCHIBALD FORBES

CASSELL & COMPANY, Limited
104 & 106 *FOURTH AVENUE, NEW YORK*

Press W. L. Mershon & Co.,
Rahway, N. J.

12 Fulham Park Road
London 6th Oct '85

Messrs Cassell & Co Limited,
La Belle, Sauvage,
London.

Dear Sirs,

In reply to your letter of the
21st instant, I beg to inform you
that you are at liberty to publish
"my" Life of the German Emperor"
in the United States as the only
edition authorised by me.

I am, Dear Sirs.

Yours faithfully,
Arthur Forbes

To

L. R. M.

PREFACE.

At half-past eight o'clock, on the morning of Friday, the 9th of March, William, King of Prussia, and German Emperor, the subject of this biographical sketch, died. Had he lived thirteen days longer he would have completed his ninety-first year. His death came unexpectedly at last; for he had lived so long and had recovered so often, with surprising rapidity, from previous similar attacks, that the world hesitated to believe, when the news was flashed, that he was no more.

The present narrative of the Kaiser's life scarcely needs a word of introduction. It was written, as far as the thirteenth chapter, by Mr. Archibald Forbes, the great war correspondent, than whom no one could have been better qualified to give the story of the splendid events and heroism of the life just ended, through which King William of Prussia was enabled to win unity for Germany, and for himself and his heirs the proud dignity of German Emperor.

Mr. Forbes had the opportunity, during the Franco-German war, of accompanying King William on the campaign through Alsace and Lorraine, up to the walls of Paris, and his account of that portion of the dead Emperor's life has, consequently, great value, as being not only the work of an historian, but of a special correspondent, fitted by long training and natural ability to give pictures of the great scenes he witnessed with artistic and thrilling accuracy.

Unfortunately, Mr. Forbes was prevented, by the state of his health, from completing the story of the imperial life, which, however, he carried through the greatest epoch of German history, up to the time when the victorious German troops returned home and were welcomed at the

Prussian and other capitals. In view of Mr. Forbes's illness, the completion of the work, containing the story of the emperor's life up to the end, was entrusted to Mr. John P. Jackson, who has given in concise form the narrative of the peace-years that followed the Franco-German war, during which the aged ruler's efforts were directed by a sincere wish to be able to leave to his successor an Empire untroubled by internal difficulties.

By the death of Kaiser William, the successorship to the royal and imperial thrones of Prussia and Germany falls to his eldest son, so long known as the Crown-Prince or "Unser Fritz," who ascends the throne as Frederic III. His consort, the new Empress, Princess Royal of England, the favorite daughter of the late Prince Consort, is a woman of noble character, who has exercised a beneficial influence upon her husband, and who, it is generally admitted, has done much towards implanting in the new Emperor's mind the love of constitutionalism, which, if he lives, will gradually take the place of the absolutism and militarism that has almost necessarily characterized the reign of the dead Emperor.

The dead Emperor's last thoughts were with his eldest son. During the night he bade farewell to all around his bedside. To Prince Bismarck he said : "Thou hast done well !" To Prince William he said : "You must treat the Czar of Russia with the utmost consideration." He listened earnestly to the prayers of the Court Chaplain, Dr. Koegel, and said : "It is well to have service, for it is Lent." When Dr. Koegel read the twenty-third Psalm, "The Lord is my Shepherd," he simply murmured : "That is wonderful." He then fell into a sound sleep, from which he never roused, except for a few minutes before his death, when he exclaimed, thinking of the sufferer at San Remo : "Fritz, dear Fritz !"

THE PUBLISHERS.

CONTENTS.

CONTENTS.

THE ELECTORS OF BRANDENBURG AND THE KINGS OF PRUSSIA.

(1) FREDERIC I. (1417—1440).

JOHN, "Alchemist." (2) FREDERIC II. (1440—1471). (3) ALBERT, "Achilles" (1471—1481).

(4) JOHN, "Cicero" (1486—1499).

(5) JOACHIM, "Nestor" (1499—1535).

(6) JOACHIM II., "Hector" (1535—1571).

(7) JOHN GEORGE (1571—1598).

(8) JOACHIM FREDERIC (1598—1608).

(9) JOHN SIGISMUND (1608—1619).

(10) GEORGE WILLIAM (1619—1648).
(Sister married Gustavus
Adolphus, of Sweden.)

(11) FREDERIC WILLIAM (1648—1688).
The "Great Elector."

(12) FREDERIC III. (1688),
Crowned King of Prussia, as
I. FREDERIC I. (1701—1713).

II. FREDERIC WILLIAM I. (1713—1740).

| III. FREDERIC II. (1740—1786). | AUGUST WILHELM. |
| The "Great." | |

IV. FREDERIC WILLIAM II. (1786 1797),
The "Fat."

V. FREDERIC WILLIAM III. (1797—1840).
(Married Louisa of Mecklenburgh-Strelitz.)

VI. FREDERIC WILLIAM IV. (1840—1861).

VII. FREDERIC WILLIAM LEWIS. (1861—1888.)
WILLIAM I., German Emperor.

VII. FREDERIC III., German Emperor.

THE FAMILY OF WILLIAM I.

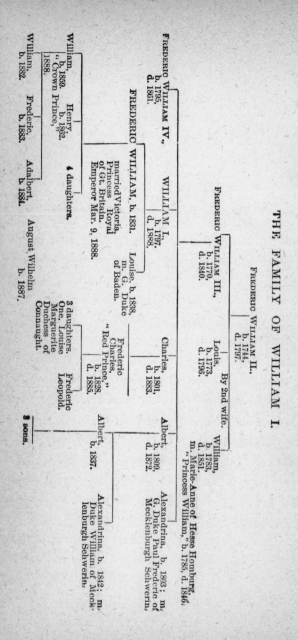

FREDERIC WILLIAM II.,
b. 1744,
d. 1797.

By 2nd wife.

William,
b. 1783,
d. 1851;
m. "Marie-Anne of Hesse Homburg,
Princess William," b. 1785, d. 1846.

FREDERIC WILLIAM III.,
b. 1770,
d. 1840.

Louis,
b. 1773,
d. 1796.

FREDERIC WILLIAM IV.,
b. 1795,
d. 1861.

WILLIAM I.,
b. 1797,
d. 1888.

Charles,
b. 1801,
d. 1883.

Albert,
b. 1809,
d. 1872.

Alexandrina, b. 1803; m.
G. Duke Paul Frederic of
Mecklenburgh Schwerin.

FREDERIC WILLIAM, b. 1831,
married Victoria,
Princess Royal
of Gt. Britain.
Emperor Mar. 9, 1888.

Louise, b. 1838,
m. G. Duke
of Baden.

Frederic
Charles,
"Red Prince,"
b. 1828.
d. 1885.

Albert,
b. 1837.

Alexandrina, b. 1842; m.
Duke William of Meck-
lenburgh Schwerin.

William,
b. 1859.
"Crown Prince,"
1888.

Henry,
b. 1862.

4 daughters.

3 daughters.
One, Louise
Marguerite
Duchess of
Connaught.

Frederic
Leopold.

8 sons.

William,
b. 1882.

Frederic,
b. 1883.

Adalbert,
b. 1884.

August, Wilhelm
b. 1887.

WILLIAM OF GERMANY.

CHAPTER I.

ANCESTRY AND PARENTAGE.

UP among the Swabian Alps, within an hour's
drive of the dull and dilapidated town of Hech-
ingen, the rugged, fortress - crowned crag of
Hohenzollern rears its precipitous sides. The fort
on its summit is quite modern, and except the
chapel, there is scarcely a fragment left of the
ancient castle that was the nest of the Black Eagle
—the cradle of the Royal Family of Prussia, whose
head became the first German Emperor. He is a
bold man who would fix the date of the actual
origin of any family; for there must always have
been ancestors before ancestors. One biographer
considers he has proven a link between the Hohenzollerns and the noble Italian family of Colonna;
but a genuinely enthusiastic German is bound to
accept the genealogical tree of the Elector,
Albert Achilles, who assigns as its root one of the
fugitives who fled from Troy with Æneas. The

B

house first steps out into more definite history when, about 1273, a Count of Hohenzollern became by a fortunate marriage, Burggrave of Nuremberg, and was elevated to the rank of a Prince of the Holy Roman Empire. With rare exceptions, the Hohenzollerns have been a thrifty race; and when, in the beginning of the fifteenth century, Kaiser Sigismund found himself troubled by heavy debt, the great-grandson of the Hohenzollern Frederic who had been the first Burggrave of Nuremberg, was ready with a loan of a hundred thousand gulden, taking the Mark of Brandenburg as his security. Kaiser Sigismund not finding it convenient to discharge the mortgage, it was amicably arranged that the worthy Burggrave should foreclose; and so, in 1417, the formal investiture took place, and Frederic VI. of Hohenzollern and Nuremberg became Frederic the 1st Elector of Brandenburg.

Elector succeeded elector; and most of the electors were men of character and vigour. Frederic the second Elector disciplined the people in the same masterful fashion as his father had brought the barons into hand. Albert " Achilles " (1471–1486) was a great soldier, the successful commander for the empire in many wars; but he was statesman as well as soldier—his statecraft being for the behoof of the Hohenzollern race. One of his

expedients to this end was the establishment of the
law of primogeniture; this act of his Hallam calls
the earliest formal promulgation of that principle.
His successor, John " Cicero " (1486–1499), earned
his by-name by his eloquence, but he could do as
well as talk.   He ruled with a strong, occasionally
a ruthless hand; and, unlike a recent English
Chancellor of the Exchequer, he was able not only
to decree a beer-tax, but also to levy it.   Joachim
" the Nestor " (1499–1535) proved his wisdom by
his care for learning. He founded the University of
Frankfort on the Oder, reformed the parish schools,
and remodelled the legal system of the Electorate.
John George, " the Steward " (1571–1598), nursed
it into great prosperity, cleared off incumbrances
on the revenues, and developed a thrift that bordered
on penuriousness.   In John Sigismund's time
(1608–1619), the Duchy of Prussia, coming to
them on the failure of direct heirs of Albert of
Hohenzollern, who was the last grand master of the
Teutonic knights, the subjugators and proprietors of
the territory, and who, on the Reformation, had
secularised the order, and constituted Prussia a
duchy, with himself as its duke, fell to the Electors
of Brandenburg and materially increased their consequence.

His son, George William (1619–1648), an

B 2

unsatisfactory Hohenzollern even had conditions
been favourable for him, fell upon the evil days of
the Thirty Years' War, and suffered, he and his be-
longings. Neutrality, which was the policy he tried
to follow, had not become one of the fine arts in those
days; and Brandenburg, perilously near as it was
to the centre of the great cockpit, was—to break the
metaphor—roughly bruised between the upper and
the lower millstone. Mansfeld, Tilly, and Wallen-
stein had a fine contempt for George William's
neutrality, and Gustavus set his cannon in array
against Berlin because the neutral Protestant had
hindered his relieving march on Protestant Magdeburg. The "Great Elector," Frederic William
(1648–1688), was a quite different stamp of man
from his immediate predecessor. As the ally of
the Swedes, he signally defeated the Poles at
Warsaw, and so secured for himself a recognition of
the complete independence of the Duchy of Poland.
As the enemy of the Swedes, he defeated them in
the memorable battle of Fehrbellin, which takes
rank in the annals of the army which won it, with
Rossbach and Königgrätz. All that can be said of
Frederic III., the "Great Elector's" son and successor, is that he succeeded in achieving the Royal
dignity for himself and his successors (1701), that
he encouraged learning; and that he begat King

Frederic William I., the stern and despotic disciplinarian who bullied his son, tyrannised over the kingdom which he made prosperous, created in his army the iron discipline that stood Frederic the Great in so good stead, and furnished a theme for Carlyle's immortal description of his manner of life. Of Frederic the Great himself there is no need to say anything, because Carlyle has said of him all that is possible to say.

The great King died in August, 1786. He had raised Prussia to the position of a first-class power; he left it, to quote Lord Beaconsfield, "regarded if not respected," thriving, well allied, in fine subordination to an autocratic but not tyrannical sway. Although the stern lesson of the Seven Years' War had taught Frederic that prudence goes farther than valour, and although in the latter period of his reign he used to say that his best regiment was his "yellow dragoons," yet the Prussian army, as he left it, was the finest fighting machine then in existence. Thrift was the maxim of the nation, and seventy-two million dollars lay accumulated in the treasury.

Barely a year after "der alte Fritz" had been laid to rest in the garrison church of Potsdam, Mirabeau left Berlin, thus recording his estimate of the state of Prussia: "The revenue falling off, expenses increasing, genius slighted, blockheads at the helm ; this Prussia is rottenness before maturity." Frederic's nephew and successor, Frederic William II., reigned eleven years, and Massenbach records the general saying when he died—" It is well for him and well for us that he is no more. The State was near its dissolution." When the debauched monarch's son and successor came to the throne, he found not only that the great Frederic's 72,000,000 accumulated dollars were clean spent, but that there was a national deficit to boot of nearly 50,000,000 dollars. The morality of the nation was at the lowest ebb, the *morale* of Frederic's army had seriously deteriorated, and Prussia had lost caste among the nations.

Frederic the Great had not watched for nothing the habits of the nephew who was to succeed him, and forecasted events with singular accuracy in his parting words to his old minister Hoym : " Let me tell you how matters will be after my death. There will be a merry life of it at Court. My nephew will squander the treasure, and allow the army to degenerate. The women will then govern, and allow the State to go to rack and ruin." A like foreboding he expressed to his grand nephew who was afterwards Frederic William III., in their last talk on the Sans Souci garden-seat: " I am afraid," he said, "that things will after my death go *péle-méle.*" But then he was probably referring rather to the future of Europe than to the future of Prussia only, for he continued with singular prescience : "There are elements of ferment everywhere, which the rulers, especially in France, are unfortunately fostering instead of appeasing and extirpating them. The masses are already beginning to make a move, and if this comes to a head it will be ' the devil let loose.' "

The great Frederic's successor, Frederic William II., vulgarly known as "the Fat," was already forty-two years of age when he came to the throne. He had been Prince of Prussia, the usual title given to the heir-presumptive when not the son of the reigning king, since the age of fourteen. From his youth he had been sensual, reckless, and weak —a most discreditable and indeed infamous Hohenzollern. At the age of twenty-five he had divorced his first wife, his own first cousin, and sister to the Duke Charles of Brunswick who commanded and fell at Jena. Immediately after the divorce he married the Princess Louise of Darmstadt, who became the mother, with other offspring, of his successor, Frederic William III. Both wives he outraged in the openest and most brutal fashion. As prince, his life was a foul and glaring scandal. Of him as king this is what Massenbach records : " He bears the greatest resemblance to an Asiatic prince, who, living within his harem with his slaves of both sexes, leaves the business of the State to his viziers. The wall, twelve feet in height, by which the new garden in Potsdam is enclosed, reminds one of the enclosure of a seraglio." The Pompadour of Frederic William II., Countess Lichtenau, born Wilhelmina Euche, was the daughter of a man who had been a trumpeter, then a pothouse-keeper, and later a performer in the private band of Frederic the Great. Her nominal husband, the flunkey Rietz, was the pander at once and the bosom friend of the degraded king, who was a sensualist first, then a maudlin devotee with a propensity towards harsh intolerance, a super-stitious Rosicrucian, and a victim to every quack who set up for a professor of the occult sciences. Ruled, victimised, and befooled by his mistress-in-chief, duped by his minister Bischofswerder, Frederic William lived detested and died unlamented.

Yet even in such a reign as this the kingdom of Prussia did not cease to grow. The " Great Elector," dying in 1688, had left a territory having a population of but one and a half millions. Frederic William I. had added part of Pomerania to the young kingdom, and left to his son, Frederic the

Great, a state of 47,770 square miles with 2,500,000 inhabitants. Frederic the Great added Silesia, and this acquisition, with the large territory gained in the first partition of Poland, increased Prussia to 74,340 square miles with a population of over five and a-half millions. And under Frederic William II.—*roi fainéant* and degenerate Hohenzollern as he was—the state was enlarged so greatly by the acquisition of the principalities of Anspach and Baireuth, as well as by the vast territory added to it by the second and third partitions of Poland, that at his ignoble death in November, 1797, the kingdom of Prussia had an area of nearly 100,000 square miles, and a population of about nine millions.

Frederic William III., the eldest son and successor of the "Fat" Frederic William, was in his seventeenth year when his grand-uncle the Great Frederic was laid in the Potsdam crypt. Mirabeau, a little later, recorded the following estimate of his character: "The Crown Prince will soon deserve the attention of the world. Not because his great-uncle has drawn his horoscope with the words 'Il me recommencera,' but because everything that is heard of him shows that he is a fine character, although his manners are not pleasing. He is awkward, but everything in

him has a decided stamp. He is uncourteous;
but he is true. He demands the reason of everything. He is hard and tenacious, even to rough-
ness; but he is not incapable of deep feeling and
tender attachment. He knows very well whom to
respect and whom to despise. His aversion to his
father amounts even to hatred, which he is at no
pains to conceal. On the other hand, his veneration for Frederic the Great borders on adoration.
This young man may have a great future before
him." Not to him however was the great future
to come, but to his second son, Frederic William
Lewis, better known to us as WILLIAM, first German
Emperor and seventh king of Prussia.

If O'Meara is trustworthy, Frederic William
scarcely impressed Napoleon so favourably when
the sovereigns met at Tilsit. "The Emperor
Alexander and the King of Prussia, especially the
latter," so O'Meara reports Napoleon as telling
him, "were completely *au fait* as to the number of
buttons there ought to be in front of a jacket, how
many behind, and the manner in which the skirt
ought to be cut. Not a tailor in the army knew
better than King Frederic William how many
measures of cloth it took to make a jacket. In
fact," continued Napoleon, laughing, "I was
nobody in comparison with them. They continually

tormented me about matters belonging to tailors, of which I was entirely ignorant, although, in order not to affront them, I answered just as gravely as if the fate of an army depended on the cut of a jacket. When I went to see the King of Prussia, instead of a library, I found that he had a large room, like an arsenal, furnished with shelves and pegs on which were hung fifty or sixty jackets of different patterns. Every day he changed his fashion and put on a different one. He attached more importance to this than was necessary for the salvation of a kingdom." But then it must be remembered that there certainly was no love lost between Napoleon and Frederic William.

The truth is that the Emperor's father was a very ordinary sort of person, rather given to temporising until braced by stronger wills and stouter hearts; brave enough personally, but rather a Herr von Knopf than a soldier; quite without pretensions to being a general, and destitute of any real insight into the art of governing. It is to be said of him that he was honest, was a true Prussian at heart, and when taught by misfortune, sufficiently modest to recognise the worth of staunch patriots and astute and resolute adherents, who discerned by what exertions Prussia was to be rescued from the abject plight into which she had been plunged by ill-fortune and a short-sighted regard for expediency in preference to principle.

Probably from indifference, Frederic William II. had allowed his son full freedom in the choice of a wife; and the latter's union with Princess Louisa of Mecklenburg-Strelitz—they were married in 1793, when the prince was in his twenty-third year, she just seventeen—was a marriage of pure and enduring affection. Louisa was a woman of a very noble character, which developed under misfortune into real heroism. Accomplished, graceful, winning, and natural, her beauty has been commemorated for us on Tischbein's canvas and in Schadow's marble. Her virtues, her courage, her grand endurance of misfortune, illuminate the sombre record of Prussia's tribulation and humiliation. Hardship, grief, and anxiety wrought her premature death, ere yet the sun had broken through the clouds that made so gloomy the last years of her short life. But Louisa will ever stand prominent in the not over-crowded gallery of Teutonic heroines.

On the 22nd March, 1797, it was that this noble woman, true wife, and devoted mother, gave birth to the man-child, who nearly three-quarters of a century later was to accomplish the fulfilment of German unity; bidden by all Germany to take up the title of GERMAN EMPEROR.

CHAPTER II.

CHILDHOOD AND BOYHOOD.

How the bloated debauchee was brought into Berlin for the ceremony from his "orgies" and his quacks in Potsdam is not on record; but it is recorded that Frederic William II. stood first godfather for his fortnight-old grandson, and held that youngster over the font to be christened in his father's palace in the Unter den Linden of the Prussian capital. Before the year (1797) was out the orgies and the quacks had made an end of Frederic William II., and his son Frederic William III., the recently christened baby's father, reigned in his stead.

The best-intentioned man in the world, the new king determined by frugality to attempt the reparation of the impaired finances of Prussia. Not only did he and his Louisa resolve to live on the former's income when Crown Prince; they continued to reside in the heir-apparent's palace, and avoided all pomp and state. Now and then, in the

records of the time, the name of the little Prince
William crops up. His earliest public appearance
was, it seems, in 1802, when only five years of age,
on the occasion of the presentation of a municipal
banner by the Queen to the burghers of Berlin,
when the young gentleman is reported to have
" hammered a nail into the flagstaff in his turn, and
displayed the greatest interest in the whole pro-
ceedings." He could have been little older when
he participated in a juvenile masked ball given by
the Lord-Marshal von Massow, at which a swarm
of masks, among whom were Prince William and
his elder brother the Crown Prince dressed as little
sailors, suddenly gathered round the Queen, and a
small Cupid, aged four, tendered her Majesty an
arrow with the precocious compliment *"De vos yeux
à tous nos cœurs."* Of course, as a Prussian prince,
it behoved him nominally to join the military
service at the earliest possible date, that probably
being fixed by his fitness to be inducted into nether
garments of the " unmentionable " pattern ; and at
the age of six, he with his brother the Crown
Prince and their cousin Prince Frederic, were presented to the Queen by her royal husband, who
described this formidable contingent as " three new
recruits for the Prussian army." Prince William's
uniform on this occasion was that of the Rudorf—

subsequently Zieten—Hussars—the famous " Red
Hussars " whose name is familiar to every military
reader.   In 1804 he and his brother began their
military exercises under Sergeant Bennstein of the
Guards, who drilled them daily until they became
thoroughly instructed in the rudiments of military
training.   Prince William's earliest tutor was
Privy Councillor Delbrück, who was succeeded by
Ancillon and Professor Reimann.

Taken one with another, the lives of royal
people have probably been as full of vicissitude and
risk as have been the lives of those among their
subjects who have made it most their aim to seek
for adventure.   The Napoleons may be put out of
court, as they were parvenus among royalties.   But
how full of strange experiences are the records of the
later Bourbons of France, of Spain, and of the Two
Sicilies !   The Hapsburgs have had their ups and
downs, and the story of the House of Romanoff
reads like a gruesome romance.   The present
royal family of Great Britain have had an exceptionally colourless experience in comparison with
Continental royalty, yet Queen Victoria has been
under fire more than have been men among her
subjects on whose breasts are decorations bestowed
on them for participation in a campaign.   William
of Germany's purple is assured, but who among us

can look back on a life so marked by vicissitude as was his?

The bright child life, with its juvenile balls and its Red Hussar uniforms, while as yet William was too young to understand the meaning of the strange, rough, sudden change, was to give place to years of discomfort and even of penury. The little fellow stood at the window of his father's palace to witness his "Red Hussars" march out on their route to Jena, and no doubt admired the gallant show they made. The drills were stopped, for Sergeant Bennstein had to go to the war with his regiment; it is not recorded whether he ever came back, or fell on the field that drank the blood of so many of Prussia's best and bravest. Poor flaccid Frederic William had temporised and finessed himself into a dead angle, and Napoleon had played with him and humbugged him until he had got conveniently ready to fall upon and annihilate him. It is difficult to feel any particular sympathy with this limp Hohenzollern, who had evinced the family predilection for obtaining additional territory—honestly preferably, other things being equal, but territory anyhow. What his devices brought him to was the loss for the time of half the territory his father had left him. He would fain not have fought, but the nation had got its

back up, and was too strong for him. It remembered the Great Frederic and his victory of
Rossbach, and it believed that another Rossbach
awaited the Prussian arms. "Ah! with the
Austrians," exclaimed the younkers of the Guard,
"it was easy work for Napoleon, but wait till he
tackles the Prussians!"

Well, he tackled the Prussians, and he found
it on the whole rather easier work with them than
it had been with the Austrians. The rottenness
that Mirabeau foresaw had been eating close to the
vitals of the nation, and of the army which the Great
Frederic had left so sound. The army, indeed,
could march past with a front like a wall, but it
had been forgotten that no victory was ever won
by marching past. "There is no doubt," wrote the
shrewd Droysen, "that as far as drill went, it was
in a state of perfection which surpassed even the
performances of the old Dessauer. There never
was more painful attention to the uniform length
of the pigtails and the equal distance between the
feet. The battalions were converted into com-
passes, which were moved to and fro on the ground;
some inspectors-general—if we may believe Massenbach—in order to be more sure of the lines of
the divisions marching at right angles, caused a
sort of astrolabe for ready use to be fixed to the

C

sabres of the colour-sergeants, not to mention other
equally ingenious contrivances. But in the midst
of this superabundance of subordinate excellence—
of this greatness in small things, some people un-
easily began to be aware that the army was sadly
deficient in certain points to which the army of
Napoleon owed its growing glory." This mis-
directed punctiliousness was a symbol of degeneracy,
yet it was also an indication of the existence of
discipline. And that discipline it was, the inheritance from the Great Frederic yet left, which so
materially contributed to the effective rehabilitation
of the Prussian army so soon after it had virtually
ceased to exist. The foundations for the new
superstructure remained extant.

It is to-day as difficult to imagine the Prussian
military organisation collapsing after a single defeat, as to conceive of Prussian officers displaying
their heroism by sharpening their swords on the
doorsteps of the ambassador with whose nation war
may be imminent; yet both phenomena occurred in
1806. Louisa had gone to the front with her husband, and remained by his side until the eve of
Jena. That night she spent in Weimar, and on
the day of Jena, with the distant thunder of the
battle ringing in her ears, she started through the
Hartz Mountains for Berlin, acting on the advice

of old General Rüchel. She reached the capital
only to find the ill news there already, everything
in confusion, and her children already sent off to
Schwedt on the Oder. Thither she followed them,
travelling with all speed, to weep over them, and tell
the bewildered infants that her tears were for the destruction of the army. Schwedt was not safe, so she
carried her dear ones farther to Stettin, sending
them on thence to Dantzig while she herself went
to join her husband at Cüstrin. That fortress
threatened, the royal couple left it—Ingersleben
pusillanimously surrendered it immediately after to
a handful of French hussars—and they retired to
Königsberg, where the parents and the children
were re-united for a short time, and where on the
1st January, 1807, Prince William received from his
father his first commission in the army. In his case
the customary age of ten at which Hohenzollern
princes enter the army was anticipated by three
months, owing to the exigencies of the family's
nomadic condition. From Königsberg they went
to Memel, where the children lived for some time,
although their parents had occasionally to leave
them. Friedland brought about the negotiations
and the treaty of Tilsit, and Louisa accompanied
her husband to that place, anxious to entreat for the
mitigation of Prussia's doom. Boyse avers that

Talleyrand, apprehensive of her influence, tried
every possible means to set Napoleon against her
coming, but unsuccessfully.   There is considerable
testimony to the effect that the conqueror desired
to soften by courtesy and attention associations
which must have been very bitter to poor Louisa.
Napoleon could behave like a gentleman ; he could
also write like a cad. Witness his letter to
Josephine, quoted by Las Casas : " The Queen of
Prussia is really a charming woman. She is fond
of coquetting with me ; but do not be jealous, I am
like oil-cloth, along which anything of this sort
slides without penetrating.   It would cost me too
dear to play the gallant."

The most sombre period for the forlorn family
was their stay in damp, unhealthy Memel. Regular
instruction was not to be procured, but a young
man named Chambeau, of the French colony in
Berlin, had accompanied their flight and taught all
the children to the best of his ability.   Their mode
of living was not only simple as that of the
burghers among whom they dwelt, but positively
meagre ; all outward show was abolished, and priva-
tions were endured that, as Fraulein von Grimm
quaintly has it, " would have been felt even by a
bourgeois."   To live even thus the poor King had
to borrow money from the Mennonites. The

smallest expense had to be thought about twice.
Princess Charlotte sorely needed a dress; the King
could give her only five dollars towards it. It was
natural that strangers should be rigorously excluded
from the observation of penury so harsh. Guests
were hardly to be entertained when money was not
always forthcoming for the daily household expenses, and when the royal table was supplied, and
that rather precariously, with coarse food served
on common earthenware.

The treaty of Tilsit reduced the kingdom of
Prussia by about one-half, but the peace it brought
enabled the royal family to leave Memel and
return to Königsberg, where the historic old palace
formed a pleasanter residence than the Memel house,
where education and companionship were available
for the young people, and where a circle of people
of culture more than compensated for the absence
of a ceremonious court. Frederic William might
have done better for himself for the moment had
he lowered himself to take a place in Napoleon's
parterre of princes, but there was too much of the
Hohenzollern blood in him for such degradation.
Personal and family sacrifices he made for his kingdom with a fine readiness. To assist the Prussian
military reconstruction, he sent his plate to the mint
and his crown jewellery to the Hebrews. When

the French laid a military contribution on Prussia
of 146,000,000 francs as the condition of evacuation, he had half the requisition charged on his own
family domains.   Misfortune braced the character
of Frederic William III.   As for the royal
children, the residence in Königsberg, with its
absence of ceremony and pomp, did much to warm
and nourish their hearts and minds, efface affectation
and pride, and make them natural.   Here they
found the rare privilege for royal children in those
days, of enjoying unmolested the unfettered happiness of childhood and youth.   In the garden
they played at ball, gathered flowers, caught butter-
flies, and were freely brought in contact with young
companions not of their own rank ; a species of asso-
ciation of great advantage for adults as well as
children, when the individuals of higher rank have
modesty and candour, and those of lower are not
toadies.

Prince William had been made a second lieutenant in the end of 1807.   He had been a delicate
and feeble infant, and a weakly and backward child ;
but in his boyhood at Memel and Königsberg,
young as he was, he took part in some of the
drills and exercises in which his regiment engaged,
and his health and development progressed under
the exertion.   Writing to her father on the boy's

eleventh birthday, his mother thus spoke of him: "Our son William—permit me, venerable grand-papa, to introduce your grandchildren to you in regular order—will turn out, unless I am much mistaken, like his father, simple, honest, and intelligent. He resembles him most of all, but will not, I fancy, be so handsome." William turned out a much handsomer man than his father, and the Queen's succinct characterisation, "simple, honest, and intelligent," was neat, true, and effective.

Long months elapsed while the royal family of Prussia continued to reside in Königsberg, during which time negotiations were slowly progressing for the evacuation by the French troops of what of Prussia the treaty of Tilsit had left. The arrangements were not concluded until after the conference at Erfurt, in October, 1808; and when the general evacuation did occur, three of the principal Prussian fortresses still remained garrisoned by Napoleon's soldiers. Louisa had made a last appeal to the conqueror for the restoration at least of Magdeburg, "supplicating, not as a queen, but as the mother of her people." The petition was unsuccessful, Napoleon, it is said, sending her by way of refusal the map of Silesia tied round with a gold chain to which was suspended a golden

heart. On the 3rd of December the French troops
left Berlin on their long march to Spain ; and on
the 10th the first Prussian soldiers re-entered the
capital.   But it was not until the 23rd, after a visit
to St. Petersburg, where the Emperor Alexander
strove to make them forget the misery of the recent
years in "festivals, shawls, and furs," that Frederic
William and Louisa again took up their residence in
Berlin, after a melancholy and miserable absence
from it of three years.   Next day, Christmas eve,
Prince William returned in military fashion, marching into Berlin with his company of guards.   This
was scarcely one of his triumphal entries.   Yet
the home-coming had in it an affecting and chastened
happiness for the long-harassed family.   The
Berliners, whose cheers for Napoleon had been but
"from the teeth outwards," were now genuinely glad
to have the Hohenzollerns back among them again.
They presented a new equipage to the Queen, in
which, with her eldest daughter and one of her
younger sons by her side, she drove down the
Unter den Linden.   It was the anniversary of the
day when she had first traversed that thoroughfare
the loveliest and the happiest of brides.   The noble
lady had seen and shared in the tribulation of
Prussia ; she was not to witness its emancipation.
Seven months after the return to Berlin she died

in the castle of Hohenzieritz, when on a visit to
her father at Strelitz. Her husband and her two
eldest sons arrived in time to be with the wife and
mother when she breathed her last. They took
the body back to the Berlin she had loved and
grieved for ; and the young Prince William, as he
had stood by his mother when the life went out of
her, now stood by her coffin when, on the sixteenth
anniversary of her first entrance into the capital, it
was placed in the mausoleum at Charlottenburg.
That tomb, the son for whom his mother did so
much—that son on whose character the mother left
the impress of her own—rarely failed during all the
years of his prolonged life to visit on the anniversary of the death of its loved inmate. It was long
ere the lad, still delicate from the ailments of his
childhood, recovered from the shock of the sudden
loss of one so dear. Distraction was provided for
him in his military studies, to which he now
devoted himself with great industry under the
direction of Major von Pirch, qualifying for general
efficiency by taking duty in turn with all arms.
A section of a field work traced by him and constructed under his superintendence in the year
1811—he was then only fourteen—may still be
seen in the park of Babelsberg. When that residence came into his possession by inheritance, Mr.

Kingston relates in his short but interesting narrative, that William gave orders for the restoration
of the earthwork of his boyhood to its pristine form,
and its maintenance as a souvenir of his *début*
in the art of military engineering. During the
interval of half a century, large trees had grown
over the surface of the *Schanze*. "He," says Mr.
Kingston, "would not allow those trees to be
removed, and they remain there till the present day,
projecting at all sorts of angles from the grassy
slope of the neatly finished earthwork, and cropping
up in some places from the bottom of the deep
trench surrounding its flanks and faces."

The maxim of Kant the Königsberg philosopher
—"What a state has lost in outward importance
must be replaced by inward development," was not
thrown away on Prince William's father. Already,
during the stay of the royal family in that city of
exile, the interior re-organisation of the realm had
been discussed and planned. The King back in
Berlin, the time had come for the practical commencement of the reforms.

Able men offered for their conduct. To Scharnhorst and Gneisenau fell the leading share of the
re-organisation of the army. Finance and civil
administration were the duties first of Stein, and
when Napoleon had enforced the retirement of that

"first statesman of Germany," Hardenberg, in many respects the prototype of Bismarck, came into office as State-Chancellor. Not one of those men was a Prussian; it must be said of that kingdom that it has not been prolific of great men. Scharnhorst had been a half-starved Hanoverian lad. Gneisenau, born an Austrian, had sung for coppers in the streets of Erfurt, and gone to America in one of the "Hessian" regiments which England hired to assist in the vain endeavour to crush the revolt of her transatlantic colonies. The treaty of Tilsit forbade Prussia to keep in arms more than 42,000 men, but no stipulation was made as to how long the men should serve; so Scharnhorst, while keeping the letter of the treaty, evaded its spirit, by the introduction of what came to be known as the Krümper system. Under it new levies were made every year; a certain proportion of trained soldiers were yearly sent home after a few months of service, and recruits were brought into the ranks in their place, to be drilled in their turn, sent home, and replaced by fresh recruits. Thus early the scheme of the Landwehr and the Landsturm had been conceived by Scharnhorst, and the foundation laid of its development. To the exertions of the military commission of which he was the head and the spirit, was due the extraordinary phenomenon

that in August, 1813—barely five months after the
declaration of war against France in March of the
same year absolved Prussia from the restrictive sti-
pulations of the treaty of Tilsit—Prussia stood possessed of an army of 250,000 men, of whom 170,000
were ready to take the field, while the remaining
80,000 formed reserve and depôt troops and supplied garrisons. The world has known no more
wonderful feat of rapid, efficient, and systematised
organisation.

Frederic William, however, lacked the boldness
to strike the keynote of the " War of Liberation."
He was still Napoleon's henchman when the Moscow campaign began ; and the family spirit of land-
hunger stirring in him could not resist the bait
Napoleon held out, that the Russian Baltic provinces to be occupied by the force he was to
contribute to the *Grande Armée*, should be given to
Prussia as the reward of Prussian co-operation.
Perhaps Frederic William conceived he could not
well help himself in the one sense, and so might as
well help himself in the other ; but as the result of
the compact, three hundred of his officers, stirred to
patriotic wrath, left his army, among them Scharnhorst, Gneisenau, Boyen, and Clausevitz — the
very salt of that army. Yorck, "the old Isegrim,
sharp as hacked iron," commanded the Prussian

contingent that marched out to degradation. The " quiet, cool man, who did not meddle with politics," nevertheless committed the act which forced the hand of his sovereign ; it must be owned at a significant crisis—when Napoleon was staggering back from Moscow. Yorck refused obedience to the order that he should aid in covering the French retreat. Nay, more, he made with the Russian general a convention of neutrality ; and in a remarkable letter to the King he announced his conduct; ready in the event of condemnation to " receive the bullet as calmly on the mound of sand as on the battle-field on which I have grown grey."

Berlin was still in French occupation. But the Diet of the province of Prussia proper acclaimed the act of Marshal Yorck. Frederic William hurried to Breslau ; Scharnhorst and Blücher had arrived there before him. The nation had caught fire and was in a blaze of patriotism. Prince William, a lad now of fifteen, went to Breslau with his elder brother and father; and heard in its streets the trumpet of the resurrection of his country's independence. He read his father's proclamation to the young men of Prussia calling them to arms ; and must have thrilled with the consciousness that the words of fire spoke not less

to him than to others. He rode out with his
father and brother to welcome Czar Alexander
coming from Kalisch to congratulate his brother
monarch, and to pledge with him mutual co-operation *à outrance,* for the grand common object of
both sovereigns and both nations.

William had participated in the wretchedness
of the bondage ; he saw the birth of the struggle
for Liberation ; in that struggle he fought. Ere
he died he must have realised that there is a con-
solation for the failed vigour of old age in the
grand range of retrospect which it affords.

CHAPTER III.

YOUTH ON CAMPAIGN.

PRUSSIA was in fierce earnest to emancipate herself from the oppression of Napoleon, and Alexander of Russia rejoiced to welcome the new and enthusiastic ally. But Napoleon was not the man to be driven from the fruits of his conquests by mere force of royal proclamations promising to the German nation liberty from foreign oppression. Those proclamations had to be followed up by resolute and persistent fighting; and many a bloody battle had to be fought ere the conqueror of Europe, under stress of arms, was to quit German soil and retire across the " German Rhine."

The hour of revolt had however struck, and the man of the hour was ready and eager. Blücher was now an old man of seventy, but there was plenty of fight still left in the stalwart veteran. He had been a man of war from his youth. His soldier life had begun under the great Gustavus in the Seven Years' War. He had struggled against

fate at Jena, and writhed under the humiliation of
having been a prisoner-of-war in the hands of
Napoleon, forced as he had been to surrender the
fortress of Lübeck. The passion of his later life
was a furious hate against the French in general,
and against Napoleon in particular. Professor
Arndt, who saw him at Breslau on the eve of the
declaration of the War of Liberation, thus sketches
old "Marshal Vorwärts," the name his soldiers
gave Blücher after his victory over Macdonald at
the Katzbach. " Notwithstanding his advanced age,
Blücher had a noble figure, was tall and active,
with fine well-rounded limbs like those of a youth.
Most striking of all was his face ; his brow, nose,
and eyes might be those of a god ; his mouth and
chin were those of a common mortal. His eyes, of
a rich dark blue, were capable of a very merry expression, but they often suddenly darkened in a
terrible sternness and anger. Indeed, the old hero,
soon after the disasters of 1806–7, had been for
some time out of his mind, in which state he would
thrust his drawn. sword against the flies and spots
on the wall, yelling out ' Napoleon ! ' His mouth
and chin, however, were rather ignoble—here the
cunning of the hussar was always lurking with
somewhat of the expression of a fox watching for
its prey." Blücher seems to have had just two

virtues.   He was not a great general, but he was
the type of a fine soldier.   He was a single-hearted
man of his word.   For the rest, he was a dissolute
old reprobate, with the weakest imaginable sense
of self-respect.   The old savage smoked his pipe in
the drawing-room of St. Cloud, and threw it at the
head of a French diplomatist.   He played in his
shirt-sleeves at the gambling tables of the Palais
Royal, puffing at his long pipe and drinking great
jorums of hot strong punch.   Most people know
from what point of view it was that the British
metropolis moved him to admiration.

The first short campaign of the allies in the
early summer of 1813 was scarcely auspicious.
Napoleon won the battles of Lutzen and Bautzen,
recovered Dresden and Hamburg, and the line of
the Elbe was again in his hands.   But he was forced
to recognise that, although he had been victorious,
the fighting had taken on a new character.   Blücher
had dared to assume the initiative, and his cavalry
charge on the night of Lutzen had shaken the
French guards.   The allies retired leisurely and in
good order from the fields in which Napoleon's
superior skill had worsted them.   Napoleon no
longer made prisoners or took cannon.   " Great
victories without trophies !" wrote a French com-
mentator, significantly—" all the villages set on

D

fire, and their conflagration barring the way." The
armistice of Pläswitz gave the allies breathing time,
and the accession of Austria added 150,000 men to
the hosts confronting Napoleon, which by the end
of the year numbered little short of half a million.
Before that time Napoleon had sustained tremendous reverses. Blücher had all but annihilated
Macdonald at the Katzbach. Bernadotte and
Bulow had beaten Oudinot at Gross-Beeren. Van-
damme, mobbed by numbers, had to surrender on
the heights of Culm. Napoleon's victory at Dresden had cost him nearly as dear as a defeat would
have done. And finally the three days' fighting
around Leipsic in October had culminated in that
terrific twelve hours'-long struggle which enforced
on Napoleon the necessity of recrossing the Rhine
into France.

Prince William had not shared in the campaign
which drove Napoleon back across the Rhine. His
elder brother, the Crown Prince, rode in the posse
of princes sandwiched between the three allied
monarchs and the chief generals of the allied armies,
in that triumphant cortege which rode out from
the market-place of recovered Leipsic, to review the
troops whose faces were still black with the smoke
of the battle, the embers of which were yet fiercely
aglow down by Lindenau and among the gardens

of the burghers in the fair delta between the
Pleisse and the Elster. It was only in his fifteenth
year that Prince William definitely outgrew the
ailments which had kept him weakly and physically
backward during his earlier years; and he was
judiciously left behind when his father, his uncles,
and his elder brother went away to share the fortunes of the Prussian army. On May 15th, just
while that army was falling back into the position
in which four days later it was to fight the battle
of Bautzen, he was promoted to the rank of first
lieutenant. On the 30th of October, the day on
which Napoleon cut his way through Wrede's army,
that he might make good his retreat to the Rhine
at Mayence, the day too on which Rapp surrendered the fortress of Dantzig which he had been
holding with a French garrison, Prince William
received his commission as captain. Soon after,
as aide-de-camp to his father, he joined the headquarters of the allied monarchs at Frankfort-on-
the-Main, whither they had moved forward after
Leipsic, and where they remained till close on the
end of the year.

Counsels were divided. The Emperor Francis
would have been content that Napoleon had
accepted the proffer made to him of the Rhine as a
frontier; and Metternich hinted to Napoleon his

disgust at "carrying on a war with Baskirs and
Cossacks for allies "—France was presently to find
out that they were considerably more unpleasant as
enemies.   How the Emperor Alexander vacillated
may be gathered from what Vitrolles said of him
later, in reference to the Congress of Chatillon—
"Alexander, upon the slightest reverse, gives orders
to treat upon any terms, at the first sign of success
he will listen to nothing."   How Frederic William
himself felt is doubtful, but the Prussian statesmen
and soldiers with one accord were resolute that no
terms should be made with Napoleon, and that not
he alone, but France as well should be humbled.
A council of war held at Frankfort in the beginning of December decided on a winter campaign
with Paris for its objective.

If the young Prince William were a close
student of war during this his first campaign, he
must have found it fertile of lessons, and yet more
fertile of warnings.   Napoleon's genius never shone
brighter, fighting as he was against overwhelming
odds and with diminished prestige—since it had come
to this with him, that he had for the first time to
endure and to cope with an invasion of the sacred
soil of France.   Prince William could scarcely have
failed to admire how adroit and how daring was his
strategy, how deft and nimble were his tactics ; with

what surprising suddenness his blow fell now on
Blücher, now on Schwarzenberg, now on Yorck, now
on Winzingerode; how ubiquitous and how energetic was this extraordinary man, who had not alone
to contend with the enemies in his front, but to
stimulate the increasing lassitude of his marshals,
and to stem the tide of disaffection that was
rising in his capital. Young as the Prince was, he
could scarcely have failed to discern the evils of
divided and vaguely defined command. He saw in
Schwarzenberg the nominal commander-in-chief of
the allied forces, but controlled and often thwarted
by the three monarchs who were making the
campaign with him, and who again were not in full
accord; while the old war dog Blücher accepted
indeed orders from Schwarzenberg, but honoured
them rather in the disregard of them, save when
they accorded with the energetic projects of
Gneisenau, who had succeeded Scharnhorst as chief
of staff in the army of Silesia when that fine soldier
had fallen on the field of Lutzen. He might have
noted how the feeble and timid Austrian dissemi-
nated his force so widely as in a great measure to
discount its superiority of strength; and how, on
the other hand, the great Corsican ever had his
compactly in the hand, equally ready to strike or to
elude a stroke. In a word, it scarcely could have

failed to furnish the young soldier prince with food
for reflection, that it should have taken 200,000 men
three months to march from the Rhine to Paris,
hindered thus long by the opposition of but 60,000.
Half a century later he was himself to traverse that
distance, not without hard fighting and a wide
detour, in about one-half of the time. Did he
ask himself, when this latter journey was finished,
whether it would have been made as expeditiously
had it been Napoleon the Great who had stood in
the path?

Blücher's army passed the Rhine on New Year's
eve, 1813, at Mannheim, Caub, and Coblentz; the
old chief himself, accompanied by King Frederic
William and his sons, crossing at Mannheim. The
passage was opposed, but not seriously, for Marmont had complied with the retrograde movement
of Ney and Victor, and fallen back toward the line
of the Vosges. Nevertheless, there was sufficient
fighting to give Prince William his "baptism of
fire," and to justify Tolstoi in executing a medal
commemorative of this "Passage of the Rhine."
The marshals fell back through the Vosges before
Schwarzenberg advancing from the south, and
Blücher coming on from the north. The chain of
fortresses was duly masked, and by the end of the
third week of January, 1814, the allied armies

stood with touching flanks on the great plain of
Champagne. They stood on the edge of the great
arc, of which Paris is the centre, and the rivers
Aisne, Marne, Aube, and Seine are the radii. Inside that arc, between the allies and Paris, and so
having the advantage of the " interior lines," were
60,000 French troops ; Napoleon, his prestige, and
his genius.

After some preliminary combats, the battle of
La Rothière, the first of importance in the campaign, was fought on February 1st, from which day
until the final stand on the 30th March made so
resolutely by Marmont and Mortier on the slopes of
Montmartre, it may be said that there passed *nulla
dies sine pugná.* The brunt of the fighting fell on
old " Marshal Vorwärts," who night and day kept
before him the settled purpose of pressing on to
Paris, took every opportunity to disobey orders that
interfered between him and his goal, and by dint of
this persistent resolution eventually obtained sanction for a plan of his own, which, in the words of
Major Adams, " was genial in conception, and
eventually decisive of the campaign." It is probable that Napoleon scarcely recognised the
geniality which Major Adams commends.

The monarchs and their suites had their headquarters with Schwarzenberg, and as Schwarzenberg

when Napoleon was in front of him was fonder of
retreating than of fighting, Prince William, who
was serving as aide-de-camp to his father, had
fewer opportunities of witnessing and sharing in
actual hostilities than if he had been campaigning
with old Blücher.   But occasionally, as for instance
at Rosnay, the day after the battle of La Rothière,
in the advance on Troyes a day or two later, in
Schwarzenberg's retreat towards Langres on the
23–4th February, he was engaged and under fire;
and on the 27th February the chance, which he
eagerly seized, of gaining some distinction came to
the young soldier in the course of the three days'
fighting by which Schwarzenberg forced Marshals
Oudinot and Macdonald back from Bar-sur-Aube
on Troyes.

The marshals had been following the retreating
Schwarzenberg with Napoleon within supporting
distance, when Blücher, by an independent movement toward Paris, drew off the latter to cope with
him.   Then Schwarzenberg turned on the marshals,
and attacked them at Bar-sur-Aube with the forces
nearest to his hand.   In all the campaign there was
no more desperate fighting than that which occurred
in the battle of Bar-sur-Aube on 27th February.
Napoleon's orders to Macdonald and Oudinot had
been stringent, that at any cost they should hold

Schwarzenberg in check, and hinder him from
interrupting the movement Napoleon himself was
making on Blücher. Pressed by the allies, Oudinot and Gerard, the latter of whom commanded
in the French fighting line, bade the soldiers
raise the acclamations which were wont to sig-
nalise the arrival of Napoleon. But on this
day the wonted spell of that great name failed
to work. The allied commanders, bent on carrying their point, were not less prodigal of themselves than of their troops. Both Wittgenstein and
Schwarzenberg were wounded in the hard-fought
action, whose issue was the stubbornly reluctant
retreat of the French. Repeated and devoted
charges of the allied cavalry contributed most
effectually to that result. One of the most furious
of these, delivered by a Russian cuirassier regiment with dash and sweep but at the cost of severe
loss, Prince William accompanied, and after the
charge had ridden back to rejoin his father's staff.
Just then the King noticed a Russian infantry
regiment in the allied front line holding its ground
on the slope of a vineyard against heavy odds, and
under an exceptionally heavy fire both of artillery
and musketry. Reinforcements were urgently
necessary, since, besides that the regiment was
itself in dire straits, there had gathered in the

depression behind it a great mass of wounded,
whom the regiment was devotedly covering. Sup-
ports were promptly ordered, but his Majesty,
anxious to know the name of a regiment which
was bearing itself so creditably, ordered his son,
just then riding in from his cavalry charge, to
gallop to the front again and ascertain the regiment's name, and to what corps chiefly belonged
the wounded huddled behind it. Right through
the fire rode back the Prince, found the infantry
colonel in front of his sore-tried regiment, saluted
that gallant officer in the most methodic manner,
fulfilled his errand, and brought back the information with equal coolness, clearness, and promptitude.
It was no time, in the heart of a battle and when
both were on duty, for the father to infringe military etiquette by praising the conduct of his son.
But that conduct did not pass unnoticed. A few
days later Czar Alexander sent Prince William the
Russian " Cross of St. George," a decoration never
won save by distinguished personal bravery, and
very rarely bestowed on a foreigner. On the 10th
of March—the anniversary of his dead mother's
birthday and the first anniversary of the order's
institution, Prince William was decorated by his
father with the " Iron Cross ; " more charily
accorded then than after the resuscitation of the

order sixty years later. Modest as brave, the lad
had not recognised that he had behaved with exceptional credit until this coveted distinction came
to him, when with frank simplicity he remarked to
his elder brother, "Now I begin to comprehend
why Colonel von Luck shook hands with me so
cordially the other day when I had made my
report, and why other staff officers smiled so
significantly."

As the winter weeks of bloodshed passed,
Napoleon's position became more and more desperate. Moreau's surrender of Soissons was for
him a cruel stroke of evil fortune. Still he fought
on, and gleams of possible extrication from his
myriad difficulties occasionally flashed on the hard-
pressed man. So late as March 19th, in a mo-
mentary panic caused by Napoleon's threatening
attitude, the Emperor Alexander in the middle of
the night sent word to Schwarzenberg to send a
courier to Châtillon, with orders to sign the treaty
of peace in regard to which negotiations were going
on there; his anxiety was so great that, in his own
words, "it would turn half his hair grey." But
the battle with Schwarzenberg two days later at
Arcis-sur-Aube went so badly for Napoleon that
he made the desperate resolve no longer to dispute
with the allies the road to Paris, but to undertake

a diversion in their rear across their lines of communications.

Then it was that the allied sovereigns hardened their hearts. Napoleon no longer stood between them and their goal. There was a suggestive significance in Talleyrand's taunt, " *Vous pouvez tout, et vous n'osez rien. Osez donc une fois.*" The communications might take their chance. It was on March 22nd, by a coincidence the seventeenth birthday of Prince William, that a council of war, held in the allied sovereigns' headquarters at Pougy, came to the resolution to march straight on the French capital, thus, to quote Grant's message to Sheridan, "ending the business this time before going back." Schwarzenberg struck hands with Blücher two days later, and the great hostile tide rolled on toward Paris, sweeping out of its course the 30,000 men with whom Marmont and Mortier tried to check it.

The final battle, on which Joseph Bonaparte and the Parisians looked down from the summit of Montmartre, began with sunrise on 30th May. Frederic William and his sons had spent the night before in the beautiful village of Bondy, and accompanied the columns of the Russian general Barclay de Tolly on their march across the plain of Romainville. Desperate as was the situation of the French marshals, their last fierce and resolute stand was worthy of the men whom the greatest soldier of modern times had delighted to honour. From sunrise till the sun was low in the west they fought staunchly against fate and overwhelming numbers; and ere Marmont at last was forced to ask for an armistice, ten thousand of the allied troops had by death and wounds apologised to the proud city for her impending humiliation. Amid the waving of white flags and handkerchiefs by officers galloping in all directions to announce the armistice and stop the firing, Alexander and Frederic William, the latter accompanied by his two sons, climbed the hill of Belleville and looked down on that fair city which was the queen of the world. For the first time William saw the capital with whose name his will go down to the ages. As they gazed, old Blücher was still fighting his way up the steep of Montmartre, for Mortier in his front was slow to be bound by the armistice to which Marmont had agreed. When at length the firing had ceased and he reached the top of Montmartre, the bloodthirsty old hussar, as he looked down on Paris through his glass, exclaimed, "I would rather turn my cannon on that next than my telescope." In case the chance should come, in a hitch in the negotiations for the capitulation, for the gratification of this truculent preference, he got up into position eighty-four cannon, and then lay down to sleep alongside of them. As for the sovereigns and their suites, after a long contemplation from the heights of Chaumont of the city lying at their feet illuminated by the setting sun, they rode back to Bondy to spend the night there. Bourrienne saw Marmont when he entered Paris after the fight he had waged so stubbornly. " He was scarcely recognisable; he had been fighting himself, sword in hand, and had been wounded in both hands. He had a beard of eight days' growth ; the greatcoat which covered his uniform was in tatters, and he was blackened with powder from head to foot."

Next day about noon, the Emperor of Russia and the King of Prussia made their triumphal entry into the capital of their fallen foe. Prince William, who—yet another coincidence—had been promoted on the day of the fall of Paris to the rank of major for gallantry on the field, accompanied his father and elder brother. The sovereigns and generals were followed by the Guards and Grenadiers of the allied armies. These had been mostly in reserve, and were comparatively presentable. The line troops who had fought the battles, had to remain outside, because of the squalor of

their aspect and the raggedness of their attire.
It was said of the vanguard, who for three months
had never been in a bed, never shaved, and never
changed their linen, that "they looked like
robbers." "Possibly we do," said an old line
colonel to the fine gentleman of the staff who made
that supercilious remark, "but we are ready to
back ourselves for hard fighting against all the
dapper dandies in the world." The reception of
the monarchs by the Parisians was lavishly enthusiastic; even the bare remembrance of Napoleon
seemed to have been erased from the minds of that
fickle population who had but three months before
all but worshipped him as a demi-god. The path
of the conquerors was strewn with flowers by the
conquered. The people along the route kissed the
feet of the monarchs and the hem of their garments; the troops were hindered by the proffers
of refreshments. In the Champs Elysées the procession stopped, and the troops defiled in parade
order before the sovereigns. The ceremony finished,
Frederic William and his sons went to their
quarters in the Hotel Villeroi in the Rue Bourbon,
where they lived for two months, the lads "doing"
Paris and its environs with Alexander von Humboldt as their cicerone.

It was an extraordinary time. The armies of

Europe, the sovereigns of Europe, the dethroned
sovereign of France, and the sovereign who had come
to resume the sceptre, were all crowded together within a circle of fifteen leagues around the capital.
There was a Bourbon in the Tuileries, Napoleon
was still at Fontainebleau, chafing fiercely against
the inevitable; his Empress, Maria Louisa, at Rambouillet, with the poor little King of Rome and
with Louis Bonaparte the ex-King of Holland; poor
repudiated Josephine fretting and dressing at Malmaison; and the Emperors of Russia and Austria
and the King of Prussia in Paris.

Prince William never saw Napoleon the Great.
He and his brothers and sisters had been left at
Memel with the Countess von Voss, when their
parents had gone to their humiliation at Tilsit.
It would have been scarce seemly that any of the
allied royalties should have intruded into the
gloomy privacy of that cabinet on the first-floor of
the palace of Fontainebleau, where Macdonald
found the fallen master of Europe seated in motion-
less dejection, "in a small arm-chair before the fireplace, dressed in a morning gown of white dimity,
and wearing his slippers without stockings." Such
a meeting would have had its awkwardness far more
for each and all of the monarchs than for the man
whom they had the quite recent memory of having

feigned to delight to honour.   But Meneval tells us that the Empress Maria Louisa was visited by all the monarchs during her short residence at Rambouillet, and it is probable that Frederic William presented his sons to the unfortunate daughter of the house of Austria.   The little King of Rome was in evidence in the course of those visits, and seems to have spoken his infantile mind with considerable freedom.   What comments he may have made on others of his mother's visitors is not recorded, but Meneval tells that he utterly declined to approve of his grandfather the Emperor Francis, on the specific ground that that potentate was not handsome.

Poor Josephine, in her divorced retirement at Malmaison, the allied sovereigns treated with delicacy and consideration.   Mlle. d'Avrillion says that the King of Prussia and his sons came frequently to Malmaison to pay their court to Josephine, and dined with her there several times. On these occasions Queen Hortense, Josephine's daughter, and the wife, but separated from him, of Louis Bonaparte the ex-King of Holland, was always with her mother, and assisted her in doing the honours of the house.   It is not clear, however, whether Hortense at this time was living altogether with her mother at Malmaison, or whether

E

she, with her two boys, habitually resided in the
mansion Napoleon had given as an appanage to her
husband at St. Leu, in the forest of Montmorency,
and only went to Malmaison to assist her mother
in entertaining her imperial and royal guests.   A
recent author writing of St. Leu, says : " In the year
1814 this château was inhabited by a queen without
a throne, for she was the wife of a monarch who had
abdicated, and by her two sons, the younger of
whom was about six years of age.   The Russians
and the Prussians were in Paris.   Napoleon was
waiting for the escort which was to conduct him
from Fontainebleau to Elba.   This Queen's château,
Bonapartist though the lady was, came to be looked
upon as in a sense neutral ground.   The coterie in
her drawing-room was sufficiently attractive.   Mole,
Lavalette, Flahaut, Decazes, and Garnerey the
painter, were among the visitors.   The châtelaine
herself was an attractive and beautiful woman.   It
was a dull time in Paris for the conquerors in spite
of the frequent fêtes, and not a few of the great
men among them were glad to mix in the sparkling
circle that was open to them in the château of St.
Leu.   Hither came once and again the Emperor
Alexander, with his Corsican minister, Pozzo di
Borgo.   Blücher cared more for a fight than for a
conversazione, but Prince Augustus of Prussia came

occasionally, and with him sometimes a slip of a lad in the uniform of the Prussian guards, and with the down not yet budded on his lip. This lad was then the younger son of the monarch of a second-rate state. The down came, and gave place to the heavy blond moustache. The blond moustache had turned snow-white when he over whose lip it hung came back half a century later to revive early memories at the head of half a million of men, and to be proclaimed in the château of Ver-sailles as William I., German Emperor. The lady of St. Leu was Hortense, daughter of the Empress Josephine by her first marriage, and wife of Louis, that Bonaparte who preferred Lausanne and his library to the nominal and vicarious throne of Holland. The younger of the two boys of St. Leu lived to be Napoleon III., Emperor of the French, and to send his sword at Sedan to the monarch by whose knee, when the latter was a stripling, he had stood in childhood in the château of St. Leu." Whether there or at Malmaison, it is certain that Prince William must have seen the boy whose guest he long subsequently was at Compiègne and in the Tuileries, and who yet later was his hapless prisoner-guest in the castle of Wilhelmshöhe.

Francis of Austria returned from Paris to Vienna with his daughter, but Alexander and

King Frederic paid a visit to England, and Prince William and his elder brother accompanied their father. Well might Alexander exclaim, as he landed at Dover, " God be praised ! I have set my foot upon that land which saved us all." It is true that no English army was in at the death, but it is safe to say that but for the lavish subsidies the little island bestowed on her continental allies, and the long wearing strain on Napoleon's resources exacted by the Duke of Wellington's career of success in Spain and the south of France, the allied armies would never have crossed the Rhine. It was a memorable visit. No Russian emperor had crossed the Channel since Peter the Great had been Evelyn's tenant at Woolwich, and Frederic William was the first Prussian monarch who had ever seen the white cliffs of Albion. Their majesties, brought across from Boulogne by the Duke of Clarence in a couple of men-of-war, landed at Dover on June 6th, and reached London next day. Both monarchs were the nation's guests—England was hospitable in those days—the Emperor at the Pulteney Hotel, Frederic William and his sons at Clarence House, now the town residence of the Duke of Edinburgh. Immediately on their arrival they visited the Regent at Carlton House. George was in his glory

all through this visit. He had not yet conceived
the impression that he took a distinguished part in
the battle of Waterloo, because, for one thing, the
battle of Waterloo had not been fought; but he
consistently demeaned himself as if he personally
were a full sharer in the prestige of the recent
successes. The day after their arrival both monarchs held levees, and afterwards attended the
courts which Queen Charlotte held in their special
honour. During the twenty days which the visit
lasted, the sovereigns worked as hard in sight-
seeing and festivity as ever they had done in campaigning, and Prince William participated in all
their exertions. The illustrious visitors went to
Ascot races, lunching by the way at the Star and
Garter at Richmond, and after having seen the Cup
run for, drove on to dine at Frogmore. The " Royal
Heath " never saw so many royalties as on this
occasion; the list would fill a page. On the following night, after dining with Lord Liverpool at
Fife House, they all went to the opera, and Prince
William had the opportunity of gaining some insight into the domestic relations of his royal host,
when the Princess of Wales entered the box ex-
actly opposite that which her husband and his
guests occupied, amidst the significant cheers of
the vast audience. So vast was that audience that

the inner doors of the Opera House were smashed, and some 2,000 people got in without payment.

Of course there was a trip to Woolwich, where Colonel Congreve showed his newly - invented rockets ; a review of the artillery brigade followed the inevitable collation. On the following day arms yielded to the gown. The sovereigns and their suites were escorted to Oxford by the Prince Regent ; the Prussian monarch and his sons were the guests of Corpus Christi College, which in their honour flew the Prussian eagle over its gateway. The Prince Regent, arrayed in his academic gown and cap, showed his visitors about the University, and in the Bodleian Library he was presented by the Chancellor with a copy of " Aristotle "—why this work was chosen is not recorded. The dinner, at which two hundred sat down, was served in the Library of All Souls. All the colleges sent their gold plate to adorn the board. We are told that when any favourite toast was specially acclaimed, his Royal Highness "was pleased repeatedly to wave his hand with enthusiastic delight, accompanied with a cheerful and dignified aspect." His visit to England certainly afforded Prince William frequent opportunities of taking lessons in deportment from the most distinguished exponent of that accomplishment. Next day the young soldier had the felicity of seeing his father made a D. C. L., a compliment extended also to the Emperor Alexander, the Duke of Wellington (*in absentiá*), Metternich, and Blücher. It was rather a shame to leave out the Hetman Platoff, when the University's hand was in. At that evening's banquet in the Hall of Christ Church, old Blücher was persuaded to make a speech, which he delivered "with a powerful voice and most expressive energy," but in German; whereupon the Prince Regent volunteered to act as interpreter.

Their majesties and suites went everywhere with great impartiality, and Prince William was present at grand receptions, charity school treats, corporation banquets, Humane Society meetings, reviews in Hyde Park, and "White's *fête.*" Then everybody went down to Portsmouth to witness a great naval review, and the illustrious visitors were treated to a general salute of forty-two guns from each ship, which it is narrated the Duchess of Oldenburg (the Czar's sister) "bore with much fortitude." All went on board the *Impregnable*, the Duke of Clarence's ship, where Alexander displayed much curiosity as to the proportion of water in the crew's rum. "Six-water grog, your majesty, and it would be no worse for being stronger," was the frank information given

by a tar. The Emperor took a tot, drank it, and
reported it "very good." It is also on record that
"the Sons"—capital S by the Jenkins of the
period—"of the King of Prussia drank grog with
the men with much satisfaction." Next day the
fleet, with the sovereigns aboard, went out quite to
sea, some twelve miles, under a brisk north-east
gale, which in some instances rendered unaccept-
able the refreshments served in the *Impregnable's*
cabin. It was during this visit to Portsmouth
that Prince William first met Wellington, who,
arriving in England from his army in the south of
France, had gone direct to Portsmouth, and was
awaiting the debarkation of the Prince Regent and
his guests. After a review on the Portsdown
ridge, the King of Prussia and his sons travelled
across country to Dover, and on June 27th crossed
to Calais on the *Nymphen* frigate.

Both monarchs were received enthusiastically
in England, but old Blücher kindled the wildest
fervour. His huge moustaches — "exceedingly
prominent"—moved wonder. When he went to
Carlton House, the mob swept the sentries aside,
stormed the royal residence, and crowded into the
hall. Once in Hyde Park he was so mobbed that
he had to take refuge in Kensington Palace. At
Portsmouth two sailors danced a hornpipe on the

top of his carriage.   One very comic story is told
of him.   When Oxford made him a Doctor of
Civil Law, the simple old soldier took the degree
for a medical one, and said, " You ought to make
Gneisenau an apothecary ; it was he who made up
the pills for me."—*Se non e vero,* &c.

From France Prince William accompanied his
father back to Berlin, and took part, along with
Blücher, Bulow, Tauentzien and his royal relatives,
in his first triumphal entry into the Prussian
capital.   Thorwaldsen's statue of Victory in her
Chariot was in its place again on the Brandenburg
Gate, as the conquering home-comers rode under
the arch to where, in the Lustgarten at the foot of
the Linden, the altar of thanksgiving stood in the
typical sunshine.

Prince William did not make the Waterloo
campaign in the following year.   When Waterloo
was being fought he was composing a very interesting and characteristic document.   The time had
come for the young man to be confirmed.   It is a
House Order of the Hohenzollern family, that
every member of it before his or her confirmation
shall indite a personal profession of faith, for the
satisfaction of those responsible for the moral training of the young candidate ; and it is held a point
of honour that this " profession " be strictly and

personally original, and done without assistance
of any kind. Prince William wrote his formal
Glaubensbekenntniss, and so fulfilled the family
statute ; but he added to his " profession of faith "
a composition of a wider scope, to which he gave
the title " *Lebensgrundsœtze,*" or " Life Principles."
In this self-definition—if the term may be used—
William engages in a quaintly simple wrestle with
the " Divine right " doctrine, which must have been
all but a part of his second nature, and succeeds
fairly in emancipating himself from its influence.
Every line breathes the Christian and the gentleman. Mr. Kingston will excuse the freedom taken
of using his rendering, conveying as it does so
felicitously the spirit of the German original.

" Life Principles.

" With a thankful heart I acknowledge God's great bene-
ficence in permitting that I should be born in an exalted
station, because thereby I am better enabled to educate my soul
and heart, and was put in possession of copious means where-
with to build up worthiness in myself. I rejoice in this station
—not on account of the distinction it confers upon me
amongst men, nor on account of the enjoyments it places
at my disposal, but because it enables me to achieve more than
others. In humility I rejoice in my station, and am far from
believing that God has intended, in this respect, to put me at
an advantage over my fellow-men. I am equally far from
considering myself better than anybody else on account of my

exalted station. My princely rank shall always serve to remind me of the greater obligations it imposes upon me, of the greater efforts it requires me to make, and of the greater temptations to which it exposes me.

" I will never forget that a prince is a man—before God only a man—having his origin, as well as all the weaknesses and wants of human nature, in common with the humblest of the people ; that the laws prescribed for general observance are also binding upon him ; and that he, like the rest, will be judged one day according to his deeds.

" For all blessings that may fall to my share I will look gratefully up to God ; and in all misfortunes that may befall me, I will submit myself to God, in the firm conviction that He will always do what is best for me.

" I know what, as man and Prince alike, my duty is to true honour. I will never seek honour to myself in vain things.

" My capacities belong to the world and to my country. I will therefore work without ceasing in the sphere of activity presented to me, make the best use of my time, and do as much good as it may be in my power to do.

" I will maintain and foster a sincere and hearty good-will toward all men, even the most insignificant, for they are all my brethren. I will not domineer over anybody in virtue of my rank, nor make an oppressive use of my princely position. When I shall have to need any service at the hands of others, I shall require it in a courteous and friendly manner, endeavouring, so far as in me lies, to render the fulfilment of the duty easy to them.

" But it shall be part of my own duty to do my utmost to thwart the machinations of hypocrisy and malignity, to bring to scorn whatever is wicked and disgraceful, and to visit crime with its due measure of punishment ; no feelings of compassion shall hinder me therefrom. I will, however, be careful not to condemn the innocent.

" To the utmost of my ability, I will be a helper and

advocate of those unfortunates who may seek my aid, or of whose mishaps I may be informed—especially of widows, orphans, aged people, men who have faithfully served the State, and those whom such men may have left behind them in poverty.

"Never will I forget good done to me by my fellow-men. Throughout my life I will continue to be grateful to those who shall have rendered me service.

"For the king, my father, my love is tender and respectful. To live in such sort that I may be a joy to him will be my utmost endeavour. I yield the most scrupulous obedience to his commands. And I entirely submit myself to the laws and Constitution of the State.

"I will perform all my service-duties with absolute exactitude, and while assiduously keeping my subordinates to their duty, will treat them amicably and kindly."

CHAPTER IV.

EARLY MANHOOD.

THE "Holy Alliance" had been formed, the "long peace" had set in, King Frederic William had returned to his capital, and Prince William, already almost a veteran ere he had come of age, was quietly serving with his battalion of Guards. On the 4th of November, 1815, the Prince was one of the guests at a somewhat memorable banquet in the royal palace of Berlin. The King of Prussia was entertaining his friend and ally Emperor Alexander of Russia, and several other members of the imperial family. Among these was the young Grand Duke Nicholas, who was later to succeed Alexander as the Russian autocrat, and yet later to die of a broken heart because of the disasters that befell his troops in the Crimean war. At the banqueting table there sat next to Nicholas a beautiful girl of seventeen, Princess Charlotte of Prussia, the daughter of Queen Louisa and the favourite sister of Prince William. At the

royal table there were but two guests not of
imperial or royal blood—the grey-haired Blücher
returned victorious from the last desperate wrestle
with the great soldier whom he had regarded as a
personal enemy, and Barclay de Tolly, who had
commanded the Russian army on its march upon
Paris. The rest of the Court guests—a numerous
company—were entertained in the adjoining room.
After dinner the two sovereigns suddenly rose and
bade the company drink to the toast of Nicholas
and Charlotte as a betrothed couple. Those at the
royal table had been informed of the betrothal
during dinner, but to the guests beyond in the
ante-room the announcement came as a surprise,
and they hurried into the principal banqueting
room to offer their congratulations.

At that time there seemed no prospect of the
accession of Nicholas to the imperial throne. He
was a younger son ; but then he was the younger son
of the great White Czar, and a family alliance with
a potentate so powerful was in those days a fortunate thing for poor mangled Prussia. Prince William
was a Hohenzollern, and therefore, although not yet
eighteen, quite old enough to be sensible of the
advantages of the connection ; but it had for the
young man the personal joy that his comrade and
his favourite sister had fallen in love with each

other, and that the course of true love had run smooth, flowing as it did parallel with the broader current of statecraft. Nicholas and Charlotte had met in Berlin when the former, a mere stripling, was on his way to join the army in the field in the spring of 1814, and both had confided to Prince William the mutual predilection. In later life, as the head of his house, he did a good deal of match-making, but probably this was the only love affair in which William was a confidant.

Nearly two years had to elapse before Charlotte, to use Grimm's quaint phrase, "was sufficiently prepared for her vocation." She had to go to St. Petersburg to be married ; and thither went with her as her appropriate escort, her brother Prince William. He was now a man in years; with experiences of life such as come to few who as yet are standing on the threshold of manhood. On his young breast were decorations, not alone empty honorary compliments, but won by conduct on the battle-field. He had got his promotion to the rank of colonel, had taken the command of a battalion of foot guards, and had been nominated a member of his father's privy council. The weakly boy whose childhood had been complicated by rickets and nervous fevers, was now a handsome and stalwart young fellow, broad of shoulder, deep of chest, straight and long of limb. If he could not measure inches with the young giant to whom he was to give away his sister, he had stature, thews, and sinews to have delighted the eye of that ancestor of his whose passion was for strapping grenadiers. Fairly well educated, fluent in French—then as now the Court language of Russia—gracious and graceful in manner, he was in all respects a creditable Prince to be sent to a critical court, the escort and brother of the lady who was its sovereign. The road to St. Petersburg, as far as Königsberg at least, was not wholly strange to the sister and brother; they had traversed it before in very different case eleven years previously, when the family had to flee from Berlin before Napoleon's victorious legions. All had been then misery and dismay. Now the peaceful and contented people everywhere welcomed the royal travellers with joyous shouts. Charlotte's beauty and winsomeness recalled to many the image of her mother; and all Königsberg, the home of her childhood, turned out to greet the young bride. Nicholas met the travellers at the frontier and escorted them through Russia till Pawlosk was reached, the residence of that masterful woman Maria Feodorowna the empress-mother. Fortunately the anxious Charlotte made a favourable impression on this dame; and as for Prince

William he captivated the old lady on the spot. The Emperor Alexander led that young man to his mother with the words, "Allow me to present to you my new brother." Whereupon the empress-mother promptly embraced Prince William with the genial observation, "And I also gain a son."

For poor bewildered Charlotte followed in quick succession her grand entry into St. Petersburg, her reception into the Greek church with her re-christenment by the new name of Alexandra Feodorowna, her formal betrothal according to the forms of the Russian National Church, and finally the sumptuous yet simple wedding ceremony; at all of which functions her brother was naturally present. It was his duty to hold the diadem over his sister's head, and as the ceremony lasted three hours, it may be conjectured he was quite ready for the grand banquet which immediately followed it, whereat the imperial family, seated by themselves, were served by the great dignitaries of the Russian realm.

Prince William achieved a distinct social success in Russia. Wherever he found himself, amid the stately ceremonials of the Winter Palace, in the modified stiffness of Zarsko-selo, in the charming seclusion of Pawlosk, he won golden opinions. Naturalness through life was the chief

F

characteristic of his manner, and the secret of the influence it exercised.   Grimm tells how he especially attracted the attention and won the liking of the old empress-mother, and speaks of her having been forced to recognise one difference between his training and that of her own sons.   " Prince William," says he, " was easy and active in all his movements, natural in his intercourse with society, youthful joyousness animating his whole being without any loss of his dignity as a Prince ; whereas it was difficult, nay impossible, for Nicholas and Michael, even in the most intimate circles, to descend from their imperial eminence, and to assume that genial tone which everywhere calls forth sympathy."   This is courtier-language that Nicholas and Michael had been educated into an unbending rigidity of pompous stick-hood; and were to be pitied in the isolation which their train-- ing had created.   Fortunately for themselves, since the days when Grimm flunkeyed in the imperial court there has been a sweeping change in the habitual demeanour of the men of the reigning family of Russia.   Their social characteristics now are frankness, simplicity of manner, and genial ease.

The Russian bear hugged Prince William closely, but it was a hug with the claws in sheath,

But the Russian mastiff used its teeth on him. At
Pawlosk he chanced to get severely bitten by one
of the empress-mother's chained mastiffs, and it
was thought advisable to have the wound cauter-
ised. Grimm recounts that he submitted to this
highly unpleasant operation with so cool a fortitude that the old lady, perhaps striving to salve
by flattery the misdeed of her dog, exclaimed, "It
is quite natural that he should be brave; is he
not a Prussian prince!" At a great masquerade
in the Anitschkow Palace, the Grand Duchess
Alexandra (previously Princess Charlotte) appeared
as an Indian prince, the old empress-mother as a
sorceress, and the Empress Elizabeth as a bat.
The chronicler does not specify Prince William's
character; probably we should have been told had
he appeared as a mastiff in a state of hydrophobia,
and attacked the venerable sorceress. In autumn
the Court travelled by easy stages to Moscow, and
Prince William saw the ancient capital of Holy
Russia ere yet it had wholly retrieved the desola-
tion wrought by the sacrificial flames of 1812.
After a stay of six months in Russia, during which
we are told his influence sensibly encouraged the
comparatively pleasant and unreserved tone of
society which had begun to prevail in his sister's
little court, Prince William left Russia amid

F 2

wide-spread regrets, and returned to Berlin to take up his military duties. On his coming of age in March, 1818, he was promoted to the rank of Major-General.

The Berlin of Prince William's early manhood was a very second-rate style of capital; one writer describes it as a provincial town compared with Prague or Venice. It covered a large area indeed, but the long wide streets were lined with small tasteless houses, indicating a quiet unpretentious citizenhood. The doors of few hospitable well-equipped mansions opened to admit guests to well-spread tables, or to evening receptions. By ten at night the city seemed dead—the silence unbroken save by the cry of the night watchman or the sentry's unfrequent challenge. Few strangers visited it, for it had little to show except regiments drilling mathematically on dusty parade grounds. Militaryism was supreme and arrogant; the highest civilian officials had scarcely any social status. General Müffling kept Alexander Humboldt standing half an hour before him, while he remained seated in the presence of a man whom emperors had delighted to honour. But matters were improving. The King, conscious of the need for his capital of intellectual resources, had established the University of Berlin, whose leading

light had been the philosopher Fichte. He was
dead, but Wilhelm Humboldt, the true creator
of the Berlin University, still lived, and the intellectual and scientific group comprised such men
as Frederic Wolf, Ancillon, Stäzemann, and the
physicians Hufeland and Heim. The social and
artistic Mæcenas of Berlin in those days was
Prince Radziwill, a man of fine culture and con-
spicuous talents who had won the hand of a niece
of Frederic the Great. The King pottered about
Berlin with his younger daughter in a homely
bourgeois fashion, stopping for a gossip with a passer
by, dining at two, and entering the theatre every
night at six precisely. He was a most affectionate
parent, and liked to have his family around him.
It was a great pleasure to him when his eldest
daughter and her husband, the Arch-Duke Nicholas,
came to Berlin to spend with them the winter of
1820–21; and he laid himself out to do his visitors
honour to such purpose as to receive from the
sententious old empress-mother the modified compliment, "He really does more than one could
think or expect." Among other entertainments
were a series of tableaux, illustrating Tom Moore's
poem of Lalla Rookh. The *dramatis personæ* were
sufficiently distinguished. The Grand Duchess
Alexandra was Lalla Rookh; her husband the

Grand Duke Nicholas, Alexis—fancy the stern
Nicholas attitudinising in tableaux vivants! The
sisters of Aurungzebe were the Duchess of Cumberland and the Princesses William and Alexandrina,
his sons the Crown Prince and Prince William,
and other junior members of the royal house.
Ernest Duke of Cumberland was Abdallah, little
anticipating that a young participant in the per-
formance would half a century later deprive his
son of the kingdom of Hanover. All the members
of the poem's houses of Bucharia and Cashmere
were represented by Princes and Princesses of royal
blood. Nor was the privilege of witnessing this
unique entertainment confined to the court and the
favoured few; it was repeated for the behoof of the
citizens, 3,000 of whom were afforded the opportunity of enjoying it.

In the spring of the same year (1821) Prince
William visited Italy, along with his father and
younger brother Charles. At Rome the erudite
Niebuhr, then Prussian minister to the Vatican,
conducted the King to all the objects of interest in
the Holy City, and the scholarly Bunsen acted as
guide to the Princes, the two German savants super-
seding the Roman antiquarians, usually nominated
by the papal court to attend high personages and
explain all the remarkable objects. Bunsen tells

his sister what pains he had taken to perform his
duties with credit, and adds that he attained his
aim. Both Princes he found "very observant and
intelligent;" of Prince William he speaks as " of
a serious and manly character, which one cannot
behold and perceive without feeling heartily devoted to him, and in all sincerity holding him in
esteem."

William always, save during one brief interval
to be afterwards alluded to, retained a cordial
friendship for Bunsen, who never visited Berlin
without having an interview with him. The elder
brother, Frederic William, from the first meeting
found great delight in intercourse with Bunsen,
and gave him frequent invitations to intimate
social gatherings, when the latter was called in to
communicate the results of his study and re-
search. One of such interviews, which occurred
in November, 1827, on the occasion of Bunsen's
bringing to Berlin Rafael's Madonna di Lante,
which he had purchased for the royal collection,
he describes in a letter to his wife: "The Crown
Prince and Prince William were present, also
Ancillon and General von Knesebeck. At first
Rome was the subject of conversation; but then
the affairs of Greece and Turkey were discussed,
and an animated and warm debate came on between

the Crown Prince and Prince William on one side,
and Ancillon and Knesebeck on the other.   The
views and feelings of the two princes were admirable.   The most important and delicate points of
the political situation were touched upon freely and
even daringly; but no word of passion or prejudice
was uttered.   If I were to write down the conversation as a memorial, twenty years hence it would
hardly seem credible."

CHAPTER V.

MARRIAGE AND MIDDLE AGE.

WILLIAM's youth had been spent amidst vicissitudes ; his years of manhood, until the events of
1848 broke in on their quietude, were to pass
uneventfully.   Europe was regaining prosperity
after decades of exhaustive warfare, and her states
were concerning themselves with the development
of domestic reforms, rather than with problems of
foreign policy.   Frederic William III. of Prussia
was not cursed with ambition.   He had retrieved
his kingdom's position, and now he was content to
let that kingdom prosper in repose, while he himself took life easily.   His second son was a soldier
in spirit as well as in name, and he devoted himself sedulously and unremittingly to the duties of
his profession.   As the years passed, he held
divisional commands, made successive tours inside
the realm to inspect territorial troops, and paid
visits to foreign countries on professional errands.
Promotion came to him in due course.   Before his
marriage in 1829, he had attained the rank of

Lieutenant-General, and been placed in command of the Brandenburg Army Corps.

And he had fallen in love, with the experience that for princes, as for people of lower degree, the course of true love does not always run smooth. He had given his heart to the fair daughter of Prince Radziwill, the cultured and intellectual Pole whose house in those years was the centre of Berlin society. But reasons of State forbade the marriage. The blood in the veins of the Princess Radziwill was only half royal; her mother was the niece of Frederic the Great, her father was a prince, indeed, but no scion of a royal family. Obedience is reckoned the first duty of a Hohenzollern; and William sorrowfully yielded to the paternal prohibition of the union that would have made him happy. Since he was not to marry the woman he loved, he would have preferred not to marry at all, but the *mariage de convenance* is a normal part of the princely lot. His elder brother the Crown Prince had been married for some years without issue, and poor William had to accept matrimony in the interests of the succession. His younger brother Charles had in 1828 wedded a daughter of the Grand Duke of Weimar, and there had come to Berlin with the bride a younger sister, who had found so much favour in the eyes of Frederic William that he chose her to be the wife of his second son. William yielded to the *raison d'Etat*, and resignedly betrothed himself to the good, amiable, and beautiful Princess Augusta of Weimar. Their nuptials were celebrated in the palace at Berlin on June 11th, 1829. William was then thirty-two, his bride barely eighteen. Among those present at the marriage were the bridegroom's sister Charlotte, who by the death of Alexander I. had now become Empress of Russia, her stalwart husband likewise becoming the Emperor Nicholas. The bride's coronet was adjusted by the Crown Princess of Prussia, assisted by the Empress of Russia and the Grand Duchess of Weimar. The young couple began housekeeping in the " New Palace " on the Linden, which was to be their Berlin residence during all the years of their long wedded life, for William, when he came to the throne, declined to remove.

The *fêtes* were very brilliant, partly in honour of the wedding, partly in honour of the visit of the Empress of Russia to the home of her ancestors. It was in homage rather to the Empress than to the bride that the spectacular tourney of "The Magic White Rose " was held ; for Charlotte it was who was the " Blanche-fleur " dear to Prussian hearts, and who was the queen of the tournament. Among the armour-clad competitors

eager to distinguish themselves by feats of arms,
whom the heralds by the Rose-Queen's permission admitted into the tilting-yard overlooked
by her tribune, was Prince William, carrying the
banner of Brandenburg, and followed by four
knights in blue, scarlet, and silver. The four
sons of the King opened the tilting. They rode
with couched lances at shields wreathed in white
roses, then at Moors' heads, and finally, discarding
the lances, they essayed to thread on their sword-
points a series of rings. The competition was a
sort of sublimated " heads and posts." The tilting
finished—there is no record how successful was
Prince William—the knights escorted the Queen
of the *fête* to the Palace, where was exhibited a
series of dissolving views illustrating incidents in
her life.

William and his princess travelled about a good
deal in the first years of their union. In 1831 they
went into Silesia on a visit to old Gneisenau in his
country retirement at Erdmannsdorf. At Fischbach, near Gneisenau's quiet homestead, the Emperor and Empress of Russia had a residence, at
which they were then living, and the two families
saw much of each other, for the lifelong friendship
between William and Nicholas was ever warm and
firm. Excursion parties were made up into the

ravines and among the crags of the Reisen-Gebirge,
and William from the summit of the Schnee-Koppe
looked down on the country where, thirty-five years
later, Prussian armies of which he was to be Commander-in-Chief were to fight and conquer.   The
French Revolution of 1830 found William and
Augusta at The Hague, and later the ripple of
its turmoil reached the Rhine Provinces, so that
William had to march Brandenburger troops into
Cologne and Aix-la-Chapelle to avert disturbances
there.   On the 18th October, 1831, was born to
them their only son, he who as Crown Prince and
as Imperial Crown Prince commanded universal
respect and admiration for his many virtues, and
whose career in his higher sphere of influence and
usefulness will prove a fitting sequel to an earlier
life of unblemished purity, of grand manliness, of
loyal devotion to duty.

William and Augusta were among the imperial
and royal personages who, in August, 1835, con-
verged on Silesia for unwontedly important military
manœuvres in that province, and afterwards crossed
the Prosna into Russian Poland, for the sumptuous
festivities of Kalitz.   There was a quiet preliminary
time at Fischbach, but in a few days both Courts
moved into Leignitz, in the environs of which were
held the manœuvres to witness which there came,

from all parts of Europe, princes and personages who
filled the castles and country houses all around, and
crowded the balls, concerts, and State theatrical
performances But the doings in Silesia paled before the brilliancy of the imperial splendour at
Kalitz. The King of Prussia was welcomed on his
arrival there by a military band as strong as an aver-
age British infantry brigade.   Ball succeeded ball ;
on the intervening nights the best singers of Europe
sang in Italian opera, Spanish and Polish dancers
enchanted by their grace, and the highest talent
of the Berlin stage performed in favourite dramas.
Around Kalitz a great army which had been
gathered from all parts of the Russian empire,
engaged in manœuvres, reviews, and sham fights of
exceptional realness.   In the Kalitz camp were to
be seen "Cossacks, Circassians, Grusinians, Tscher-
kessen, and Mussulmans, in every imaginable
costume,—primitive-looking forms, with sunburnt
faces and glossy black hair and beards, armed with
pistols, scimitars, and daggers, their heads covered
by turbans or fur caps; others wore glittering
silver helmets and coats of mail made of links of
steel ; and while some invoked Allah, from the lips
of others resounded hurrahs."

In the early part of 1840 William visited
St. Petersburg in command of a detachment of

Prussian troops, on the errand of participating in the inauguration of Czar Alexander I.'s memorial column. He went as the representative of his father, for Frederic William was too old and frail for a journey so arduous. His ailments increasing as the year advanced, the King had to delegate to his second son all the arrangements connected with the laying of the foundation stone of that monument to Frederic the Great, with which every one who has visited Berlin is familiar. The hand of death was on the old monarch, and he could stand only for a few minutes at his window to look on the little remnant of veteran comrades of "der alte Fritz" standing around the spot, where with much ceremony was laid the foundation stone of the monument to the great warrior who had so often led Prussian soldiers to victory. A week later, on 7th June, 1840, there died the homely, well - meaning old sovereign whom his subjects loved; and the reign began of his eldest son, Frederic William IV., a man as well - meaning as his father, of a more liberal nature, a loyal student of art, but lacking the firm will and the strong hand to guide wisely the destinies of the country he ruled through the troublous years of revolutionary turmoil that were soon to come.

By the death of his father, William became

heir - presumptive, and took the titular rank of
"Prince of Prussia." Nominated by his brother,
the new King, to the Governorship of Pomerania,
he held that office for some time; and during a
visit which the King paid to England in 1842, the
functions of Regent were entrusted to him.

The agitation for a Constitution had commenced
in Prussia with the accession of Frederic William
IV. The Government was an absolute monarchy;
but as regarded local provincial affairs, a species of
"home rule" obtained in the limited administrative
jurisdiction of the Provincial Diets. In so far as
Prussia was not governed direct from the throne,
the principle of decentralisation, of which we now
hear so much, was in full development. The movement in favour of a National Parliament, the King
was understood to regard favourably; the Prince
of Prussia did not recognise the particular need
for a Constitution, and took umbrage at Bunsen's
advocacy of that reform. A reconciliation took
place in 1844, when Bunsen, who was then
Prussian minister to England, visited Berlin and
had an interview with the Prince, which he thus
describes in a letter to his wife: "The Prince
spoke with me for more than an hour; in the first
place about England; then on the *great* question,
the Constitution. He asked my opinion on this

matter.   I replied that I had come rather to learn and hear than to offer an opinion; but this I could well perceive, that it would be impossible longer to govern with provincial assemblies *alone*—it would be as if the solar system should be furnished with centrifugal power only.   The Prince stated to me his own position in relation to the great question, and to the King, with great clearness, precision, and self - command."   Bunsen does not mention whether the Prince was converted by his "solar system" argument; but William determined to give up his project of going to Russia with the Emperor Nicholas, who had been visiting western Europe; and instead to go to England and make a tour through that country, with Bunsen as his guide, perhaps to study there the working and results of free institutions.   William was in England when the Duke of Edinburgh was born, and a special parade of the Household troops was held in Hyde Park as a compliment to him.   Then, with Bunsen as his "guide, philosopher, and friend," he went on a round of visits to great houses in the provinces.   Bunsen writes from Badminton on August 30th :—

   " . . . At length, on the twelfth day of the journey, a day of rest in this truly royal country-seat! We have seen Edinburgh (the magnificent)

G

and Glasgow, the lakes, and Liverpool (before this tour we had been at Portsmouth and at Oxford), the splendid seat of Chatsworth (more than royal), Stowe, Warwick Castle, Lowther Castle, Belvoir. To-morrow to the Queen, and on 4th September to London, where the Prince will embark. The journey was a refreshment, and a great event. The Prince of Prussia has taken an affection for England ; admires her greatness, which he per- ceives to be a consequence of her political and religious institutions. . . . I am always alone with the Prince in the carriage, except Captain Meynell, who, not understanding German, is no check on our conversation." Poor Captain Meynell, what he must have lost !

Bunsen quotes a curious passage in a letter to him from King Frederic William, in relation to this visit. " To William all that is cordial and affectionate ! Talk over with him all things as much as possible—politics, Church matters, the arts, Jerusalem in particular. I have begged him, on his part, to discuss everything unreservedly with you ; that will be most useful and very necessary." On the whole, perhaps, Captain Mey- nell was not greatly to be pitied.

Bunsen appears to have done his bear-leading with assiduity and skill. He is reported by his

wife, whenever he brought the Prince into contact
with distinguished persons, to have led up indus-
triously to topics on which they might be moved
to utter opinions, which he then translated into
German for the behoof of his Royal Highness.
The Duke of Wellington was unwontedly com-
municative on military subjects, but only one of his
answers to Bunsen's catechism is remembered, a
reply concerning military regulations. " I know of
none," said the great Duke, " more important than
closely to attend to the comfort of the soldier;
let him be well clothed, sheltered, and fed. How
should he fight, poor fellow! if he has, besides
risking his life, to struggle with unnecessary hard-
ships? Also, he must not, if it can be helped, be
exposed to the balls before he is fairly in action.
One ought to look sharp after the young officers,
and be very indulgent to the soldier." The obser-
vations as we read them, suggest the idea of
having been paraphrased freely.

King Frederic William IV. was far from being
a dull man. He did not keep his eyes closed
against the signs of the times, and he recognised,
earlier than did most of his brother monarchs, the
stirring throughout Europe of the aspirations
of the peoples for liberty. In the Prussian
character are united a love of freedom and a certain

G 2

veneration for the settled order of things which
have in every age marked the Teutonic race,
and which, by separating the aspiration for liberty
from a craze for headlong innovation, have made
the progress of liberty sure, if slow, and its ultimate triumph sounder. A desire for national
liberty is a natural concomitant of national prosperity and the universal diffusion of education.

Since 1815 the population of Prussia had swelled
from ten to sixteen millions, and its industry and resources had advanced in a still greater proportion.
With the enjoyment of peace and prosperity had
naturally grown up a general desire for free institutions, such as were observed to be enjoyed by
other countries in a similar condition of civilisation
and advancement. In Prussia education was
enforced by the State ; an educated people are a
thinking people, and to a thinking people des-
potism, however benevolent, becomes intolerable.
Frederic William felt the throes of the upheaval,
and he strove at once to allay their intensity by a
modicum of concession, and to posture as the
prominent figure on the apex of the upheaval. In
the spring of 1847 was published a royal decree,
which, with the ordinances accompanying it,
formed a Constitution after a fashion. The Provincial Diets were fused into a National Diet, with

very restricted powers; the Sovereign did not cease to be absolute. In the curious rambling speech he made at the opening of the first United Diet, the King made this, at least, clear enough. "No power on earth," said he, "will ever succeed in moving me to change the natural, and in Prussia's case the imperatively necessary relation between prince and people, into something merely conventional or constitutional; and I say once for all, that I will never suffer a written sheet of paper to force itself in, as it were, a second providence, between our Lord God in heaven and this people, to rule us with its paragraphs, and to replace by them our ancient and time-hallowed reliance on each other. If other countries find their happiness in another way than we in the way of 'manufactured and granted' constitutions, we can indeed regard their happiness with brotherly approval. But we furnish the example of a happy country whose constitution has been made, not by sheets of paper, but by the centuries, and by the exercise of an hereditary wisdom without a parallel."

Those were brave words, but Frederic William was to talk in another key ere the "centuries" had been swelled by another twelve months. The "Constitution" of 1847, such as it was, satisfied nobody. The sturdy old Absolutists looked with grave foreboding on the concession. The Liberals recognised in the new patent only the starting-point of a progress which would find its meet end in a modern constitutional monarchy. The Ultras regarded it as an obstacle in the path of their revolutionary designs, and would have been glad of its rejection.

As for Prince William, he took his seat in the Assembly of the Three Estates, and his popularity was not increased by the vigorous opposition he offered to what a Prussian writer terms " the insolent pretensions of the modern parliamentary spirit."

CHAPTER VI.

EXILE AND COMMANDER.

BEFORE the first month of 1848 had ended, the "Citizen King" had walked out of the Tuileries, France had consummated another revolution, and the Republic was established. The fire kindled in France spread far and wide; and a *sauve qui peut*, in divers fashions, set in with great severity among the sovereigns of continental Europe. Frederic William of Prussia had tried in vain to curb the storm; now he made a fine time-serving effort to ride the whirlwind. On the 13th of March a great popular meeting of Berliners, tumultuous and disorderly, clamoured loudly for reform, and gave convincing demonstration that the citizens of the capital, at all events, refused any longer to be pacified by ambiguous promises of which there had been so scanty fulfilment. It was on this occasion that the first collision occurred between the military and the populace. For five days Berlin was a prey to disorder. The mob were free to work their lawless will, for the restraints attempted to be put on

their excesses were of the feeblest kind. Frederic
William was in a state of vacillation, and while he
wavered to and fro, his capital was suffering.

At length he took his resolution, if the term
can be used in relation to a person who had so little
resolution; he determined to out-trump the hand
of the agitators. On the 18th he issued a remarkable proclamation, pronouncing for the transforma-
tion of Germany from a bundle of separate states
into one great Federal whole. He pronounced for a
Pan-German parliament, for a Pan-German army, for
Pan-German laws, for the abolition of customs duties
between the states, for uniformity of currency,
weights and measures, and for liberty of the press all
over Germany. This was a large order; if it could
have been fulfilled, the unification of Germany with
the King of Prussia for its emperor would have
been accomplished thirty years in advance of the
ceremony in the Galerie des Glaces of Versailles.
But the ink of this sweeping pronunciamento was
scarcely dry ere Frederic William was to experience
a rude confirmation of the truth, that those who
aspire to sway events by the support of the democracy have to submit to become the puppets of its
will. For a moment it seemed that he had played
the winning card. On the evening of the 18th an
immense crowd of citizens had assembled in front

of the palace, to thank the monarch who had so well interpreted the popular aspirations, and loud acclamations greeted him when he came on the balcony to thank the people for their appreciation of his anxiety to meet their wishes.

But the implacable revolutionists regarded with disgust this good understanding between monarch and people, and saw their way to break it up by provoking a collision between the citizens and the troops. Half a dozen shots fired into a squadron of cavalry drawn up under the windows of the palace—the King had been a trifle distrustful of his turbulent Berliners—sufficed to raise civil strife. The cavalry moved forward to clear the square, but at a walk, with sheathed swords ; their moderation, however, was thrown away. Already barricades were being erected within sight of the palace. The infantry fired a few shots ; retaliation came in a general discharge of musketry by the mob, of which the leading spirits were the students of the university. A battalion of regulars changed sides and fought with the populace. A sanguinary conflict set in, and was stubbornly maintained. A Prussian mob is always formidable, because the whole nation has been trained to arms, and the insurgents on this occasion had among them an exceptional number of old soldiers,

who were as well versed in arms as were the troops
to whom they were opposed. The conflict lasted till
long after nightfall, carried on by the light of burning houses, which had been broken into, sacked,
and then fired. This fierce street-fire cost sixty
lives, and reduced the King to a state of abject
pusillanimity. He surrendered all along the line.
He apologised to his " beloved Berliners " for the
hostile acts of his troops; he dismissed his
ministers, and replaced them by a cabinet of known
Liberals ; he proclaimed a general amnesty for
political offences, and so released as well the persons
in custody for their share in the insurrection, as
a number of revolutionary Poles previously incar-
cerated. He rode about the streets bedecked with
the German colours, and avowed his pride in the
" powerful manifestation of public opinion " that
had made him for the time but a king at will. The
bodies of the citizens who had been killed in the
affray were paraded with great pomp before
the palace, and the King had to salute, hat in
hand, the corpses of men who had fallen in an
insurrection by the hands of the troops striking in
the cause of order. Finally he withdrew from
Berlin its garrison of regulars, and committed the
capital to the care and protection of a Burgher
Guard.

Yet another act of surrender to the mob-rule did the agitated monarch commit. His brother, the Prince of Prussia, had become the arch-object of detestation on the part of the demagogues. A known and professed supporter of absolutism, all sorts of charges were hurled against him, to some of which reference will presently be made. The windows of his residence had been broken, and repeated attempts had been made to storm it. The clamour against him surged so high that the King succumbed before it; perhaps hoping as well to make a little capital out of his compliance. On the morning of the 19th William was ordered to quit Berlin within twenty-four hours, and to leave the kingdom as early as possible. The same night the Prince went to Potsdam, where he spent with his family a few days, one of which was his birth-day. It was scarcely a pleasant present his royal brother sent him, in the official announcement of his impending departure for England. But William was not a man given to murmuring; he made no remonstrance against the banishment imposed on him in deference to the clamour of the mob, and on the 27th he arrived in England, having travelled to Hamburg, and made the voyage thence as a passenger in that honest old tub the *John Bull* steamer.

Later Prussian writers are extremely solicitous to exonerate William from any share in the military dispositions during that stormy week of the " Red Year." Why they should take so much trouble is scarcely apparent. Both as a soldier, and as the first subject of the realm, it would have consisted with his duty to have done his utmost to combat anarchy. Prussian officers whose names became distinguished in the annals of Prussian wars, were actively concerned in the course of their duty in the attempts to thwart the lawlessness of the Berlin mob. Manteuffel bade the cavalry charge, Steinmetz led his battalion to attack the people, Vogel von Falckenstein was wounded in the affray. None of these men shirked the acknowledgment of having performed acts of simple duty, or were thought the worse of afterwards, because they had been true to their soldier-oath. If William had been in command of the Guard Corps when the disturbances occurred, it may be taken for granted that he would not have asked himself twice whether he should strike, and strike hard, in the cause of order. But as it happened, he was in Berlin during the riots in a wholly unofficial capacity. As an officer he would have even thus been at the disposition of his sovereign, had that sovereign called for his services; but they were not requisitioned, and he therefore remained simply a spectator of events. Some of the charges party rancour put forth against him carried their own refutation; as for instance, that it was at his instance the prisoners taken during the street-fighting of the 18th received ill-treatment. The accusation that from his window he had, by waving his handkerchief, given the signal for the cavalry to attack the mob, fell to the ground in face of the fact that his palace was invisible from where the dragoons stood drawn up.

The Rhine provinces had caught from adjacent France the infection of anarchy, and disturbances had occurred there before they broke out in Berlin. As a man who had some experience in coping with this sort of mischief, the Prince of Prussia had been appointed to the western Governor-Generalship, with his headquarters in Cologne. Berlin was perfectly quiet when this appointment was made, and continued so on the morning of the 12th, when William, about to quit Berlin for his new sphere, bade•adieu to the officers of the Guard corps, command of which he had ceased to hold. He was still in Berlin during the week of trouble, but it was not his place to give orders to troops commanded by another, nor did he do so. Punctiliously, as some might hold, over punctiliously, he had even in emergency and when urgently applied to, resolutely refused to intervene. On the evening of the 18th, an officer, who saw how important it was that the Frederic Bridge should be held against the raging populace, and who had in vain addressed himself to the Governor of Berlin and to the minister of war, made an appeal to William to order a detachment on the service. He would not budge from his attitude of non-interference. " You are right," said he, " the bridge ought to be held, but I cannot give you the order." Rightly or wrongly, he would not go one hair's-breadth outside the line of strictest duty. Yet if he had swept the Berliners off the Linden with grape-shot, and slivered half a dozen pursy burghers with his own sword, he could not have been more fiercely vituperated.

The scapegoat of monarchy *in extremis* betook himself to England; his previous study of her free institutions had brought forth no visible fruit. He came on this later visit to find them stable and sure, while all over Europe the pillars of absolutism were toppling headlong. On the morning of March 27th, at eight o'clock, the Prince arrived quite unexpectedly at the Prussian Legation in Carlton House Terrace. No intimation of his intended visit had been given, though the newspapers had announced his departure from distracted Berlin two days previously. The Prince waited on Queen Victoria at Buckingham Palace—he was the bearer of a communication to her from his brother—but did not see her, for Princess Louise had been born on Berlin's " bloody day." Visits of ceremony were paid him by the Prince Consort, the Duke of Cambridge, the ambassadors of the European powers, and by the Duke of Wellington, who paid him the compliment of wearing a Prussian uniform. His advent rather disorganised the domestic arrangements of the Bunsens, for he consented to take up his residence in the Legation, and it was turned upside down to furnish him with fit accommodation. Members of the family were billeted out in all directions, and the only inmate who remained besides the minister and his wife was the first secretary, Count Lowenstein. The baroness writes, two days after William's arrival :—

" I think all the business of accommodating the Prince has been well got through ; if on the one hand one has trouble, on the other hand one is saved trouble; for of course no visitors are let in, and thus we can remain quiet. We had sent out invitations for a series of Tuesday receptions, and intimations putting these off had to be hurriedly sent out. The Prince to-day dines with the Duke of Cambridge.

He came to breakfast with us all at ten o'clock, and
was very amiable. F. had fetched an arm-chair,
but the Prince put it away and took another, saying,
'One ought to be humble now, for thrones are
shaking.' One longs to perceive how a bridge can
be constructed for his return home. He expresses
much concern and scruple for the trouble he occasions, but now that the arrangement has been
made, it is infinitely preferable that he should be
here, rather than his having to hire a place of
abode."

At the dinner-parties which the Bunsens gave
in honour of the Prince, we are told that "he was
censé to receive the guests himself," the house of the
Prussian Legation being, in the first place, his
residence. The 10th of April was the day on
which occurred what was to have been the great
Chartist demonstration. Bunsen, at Lady Palmerston's on the previous Saturday night, had
brought his Prince up to the Duke of Wellington,
to hear of the manner in which the victor of
Waterloo meant to cope with a demonstration
which seemed to threaten an outbreak similar to
that which had made the heir to the throne of
Prussia an exile from the Fatherland. "Your
Grace," said Bunsen, "will take us all in charge,
and London too, on Monday?" "Yes," replied

the Duke; "we have taken our measures, but not a soldier nor a piece of artillery shall you see, unless in actual need. Should the police—the force of law—be overpowered or in danger, then will come the time for the troops. But it is not fair on either side to call on them to do the work of police—the military must not be confounded with the police, nor merged in the police."

While William was having an anxious but a sociable time in England, visiting at Osborne, spending the Easter week at Strathfieldsaye, and touring through the Lake country and Scotland, strange doings were being enacted in Berlin. Over the royal palace floated no longer the black and white banner of Prussia, but the tricolor of black, red, and gold. In place of the stately Prussian Guards, portly citizens were burlesquing military duties in plain clothes and pipe in mouth. The King remained in Berlin in a species of contemptuous toleration, as a sort of tap through which to draw concessions to democracy. But the nation was beginning to show that Berlin is not to Prussia what Paris is to France. That the provinces were not in full accord with the capital was first manifested with respect to the exiled Prince of Prussia. Berlin maintained all its virulence against him; and his name was expunged from the Liturgy

H

in the metropolitan churches.   But in the provinces, where he was best known, a clamour arose
for his return.   Pomerania urgently petitioned;
the West Prussians grimly threatened to lay Berlin
in ashes if he were not back by the end of May.
A song had been written in his honour, which was
sung in every barrack-room.   The minister Camp-
hausen advised the King to recall his brother.
When this became known, Berlin raged furiously;
the walls were placarded with vituperative hand-
bills.   Twelve thousand Berliners massed in the
Thiergarten and marched down the Linden in
procession, to inform the minister that the people
would not consent to the Prince's return.   But he
was sent for all the same.   In truth, the impression
was dawning that men of his stamp would soon be
wanted in Prussia.

The recall reached him on the 27th May, and
he started at once, escorted to the coast by his host
the minister, whom and the Baroness Bunsen he
had "thanked most kindly and touchingly for
kindness received."   The Prince's parting words
were that "in no other place or country could he
have passed so well the period of distress and
anxiety which he had gone through, having found
so much to interest his mind both in the country
and in the nation."   He is described as having

bestowed close study on the principles and working of the British constitution. Wherever he went during his short two months' stay in London, his manly frankness and unaffected courtesy created a most favourable impression. The Baroness Bunsen speaks enthusiastically of the manner in which services were acknowledged as " kindness," which were but the fulfilment of bounden duty; and of "the dignity, the cheerfulness, the gracious kindness, the constant regard for others' convenience, which marked from first to last the Prince's demeanour." He did not hurry in his journey; awaiting instructions and answers to letters at various points *en route*.

The King, on the 22nd, had opened the first session of the new National Assembly—a parliament whose members were elected on the household franchise suffrage, so swiftly had reform marched in Prussia—and had submitted to it a constitutional programme which was broad enough to have satisfied all honest aspirants for real freedom. In a letter written to his brother on his way through Brussels, William, with a certain dryness, accepted the new departure. "I beg," he wrote, " respectfully to inform your Majesty that, in accordance with the commands imparted to me, I have quitted London and am at present on the Continent. I deem this a

H 2

most opportune moment for giving renewed expression to the sentiments, already well known to your Majesty, with which I return to my native country. I venture to hope that the free institutions, to found which still more firmly your Majesty has convoked the representatives of the people, will, with God's gracious aid, become more and more developed to the benefit of Prussia. I will devote all my powers sincerely and faithfully to this development, and look forward to the time when I shall accord to the Constitution, about to be promulgated after conscientious consultation between your Majesty and your people, such recognition as shall be prescribed to the Heir-Apparent by constitutional charter."

A few days later his arrival at Wesel was greeted by an enthusiastic public reception, to which he responded under the influence of great emotion. "It is painful," said he, "to be misunderstood. A clear conscience only has carried me through this sad time, now ended; and it is with a clear conscience that I return to my country. I have always hoped that the day of truth would dawn—and it has dawned. Many things have been changed in our native land. The King has willed this: the King's will is sacred to me. I am the first of his subjects, and I honestly acquiesce in the new order of things.   But right, order, and law must have sway, not anarchy—against this shall I struggle with all my might.   That is my calling in life.   Whoever has known me, has known how ardently I have loved my country."

It was to a strange Berlin that William returned on the 8th June.   There was no Court, for the King had gone to Potsdam out of the turmoil. Most of the great houses on the Linden were empty, and a private carriage was seldom seen, for all the gentry had quitted the distracted city.   At the street-corners popular democrats with strident voices expounded the principles of democracy to noisy crowds.   "Flying booksellers" ran about crying broad-sheet manifestoes, put forth by the leaders of the popular movement.   "How melancholy does Berlin now appear to me!" cried Wrangel, returning in September from Sleswig-Holstein.   "Grass is growing in your streets; your houses are empty; your shops are full of goods, but there are no purchasers; your industrious citizens are without work, without wages, without profits."   It was through a capital in this plight that William, accompanied by a single aide-de-camp, drove to the Opera-house, where the National Assembly was in noisy session.   He might be unpopular in Berlin, but a constituency in Prussian Poland had returned him to Parliament by a sweeping majority, and he was on his way to take his seat, as his first act on returning to the city from which mob-clamour had ejected him. At the sight of him, and of the Prussian uniform so detested by the revolutionists—for William was a soldier, and had not truckled to dress himself in civilian attire—the serried benches of the Left greeted him with vehement hissing. They ostentatiously kept their seats—those gentlemen of the Left; the Right was but a handful, but it rose in a body to show respect to the heir to the Crown. A vehement radical had possession of the floor, and kept it obstructively in the face of the House's anxiety to hear the Prince of Prussia, who quietly waited until Herr Temme had talked himself out. Then the Speaker announced that " the member for Wirsitz desired to speak on a personal matter," and the Prince rose. He had not the discursive fluency of his brother; when it seemed to William that he had anything to say, it was his way to liberate his mind in the fewest words that would express his meaning. On this occasion he simply said that he had come to declare his honest and loyal acceptance of a Constitutional Government, since the King had thought fit to adopt that form of rule; and expressed the hope that the new legislative body would act steadfastly on the grand old Prussian motto, " With God, for King and Father-land." The feeble Right cheered him vociferously ; the democratic Left responded to his utterances in hisses and hootings. Having said what he came to say, William left the National Assembly to its devices, and went away to Potsdam to live there in seclusion with the family to whom he had come back from exile.

In Berlin things went from bad to worse. Cabinet succeeded cabinet, only to go down before the factious violence of the Assembly. A few days after William had taken his seat, a mob attacked the arsenal, overpowered the feeble resistance offered by the Burgher Guard, stormed the place, and pillaged the immense stores of arms which it contained. It may be assumed that William did not hesitate to express his opinion on the state of affairs, and to make suggestions of a remedial character. For the moment not much could be done, for divers reasons ; but the armistice of August placed at the King's disposition some thirty thousand staunch troops who, under Wran-gel, had been engaged in Sleswig in a rehearsal of the campaign of 1864. They and other troops were concentrated in the vicinity of Berlin ; and the military command in the Marches of

Brandenburg having been entrusted to Wrangel, that plain-spoken old fighting-man lost no time in informing the Berliners that any attempt at insubordination or sedition would find in him a stern and uncompromising opponent. He spoke his mind in a series of jerky sentences: "I shall re-establish order when it is disturbed, and support the laws when they are infringed. Should the Burgher Guard fail to keep order, we will enter; and we will succeed. My troops are staunch; their swords are sharp and their muskets loaded. . . . No reaction, but to protect liberty; for the laws and for freedom."

The Berliners were stiff-necked, and took no heed of Wrangel's warning. Law and order were in abeyance; the working classes were idle and starving; the jails had been thrown open, and 8,000 convicts were at large. The rabble joined in desperate attempts to destroy machinery; barricades were erected and lives lost. Parliament amused itself in passing resolutions abolishing the nobility and declaring universal equality; yet it did not move fast enough for the revolutionary mob, who broke in upon its deliberations, carrying ropes and nails for the encouragement of the Conservative members by the summary argument of hanging them. It was evident that a new revolution was

imminent, in which the throne and the constitution
would alike be overthrown, and a republic established on their ruins. Frederic William, strenuously
counselled, was stirred to decisive action. A Conservative Government was formed, with a resolute
nobleman at its head, who promptly served on the
Parliament a royal decree, transferring its place of
meeting from the capital to Brandenburg, and
meanwhile suspending its deliberations.

The Assembly, by its majority, vehemently protested against this edict, and resolved to remain in
Berlin and sit in permanence. A detachment of
thirty gallantly remained in session all night.
When the members who had slept at home began
to arrive in the morning, they found the building
surrounded by regular troops, with Wrangel in command. Asked how long he intended to maintain the
cordon, he replied : " For a week, if necessary ; my
troops are accustomed to bivouac. Anybody is
free to withdraw, but none shall enter." The
Assembly evacuated the Opera-house under pro-
test, and met in another place, protected by the
Burgher Guard in great strength, and applauded by
the mob for their firmness. A royal proclamation
dissolved the Burgher Guard, thirty thousand
regular troops were marched into the capital, and a
state of siege was declared. Military officers entered

the hall where the Assembly was sitting, and summoned it to disperse as an illegal gathering. A violent refusal being given to the demand, the officers picked up the Speaker, chair and all, carried him out and set him down in the street. Another meeting held by it elsewhere was dispersed by the military, and when the Left threatened to go to Brandenburg and swamp the Conservative minority, the King turned the flank of the revolutionists by dissolving the Assembly altogether. The crisis was over, although it was long ere Berlin recovered from the spasm of anarchy and distraction it had undergone. A considerably modified constitution was presently accorded, which underwent further restrictions before the termination of Frederic William's reign.

This is scarcely the place for the review of the political condition of Germany at this epoch of upheaval and fermentation. Of the " Vor-Parliament " and its lusty outcome the Frankfort Assembly, of the latter's fair promise and its ultimate ignominious collapse on the mandate of the Würtemburg police-sergeant, nothing can here be said ; yet the reflection may be permitted by how narrow a chance was baulked then the achievement of German unity, while as yet the statesman who on the daïs of the Galerie des Glaces watched the triumphant crowning of the edifice he had built up with craft and blood, was but an obscure Brandenburg squire. " Do not," said the wise Welcker, at the great Liberal meeting at Heidelberg, " do not mistake liberty for license, nor suppose that because much must be remodelled, all must be overturned." If the Frankfort Assembly had but acted on that good counsel, if the violence of the revolutionist element in that body had not alienated the support of men who discriminated between license and liberty, the great work might have been accomplished while the man who twenty-two years later was to be the first German Emperor was living in his quiet Babelsberg seclusion. As things turned out, it befell him to stamp out the final flash of revolutionary anarchy into which the proletariat blazed up.

In May 1849, Baden and the Palatinate rushed into arms against constituted authority. The Grand Duke was a fugitive from Carlsruhe ; the Duchy had a ministry of revolutionists, and a revolutionary provisional government was set up in the capital of the Palatinate. The crisis demanded energetic action, and Prussia sent to co-operate with the troops of the Confederation, an army in command of which was placed the Prince of Prussia, with Count von der Groeben and Von Hirschfeld as his corps' commanders. After the battle of

Grossachsen, the supreme command of the combined operations was vested in the Prince. He acted with prompt vigour.

He had left Berlin on the 10th of June, on the 14th he was in the Palatinate, and fought a victorious action at Kirchheim Bolanden. Next day his troops stormed the Rhine-shore entrenchments of Ludwigshafen, opposite to Mannheim. From Newstadt, where he quartered on the 19th, William swept the Palatinate clean of insurgents, followed them across the Rhine, and narrowly missed cutting off the Baden insurrectionary army under Mieroslawski, on whose flank he came at Waaghäusel, while close locked in command with Hannehen's small division. Giving the insurgents no rest, he struck them again at Upstadt on the 23rd, stormed their entrenched position at Durlach on the 25th, and on the same day entered Carlsruhe, the capital of the Grand Duchy. Mieroslawski and Sigel withdrew their discomfited bands to the hill country of the Black Forest, whither they were followed by the Prince, and utterly dispersed. Part of the insurgents had thrown themselves into the fortress of Rastadt, which they continued to hold for nearly a month. The place was strong and well found in artillery and ammunition, and the heterogeneous crowd of men of all

nations that made up the garrison were of the
desperado stamp.

The Prince was humanely anxious to spare
his own troops, nor had he the desire to push
matters to extremities with the misguided garrison, mostly mere tools in the hands of their
officers. His proposal that two officers from the
defenders of Rastadt should visit the Black Forest
and the Swiss frontier, to satisfy themselves of
the dissolution of the insurgent field army, was
accepted. One of the officers who made this excursion was a Colonel Corvin, a soldier of fortune,
whose autobiography reads like a romance. Satisfied that relief was out of the question, Corvin
strove hard to make terms for the foreigners, but
surrender at discretion was insisted on. His Royal
Highness witnessed the march out of the garrison
on the 23rd of July. There is at Babelsberg a
twenty-four pound shell, from which he had a
narrow escape in the course of a reconnaissance of
Rastadt, and his quarters at Château Favorite were
within range of the fortress artillery.

Hard measure was meted out to the officers of
the Rastadt garrison, many of whom were shot by
sentence of court-martial. Arrangements had been
made to exempt the Prince from the disagreeable
necessity—all the more disagreeable to him as the

successor to the throne—of refusing the numerous
applications for mercy with which he was certain to
be assailed, by the devolution upon one of the
army corps' commanders of the duty of dealing
with the sentences of courts-martial on Prussian
subjects. Corvin grumbles in print at having been
subjected to what he considers the ignominy of
imprisonment in the house of correction, instead of
having been shot like a gentleman. His mother
wrote to the Prince begging for his intercession
with the Grand Duke of Baden on behalf of her
son, and William's reply is too characteristic not to
be quoted: " Though you avail yourself of the
accident which threatened my person to appeal to
my sympathy for your sorrow as the mother of a
son who has strayed from the right path, it was
not necessary to do so in order to move this emotion
in me. So much the more painful, then, is it for
me to be unable to support your request to the
Grand Duke of Baden, for the commutation of
your son's sentence to banishment. This reply
will be comprehensible to you when you reflect
that I saw my soldiers fall and bleed before insurgents commanded by your son. Perhaps misled,
he was one of those who continued the contest with
bitter obstinacy, and his return from exile to renew
it is not impossible. May God assist you, my

lady, in enduring your hard fate with patience. He does not send us any more than we are able to bear by submission to His will."

It was scarcely a campaign in which much renown was to be earned, but to William belongs the credit of having conducted it in a soldierly manner, and he certainly deserved the order *pour le mérite* which his brother sent him. He was home in Babelsberg by the middle of October.

There was little incident worth noting in the life of the Prince of Prussia for the next seven years. In the beginning of 1851 he paid a short visit to his sister in St. Petersburg, and in May of the same year came to England for Prince Arthur's christening, one of whose godfathers he was. In May, 1851, he superintended the solemn dedication of the monument to Frederic the Great, which had been curiously slow in finishing. In 1853 he was in England again, present at the review held by the Queen of the troops that were in Chobham camp, and at the naval review off Spithead. In February, 1854, he was raised to the rank of field-marshal; and in June of the same year celebrated his silver wedding. In 1855 he presided over the Military Commission which settled the adoption of the needle-gun as the weapon of the German infantry—it had been used to a considerable extent

in the Baden insurrection with good results.   The
1st of January, 1857, was the half-century military
jubilee of his Royal Highness, in honour of which
occasion Queen Victoria sent him the Grand Cross
of the Bath by the hands of a worthy bearer, Sir
Colin Campbell, afterwards Lord Clyde.   In the
summer of 1857 the Prince made the acquaintance
at Baden of Napoleon III., and we read of him in
September of that year sitting resignedly at the
reception by the King of the Evangelical Alliance,
which was attended by " lots of Americans, Scotch,
Australians, Hungarians, &c."   William's longevity
proves how tough was his constitution, but his
brother, the King, promptly succumbed to softening
of the brain.

CHAPTER VII.

KING WILLIAM AND THE NEW ARMY.

KING FREDERIC WILLIAM IV., never a man of strong head, had for years been growing weaker and more eccentric. The tragic events of 1848 had severely shaken his never very strong nerves. In 1850 his vacillation and feebleness had entailed on Prussia the humiliation which culminated in the Olmütz "capitulation," and in his latter years of comparative sanity the influence of the " pietistic " party had been gaining more and more hold upon him. He was a well-meaning man, and there is no evidence that there was any foundation for the insinuation conveyed in the nickname of " King Clicquot " which *Punch* fastened upon him ; but as was said of Lord John Russell, " he was not strong enough for the place." In the early part of 1857, symptoms of softening of the brain began to show themselves. That disorder so developed itself that in October, 1857, he gave a delegation to the Prince of Prussia to act as regent ; but the first commission was only for three months. Queen Elizabeth stood out as long as possible against the

I

constitution of a permanent regency, and the
Prince's temporary commission was renewed from
time to time; but it soon became apparent that
Frederic William's case was hopeless, and his
brother was formally installed as Regent in October,
1858. Ultimately the King died in January, 1861,
and his brother succeeded to the throne as William I.

In the popular mind there had been a wonderful
reaction in favour of the Prince from the fierce
rancour against him of the " Red Year." It had
come to be believed that if he were a champion of
the rights of the Crown, he was at any rate no ex-
tremist. It was in his favour, too, with the masses
that his election as Regent should have been met
with opposition by the aristocratic and pietistic
faction, of which the Queen was a partisan, and to
whose influence had been ascribed the later obnoxious policy of King Frederic William, with which
the Prince of Prussia was supposed not to be in
accord. The Manteuffel cabinet quitted office, and
the Regent replaced it by a ministry of so-
called Old Liberals, under the leadership of his
connection and friend Prince Charles Anton of
Hohenzollern and Baron Rudolph von Auerswald.
" Old Liberal," in this connection, was equivalent
to what we know as " Conservative," in contradis-
tinction to bigoted obstructive and reactionary

"Old Toryism."   But the Regent was not the kind
of man to accept a popularity springing out of
erroneous assumptions.   He was a man of indomitable resolution, or as others have phrased it, of "un-
conquerable obstinacy;" his honesty was thorough
as his firmness was unflinching; and he thought it
the straightforward line to take, to define his attitude on the threshold of his new sphere.   The
result of the elections was much in favour of the
Progressist party.   Progressist majority or not,
William was determined there should be no mistake
about the policy he meant to stand or fall by; and
in his address at the opening of the Chambers he
roundly laid it down that he "never could permit
the progressive development of the nation's inner
political life to question or endanger the rights of
the Crown or the power of Prussia."

Such were the new ruler's principles, from
which alike, through bad report and through good
report, neither hostility nor popularity ever caused
him to deviate one jot.   "For King and Fatherland;" yes, and for the Constitution afterwards,
if it would persist in claiming attention.   Fatherland and Constitution had no affinity in the sight
of the resolute old patriot, who did so much for
the former and so little for the latter.   If in those
early days of fine curt frankness he already looked

down the vista of the strange improbable future
that was to be, and had in his mind the mighty
projects whereby he was to make the Fatherland
so prosperous and glorious as to beguile its children
from caring any more, at least for the time, about
that Constitution in hostility to which he lived
and died, what a superb faith had he in the nation
and in himself! But if again the future, did he
care to look into it, was blank and misty, he was
a yet braver man, thus unwitting of expedient to
stand upright and defiant in the path of a great
popular movement. In either case, he was a
champion; in the former he meant to risk the
leadership of a forlorn hope for the sake of victory;
in the latter, he was either bat-blind or prepared
to die in his ditch rather than quit it.

Because of the imposing personality of his
great servant Bismarck, the impression has long
been all but universal, that William was only the
figure-head of the ship at the helm of which stood
Bismarck, subtle, wily, shrewd, cynical, and unscrupulous. Probably how much Bismarck has
done for William no man will ever know, for the
dead are not garrulous, and the living has a certain
modified sense of decency. But it is not easy to
deny, whether or not William consciously worked
toward the great enterprise which the political

strategy of Bismarck crowned with success, that as Bismarck certainly did a great deal for him, he at the least did much for Bismarck.   The shrewdest diplomatist has a bad and bitter time of it when the pourparlers become significantly abrupt, and he is the representative of a state that cannot fight.   It is all very well to enunciate a policy of " blood and iron," but these cheerful persuasives involve the control of a great and thoroughly effective army. The needle gun it was that achieved the United Germany, and William it was to whom Prussia and Germany owe all which armed strength, tipping the arrow of Bismarck's shrewd statecraft, has wrought on their behalf.

William had long recognised the slow deca- dence of the army which had conquered at Hohen- friedberg and Rossbach, and fairly divided the laurels of Waterloo.   Like his father, he was a soldier; but unlike his father, he was not a mili- tary pedant.   It was as he lay on his death-bed, while the Guards were marching past the palace, that the old King anxiously said to his son, " I hope the companies are following each other in proper numerical order."   It may be said with hardly a strain of the fact, that assured this was so, he died contentedly.   William was the stamp of soldier to whom it was a matter of moment

indeed that the companies of a battalion should
march past in correct sequence ; but this he did not
regard as a conclusion, but as an illustration.
Once and again he had seen his country humiliated
because her sword was rusty in the scabbard. He
knew that Austria would not have dared to put on
Prussia the affront of Olmütz, but that Austria
was aware Prussia was in no condition to resent
the indignity. A man need have neither ambition
nor visions to recognise when his country is slighted
because its army has degenerated. Since William
had obtained high rank in the Prussian army, it
had been found expedient three times to order its
partial mobilisation, and each time graver and yet
graver defects in the system had manifested themselves. Almost as soon as he accepted the reins
as regent, yet further evidence of the unsatisfactory condition of the army was urgently forced
on him by events. When in 1859 Austria was
hard pressed in the Italian campaign, with France
and Sardinia as her adversaries, the Regent was
disposed to afford her succour by an armed diversion
on the Rhine, and the Prussian army was again
mobilised. Francis Joseph preferred to submit to
the harsh terms of Villafranca, rather than con-
cede that William should have the command of
the forces which the Germanic Confederation

proposed to send into the field. Probably it was
fortunate for Prussia that she did not then come
into collision with France; Bismarck held that she
was arming herself too soon. The mobilisation of
1859 revealed more than ever the irremediable
defects of the old military system which had stood
Prussia in so good stead forty-five years earlier,
but which in the altered conditions of more modern
warfare imperatively called for sweeping reformation.

It had been one of the wise acts of the Prince
of Prussia to surround himself with officers whose
capacity had become apparent to him in the course
of his professional duties. Among those were
Moltke, who in 1858 had been made chief of the
general staff, and who in that capacity had prepared a plan of campaign in the event of the Germanic Confederation having struck in for Austria
in 1859; his own nephew Prince Frederic Charles,
Manteuffel, Vogel von Falckenstein, Hindersin, and
the singularly shrewd and clear-headed Roon.
The last had devoted much thought to the defects
of the then existing military organisation, and
there is reason to believe that the Prince Regent
had desired him to prepare a scheme for its amendment. This much is certain, that a plan based on a
memoir submitted by General Roon was adopted, and

Roon himself named war minister and charged with the arduous task of carrying it into practical effect.

The Prussian army as reformed by William on the lines laid down and carried out by Roon, is so interwoven with the story of the most momentous period of the former's life, that it is necessary to go into some detail concerning it. Three great principles characterised the military organisation by which in so short a time Scharnhorst had created a great army for the needs of Prussia in her time of strait; and which was definitely and permanently adopted on the conclusion of the War of Liberation. Those three principles were: short service, universal obligatory service, and territorial service. The last gave at once economy and convenience. The two first afforded the potentiality of having a large force available for war without the necessity of maintaining a great standing army. Prussia managed her army matters, as, indeed, to a great extent, she still does, on the same advantageous footing that a commercial company works, which has but a small capital on which dividend is payable, but large financial resources from debenture loans and money deposited. She was poor, and her population was small, but she claimed to be a first class power, and had to act up to her

pretensions.   Her wealthy and more populous com-
peers kept up large standing professional armies;
this for lack at once of men and money, Prussia
could not afford to do.   Her expedient was to utilise
her population in the double capacity of soldiers and
of civilians.   She took up annually 40,000 recruits,
who served with the colours three years, and afterwards two more in the reserve. So her standing army,
not reckoning officers and permanent organisation—
about 20,000 in all—amounted to 120,000 men,
and by calling up the reserves, could be immediately
raised to 200,000.   But to keep her place with the
other powers, it was requisite that her army should
be about 500,000 strong; so the reserves when they
had completed their two years' service as such, became Landwehrmen of the first levy for seven years,
affording a further instalment of 160,000 more;
and those seven years completed, passed for five
years more into the Landwehr of the second levy,
affording yet another contingent of about 140,000,
which brought up the grand total to about 500,000
men, of whom less than one-fourth during peace
were actually present with the colours, drawing
pay, and withdrawn from the civilian community.
This, in contrast with the large standing army
and no reserve system of the other States, was
a kind of military thimble-rig on a grand scale.

The device worked well when the nation, with one mind, was eager to rush to arms against Napoleon. But the impetus of national enthusiasm is not always to be relied upon. Subsequent mobilisations showed the Landwehr obeying un- willingly the summons to turn out; their discipline was not always satisfactory, nor did they without exception acquit themselves creditably in action. The old system involved other disadvantages. Under it the Landwehr, constituting about one half the field army, took some time to be embodied, and after embodiment were found to require a short preliminary training before being in a proper condition for active service. And thus there oc- curred delay which was found detrimental to the chances of military success in an era when short, sharp, and decisive wars had begun to be rendered possible by the increased facilities of transport. Some minor reforms had been instituted in 1850, 1852, and 1853, but those were merely in details. King Frederic William acknowledged that more heroic changes were needed, but he had not force of character to take action.

The reorganisation into which William threw himself with all his energy as soon as he had a free hand, and for which, not Prussia alone, but all Germany owes him so much, was no revolution.

Scharnhorst's principles were devoutly respected in the spirit. The double aim of the reforms was to increase the armed strength of the country, and to make that armed strength more quickly available. Since 1815 the population of Prussia had increased from ten millions to eighteen millions, but the annual contingent of recruits remained at 40,000. As the increase swelled, a larger and yet larger proportion of the young men remained unsubjected to military training in the first instance, and free from liability to be called up on mobilisation in the second, since the reserves and Landwehr consisted exclusively of men who had been three years with the colours. Thus, two evils arose; the principle of universal training and service was more and more infringed in practice, and an excessive liability to be called on for the national defence was thrown on a mere proportion of the population—that proportion consisting solely of those who had formed the annual contingents of 40,000 each. As the population of the kingdom had increased, so in almost direct ratio had its revenue swelled from fifty million to ninety-three million thalers; so that there were legitimately available means to justify an increase of the military expenditure.

At one stroke the annual contingent of

recruits was raised from 40,000 to 63,000; an increase which, as it took effect, increased the numerical strength of Prussia's standing army, including officers, &c., to 217,000; and permitted its augmentation by 117 infantry battalions, 10 regiments of cavalry, 31 companies of artillery, and 18 of engineers. The increase inflicted no added strain either on the population or the revenue. The army of 1814 withdrew for the time from civil avocations $1\frac{1}{4}$ per cent. of the country's population; the " bigger battalions " called into existence by William demanded scarcely so large a percentage. The army of 1814 had cost 35 per cent. of the current national revenue. When the strengthened army under the reorganisation had attained virtual completion on the eve of the war of 1866, William's " bloated armament" absorbed only 29 per cent. of the kingdom's revenue.

But the reorganisation plan embraced a reform which, in seeming paradox, relieved the nation from military strain, roughly in proportion to the augmentation of its military strength; and this, notwithstanding that the army of Prussia was a national, as contradistinguished from a professional army. Under the old dispensation, the Landwehrman stood almost close behind the small standing army, with nothing between him and it save the

80,000 reserve men. Even a partial mobilisation tore him from his home, and a petty campaign sent him into the field of battle. Thus the Landwehrman lived on the constant knife-edge of unsettled perturbation until the period of his liability had expired. But under the new dispensation, the fetters of his military obligations galled him infinitely less. There was now a multiplicity of buffer between him and the fear lest war should make his wife a widow and his children fatherless. First there was the standing army in augmented strength; then the new scheme lengthened the term of service in the reserve from two to four years, so that instead of two tiers of reserve men in front of him, he had now four. The Landwehrman was still liable for service as well beyond as within the confines of his country; but it would thenceforward be only in a great war that he would find himself in the forefront of the battle. As a rule, he was to do garrison work and guard the lines of communication. He was not mobilised at all in the Danish campaign. He was extensively called out in the Seven Weeks' War, but of the 260,000 Prussians who stood on the field of Königgrätz, not 27,000 were Landwehrmen. Under the old disposition of a fighting force of that strength, could it have been mustered, one-half at least would have been Landwehrmen.

The elastic efficiency of Scharnhorst's system stands out more and more triumphantly indicated as the years roll on. Almost every nation in Europe—certainly every wise nation in Europe—has adopted its leading principles, as well as the improvements devised by Roon and carried into execution under William. In virtue of the Prussian military system, the armed strength of United Germany constitutes to-day the most puissant force which the world has ever seen. The army of Prussia consisted of eight army corps when that State engaged in the war of 1866. That war brought about the North German Confederation, with an army of thirteen and a half army corps—made up of the Prussian guard, eleven Prussian territorial army corps to which were attached the contingents of the smaller States of the Confederation, the Royal Saxon army corps, and the division furnished by the Grand Duchy of Hesse-Darmstadt. The Franco-German war brought about the German Empire and the disruption from France of Alsace-Lorraine; and the army of the empire now consists of nineteen army corps. In peace time its numerical strength is but 430,000 men. Mobilisation of the reserves raises that strength to one million of fighting men, and such is the perfection of arrangement and system, that this stupendous increment can be fully attained throughout the whole empire in the space of eight days from the issue of the order. Behind the reserves are ready at call 500,000 Landwehrmen, and at the back of the Landwehr again stands the Landsturm, the last final buttress of the German military edifice.

At the opening of the session of the Prussian Parliament in January, 1860, the Prince Regent spoke with great emphasis as to the necessity for the adoption of the scheme for the reconstruction of the army, on the accomplishment of which he had resolved. The outcome of that accomplishment, he pointed out, would be that in the future the Prussian army would be the Prussian nation in arms. The object of the measure, he declared, with a significance which stood disclosed ere many years had passed, was to assure the ability of the fatherland to cope with the vicissitudes of the future.

But the Liberal majority in the Prussian House of Commons were perverse and short-sighted. They feared the power of the Crown more than they cared for the supremacy of Prussia, or the possibility of a United Germany attainable by force of arms. The ministry were lukewarm, nor was there much more real heart in the enterprise in the nominally Conservative Government, which under Hohenlohe

had superseded the Auerswald administration.
William, who had now (Jan., 1861), succeeded to
the crown, was resolute to effect the reform.   The
attitude he had taken up when as yet regent in
regard to the sacredness of the rights of the Crown,
he had maintained at his coronation when he
crowned himself with the words, " I receive this
crown from the hands of God."   To carry out the
army reorganisation scheme in its fulness must
necessarily be the labour of years, but he had
already commenced the work, and in a solemn
ceremony performed at the foot of the statue of
Frederic the Great, the reform had received a
stately inauguration by the consecration of the
banners under which the new cohorts were to
march, and, if need arose, to fight.   But the
majority in the Second Chamber stood in his path
with a resolution only second to his own.   They
persisted in refusing to vote the budgets which
included the expenditure that the reorganisation
necessarily involved.   There were two courses open
to him in this dilemma.   He might fling aside the
flimsy robe of constitutionalism he had hitherto
worn, walk in the footsteps of Cromwell, and dis-
pensing entirely with the irritating encumbrance of
a parliament, revert to the absolutism which his
brother had surrendered as the ransom of his

throne. Or, if haply there was such a man, he might find a minister strong enough, resolute enough, unscrupulous enough perhaps, to act as a buffer between him and naked absolutism, and who should effect for him the object on which he was stiffly determined, as well without a *coup d'état* as without a revolution.

Such a man there lay to his hand in Otto von Bismarck, and him in September, 1862, William placed at the head of a new ministry, in which Roon, the mainspring of the army-reorganisation, retained the place of war minister, and carried on with steadfast and unswerving perseverance the working out of his great plan. The other members of the cabinet need not be named. They were nonentities who had to be content with the duties of departmental administration. The Minister-President was the ministry. He it was whom the task confronted of thwarting a parliamentary majority—of violating the constitution—without producing a revolution. Scarcely a less arduous duty did he assume when he accepted with the Premiership the portfolio of Foreign Secretary.

Bismarck, when he entered public life, in 1847, had liberal leanings; to the extent at least of approving of the constitution promised to Prussia by King Frederic William IV. in that year. What of

J

liberalism he began life with was soon weakened
by his realisation that the Prussian liberalism of
the period had its goal in democracy; and the wild
licence which shook throne and institutions in
1848 not only stamped out his earlier predilections,
but changed him into a staunch and unscrupulous
conservative. If it was Bismarck, and not William or events, that wrought out German unity, it is
certain that not from the first was German unity
an aspiration of Bismarck. " In the Prussian army,
as in the rest of the Prussian people," he said, in a
speech delivered in 1849, " there will be found no
longing for national regeneration. The name of
Prussia is all-sufficient for it. The accents of the
Prussian National Anthem, the strains of the
Dessau and Hohenfriedberg march are well known
and beloved among them; but I have never yet heard
a Prussian soldier sing, ' What is the German
Fatherland ? ' . . The Prussian nation does not
desire to see the Prussian realm melt away in the
filthy ferment of South German immorality. . .
We are Prussian, and Prussians we desire to
remain." As Prussian envoy to the Frankfort Diet,
all his political activity was concentrated in the task
of presenting an opposition to the anti-Prussian
policy of the Vienna cabinet, and so strong was his
disgust that Prussia did not assert herself against

Austria in 1858, when the latter's hands were full in Italy, that the Prussian ministry of the day regarded his longer stay at Frankfort as impossible, and recalled him.

William and Bismarck had met so early as 1836, at a court ball, when the latter, having passed his examination in law, was serving as an assistant in the judicial department of the Berlin police. He and a brother legal official as tall as himself, were presented to the Prince, who, looking the strapping young fellows up and down with something of the eye of his ancestor, remarked, " Well, justice seems to recruit her functionaries according to the standard of the Guards ! "

Bismarck had found favour in the eyes of King Frederic William, who conceived the idea of sending him, in 1851, to represent Prussia at the Frankfort Diet. Bismarck was quite ready for the " experiment ; " when the King rather hesitated, he struck in with the observation, " Your Majesty can surely try me ; if I prove a failure, I can be recalled in six months or sooner." So Bismarck was sent, but, till he had gained some experience, only to act as First Secretary to the Embassy, General von Rochow temporarily remaining as Envoy. In the summer of 1851 the Prince of Prussia visited Frankfort, and among the functionaries who received him was Bismarck, the prospective ambassador, in the uniform of a Landwehr lieutenant. The prince commented on the anomaly that a militia lieutenant of thirty-six should be Prussia's representative at the Bund! Von Rochow gave the Landwehr lieutenant a high character for vigour and ability; and although the Prince, with strong personal goodwill to Bismarck, still harped on his youthfulness, the apprehension disappeared under the influence of close personal intercourse. The Prince conceived a real friendship for the big lieutenant-ambassador, and a year later stood godfather to Bismarck's younger son, whom Berliners best know as "Prince Bill." Relations between William and Bismarck had become very intimate; and the latter, then Prussian ambassador to St. Petersburg, had known early in 1862 that his Majesty had it in his mind to appoint him Minister-President. He was recalled in the spring of that year, probably with the intent that he should take office at once on the resignation of the Auerswald-Schwerin ministry; but the appointment was postponed —Bismarck certainly was not eager for the promotion—and he went ambassador to Paris until called back to Berlin in September of the same year.

It was an arduous duty which, at the bidding of his sovereign, the Brandenburger Junker had undertaken. The Progressists, roughly equivalent to our Radicals, were in themselves a majority of the Lower House, and were in almost rancorous opposition to him. Of the Liberals—the Whigs of Prussia—a preponderating majority were also hostile to Bismarck. He had behind him the Conservatives, it is true, but in the Lower Chamber that party had become very feeble. Untoward conditions truly, under which to accept office with the set purpose of carrying through the King's army reorganisation measures, in the teeth of the assured determined opposition of a powerful majority, and of the fact that the nation through its elected representatives had emphatically pronounced against the project.

Bismarck began as he meant to go on, with uncompromising masterfulness. His first appearance in the House as premier (23rd September, 1862) was to inform it curtly that since the adverse vote on the military expenditure for 1862 gave no prospect that the estimates under that head for 1863 would meet with a more favourable reception, the proposed budget for the latter year would be withdrawn. Next month the Upper House rejected the Commons' amendments on the 1862 budget, and passed the Government proposals in their entirety. Two days later the session was closed with a frank and explicit declaration by the premier that the Government, seeing no prospect of carrying the Lower House with it on the budget question, recognised no other alternative than to conduct the administration of the state regardless of the absence of the parliamentary sanction of the state expenditure prescribed by the constitution. In a far more violent sense than that in which the Duke of Wellington used the phrase, Bismarck in effect said, "The King's Government must be carried on."

In the next session the reproduced budget for 1863 was duly rejected, as well as the bill introduced by Bismarck for the parliamentary approval of the army reorganisation measures. The House voted an address to the Crown, explicitly denouncing the ministry for a gross violation of the constitution in the matter of the budget. Before such a pronouncement Bismarck did not quail. He significantly informed the majority that if they insisted in their stubborn opposition to the Government measures, the issue would be that the side in whose hands lay the actual power would cut the knot in its own favour. To this all but explicit suggestion that the majority were welcome to try their strength in the direction of a revolution, the answer of the House was an address to the King, demanding the dismissal of his Government, and a return on the part of him and of his ministers to a constitutional line of action.

William had the courage of his great minister's opinions. He answered this address by promptly closing the session; and that act was closely followed by an ordinance restricting the freedom of the press. In the next session parliament maintained its unrelenting hostility to the measures of the King and his minister. It went through the now accustomed formula of rejecting the military reorganisation bill as well as the military expenditure estimates. It opposed the Government policy on the Danish war question, and declined to sanction a war loan of 2,000,000 thalers, which the Crown asked for. " No surrender," was still the motto of William and his minister. The House of Lords voted everything it was asked to vote; the loan was effected, the revenues were collected, the military disbursements were made, just as if there either existed no constitution at all, or as if the provisions of the constitution were being fulfilled *au pied de la lettre*.

The session of 1865 passed, like its predecessors, without having led in the least to the settlement

of the army question. But the triumph of the
monarch and his minister over the constitution
was approaching. The policy of doing political
evil that national good might come was, for once
at least, to stand vindicated. The parliament was
dissolved on the eve of the great war of 1866, and
the general election took place amidst the fervid
outburst of enthusiasm which the earlier victories
of the Prussian arms in that campaign stirred
throughout the Prussian nation. When the new
parliament met in August, 1866, the clamour of the
rejoicings for Sadowa was still ringing in the ears
of the new members. The King and his minister,
for the first time since they had entered on the
career of unconstitutionalism, found themselves no
longer confronted by a hostile parliamentary majority. William, strong in his divine right con-
victions, would have let the dead years bury their
dead, and begrudged to pass under the Caudine
Forks of submission to the law of the land. But
Bismarck was wiser in his generation, and persuaded his master of the expediency of an absolu-
tion. The minister made the monarch comprehend, since it was unquestionable that the free-est
liberties had been taken with the constitution in
the past, and since events had rendered it possible
for King and Government to return to the safer

routine of the constitutional path, that it was a discreet concession and precaution to ask the representatives of the people to grant an act of indemnity for the past. The conquerors in the long arduous struggle could afford to be at once considerate and politic ; all the more so since it was obvious that as there had been a past, so there would be a future. The act of indemnity extinguished the conflict of years, and gave internal quietude to a nation rejoicing in a triumphant external peace. Other times, other peoples, other outcomes. Strafford went to the scaffold, and Bismarck was the most popular subject in Prussia. It might not be seemly to point the contrast between the fates of the royal masters of the two ministers.

The act of indemnity was passed by both Houses in September, 1868, and thus terminated the most momentous internal episode of William's long reign. By dint of riding roughshod over the constitution, he had created an army so swift to muster, so effective when mustered, that while yet unperfected it had prostrated the military power of a gigantic adversary in a campaign measured by days, had wiped out the opposition of a horde of minor enemies, and had placed Prussia at a bound among the most puissant of the great military powers of Europe.　The nation had acclaimed that the grand results justified the rough and illegal methods whereby those results had been made possible.　So all were content, and lawlessness was justified of her children.

CHAPTER VIII.

THE WHETTING OF THE PRUSSIAN SWORD.

IN the preceding chapter chronological order had to be violated for the sake of recording without a break the progress of the development of Prussia's reorganised army, the weapon which in conjunction with William's strong will and Bismarck's diplomacy carved out the achievement of German unity. It is now necessary to revert to William's accession to the throne of Prussia, and briefly sketch the events of his reign and life which preceded the "Seven Weeks' War."

William began his reign by asserting the royal prerogative in relation to the army. He decreed that it was no longer necessary that the royal orders respecting military matters needed to be countersigned by the war minister, thus denuding that functionary of any discretionary status. In February, 1861, the month after his accession, a special British Embassy was sent to Berlin charged with the duty of investing his Majesty with the

Order of the Garter. The ceremony of investiture
was held in the palace. There was a difficulty as
to the dress the King should wear on the occasion.
It was contrary to the order of things that the
garter should be fastened on a trowsered leg; but
there was no Prussian uniform of which knee-
breeches formed a part. The King resuscitated for
the ceremony the old ball uniform of the gardes
du corps, and was invested with the garter attired
in a red dress-coat, white knee-breeches, and white
silk stockings. Another dress problem confronted
him when, in September of the same year, he went
to Compiègne on a visit to the Emperor Napoleon.
During his stay there a parade was held of the
Zouaves in garrison at Compiègne, which the easy-
going French Emperor professed his intention of
witnessing in civilian attire. To wear mufti on a
military occasion was heresy in William's eyes—
indeed, except during his visits to watering-places,
few people save his valet ever saw him out of
uniform. But to wear uniform when his imperial
host was in plain clothes would have implied a
rebuke to the latter, and so William, for the only
time in all his long life, had to appear on a parade
ground in a black coat and a tall hat. Sedan was
avenged in anticipation.

The King went in the teeth of almost universal

public opinion in carrying out his resolve to celebrate the ceremony of his coronation. No Prussian
king since Frederic the First, Carlyle's "expen-
sive Herr," had ever been crowned; a coronation
had uniformly been regarded as a useless piece of
costliness. But William held that since his brother
in granting Prussia a constitution had seemed to
diminish the prestige of the kingly power, the
ceremony of a coronation afforded him a fitting
opportunity for making it manifest to the nation
that he refused to consider the kingship weakened
in its masterful prerogative. He went to Königsberg days before the ceremony, and in his methodical painstaking way, saw himself to all the arrangements for it. Thus on the margin of the specifica-
tion for the height of a balustrade to enclose the
stand to be constructed for the accommodation of
military officers, his Majesty wrote in his own
hand, "Lower; if I invite officers of my army to
be witnesses of a solemn act, they must be able to
see something." So, when the day before the
coronation the stage outside the royal apartments,
on which had been arranged all the representative
colours of the army, suddenly fell with a great
crash and brought down the colours *péle-méle* in
its ruin, William quietly ordered the standards to
be picked up and ranged in the coronation room

about the throne, forbidding the accident to be
spoken of " as it might give disquietude to many
very worthy people."

The ceremony was held in the chapel of the
castle of Königsberg on the 18th of October.
While the blessing was being invoked, the King
held high and firm the naked sword of Prussia
that had been tendered him by Count von
Brünneck, the chief burggraf of the kingdom.
Then with his own hands he lifted the crown from
off the altar, and set it on his head, saying in a loud
voice, " I receive this crown from God's hand, and
from none other!"—significant words which scarcely
tended to increase William's popularity among his
subjects. A few months before his life had been
attempted at Baden Baden by Oscar Becker, who
coolly pleaded amidst no little sympathy his
intense German patriotism as his justification.
Becker, however, found the plea less practically
effective in his case, than had the would-be
assassin who shot at William between Mayence
and Creuznach, when the Prince was on his way to
deal with the Baden insurrection. The latter self-
asserted " patriot " was duly acquitted by an anti-
monarchical jury; Becker was as duly executed.
How discontented were the burghers of his capital
with the policy with which William as king had

identified himself was shown in their flat refusal
to have anything to do with the festivities with
which he celebrated the centenary of the Peace of
Hubertsberg, by which the Seven Years' War had
been concluded. " The time," said the trades guilds,
"was no time for merry-making." But their
gruffness did not daunt William ; he duly commemorated Hubertsberg, listening to the same Te
Deum as Frederic the Great had commanded to be
sung. And while festivities were the order of the
day, he made the founding of a monument to his
father the occasion for gathering together all the
veterans of the wars of 1813–14 and 1815. Four
thousand old soldiers headed by old Marshal
Wrangel, marched down the Linden to where the
foundation stone was to be laid in the Lustgarten ;
the iron cross veterans leading, the lameters from
wounds bringing up the rear on wheels. Revising
the programme of this as of every other ceremony,
William made an emendation that is worthy of
notice. In the direct, rugged, perhaps one might
say brutal style occasionally adopted by Prussian
military persons, the officer drawing up the programme had written "all cripples will be driven
after the procession in carriages from the royal
stables." This sentence the royal editor crossed
out, and substituted this other, "Those who are

lame from honourable wounds received in their
country's cause will be driven in the procession in
royal carriages." The provincial veterans were the
King's guests in the large hall at "Krolls," where
he paid them a visit, drank their healths, and made
them a speech. It was rather a big dinner party
he had in the palace the same afternoon—covers
were laid for 2,400 guests, all possessors of the Iron
Cross, instituted by William's father fifty years
previously.

It is a German custom to celebrate both
public and personal anniversaries, which are com-
monly known as "Jubilees." "There are few
incidents," says Mr. Kingston, "in which a German happens to have played anything like a leading part that are not caught at as occasions for
'Jubilees' by his friends, admirers, or dependants,
that is, if he live long enough to be a person of
mark." The latter part of William's long life was
studded thick with anniversaries and consequent
jubilees. Already, in 1857, had been celebrated
the fiftieth anniversary of his entry into the
Prussian army. February 27th, 1864, was the
fiftieth anniversary of that battle of Bar-sur-Aube,
in which he had won the Iron Cross and the
Russian St. George. While his own subjects holding the former order gathered to congratulate their

king and comrade, there came from far off Russia
on the same errand a detachment from the Russian
regiment of Kaluga—the regiment to which the
young Prince had ridden on duty through the
fierce French fire on the day of Bar-sur-Aube.
His Majesty received the deputation wearing the
uniform of the Kalugas and the St. George that
had been given him fifty years previously.

But while the Kalugas were commemorating
William's soldierhood in a long-past battle in which
Prussian troops had taken part, these were now
engaged in another campaign. Austria and Prussia
had leagued their armed strength against unfortunate and gallant little Denmark. It was a contest
so unequal as to bring little martial credit to the
conquerors; the vanquished could say with Francis
at Pavia, " All is lost save honour ! " He must be
a very bold or a very reckless writer who does not
tremble when he finds himself compelled to touch
even the hem of a subject so intricate and so obsolete as the Sleswig-Holstein question, of which
Lord Palmerston used to say that there was only
one man in Europe besides himself who understood
it, and that man was dead. Only as much reference
to it will here be made as to render lucid the
sequence of events that led up to two wars in which
Prussia during William's reign was a participator.

K

The population of Holstein was almost exclusively German, that of Sleswig partially so. King Frederic VII. of Denmark had no male heirs, and by the Treaty of London executed in May, 1852, to which the signatories were England, France, Russia, Austria, and Prussia (but not the Germanic Confederation, of which the two latter Powers were members), the succession to the throne of Denmark was vested in Prince Christian of Sleswig-Holstein-Sonderburg-Glücksburg, the husband of the granddaughter of King Christian VIII. of Denmark, and the father of the Princess of Wales. This provision was intended to bring about the dynastic blending of the Elbe duchies with the kingdom of Denmark, and was guaranteed by the five Powers parties to the treaty. In November, 1863, Frederic of Denmark died, and Prince Christian succeeded to the throne of that kingdom. Already before his accession, the duchies were possessions of the Danish monarchy, but had in certain respects a separate administrative existence. This Denmark, in the year of Christian's accession, had materially infringed in the case of Sleswig, by a law which virtually incorporated that duchy with the Danish monarchy. The German Confederation protested against this " Danification " of Sleswig, and having pronounced a decree of Federal execution against the new King of Denmark as Duke of Holstein and, in virtue of that duchy, a member of the German Confederation, sent into Holstein Federal troops belonging to the smaller States of the Confederation. The Confederation, as a collective body, favoured the establishment of the independence of the duchies, and had with it the wishes probably of the great mass of the German nation. But the independence of Sleswig and Holstein scarcely suited the views of Bismarck. He desired the annexation to Prussia of at all events Holstein, because in Holstein is the great harbour of Kiel, all important in view of the new fleet with which he purposed equipping Prussia; if Sleswig could be compassed along with Holstein, so much the better.

But there were two difficulties in Bismarck's way. Prussia was a co-signatory of the Treaty of London. If he were to grasp at the duchies single-handed, a host of enemies might confront him. England was burning to take up arms in the cause of the father of the beautiful princess she had adopted as her own. The German Confederation would oppose Prussia's naked effort to aggrandise herself; and Austria, in the double character of a party to the Treaty of London and of a member of the Confederation, would rejoice in the opportunity

K 2

to strike a blow at a power of whose rising pretensions she had begun to be jealous. The wily
Bismarck had to dissemble. He made the proposal
to Austria that the two states should ignore their
participation as individual States in the Treaty of
London, and that as corporate members of the
German Confederation they should constitute themselves the executors of the Federal decree, and put
aside the minor states whose troops had been
charged with that office. Austria acceded. It was
a bad hour for her when she did, yet she moves no
compassion for the misfortunes which befell her as
the issue. She was playing her own game without
regard to principle; because she lost the game,
worsted in it by an astuter player as little troubled
by principle as herself, no condolences are due to
her.

The Diet had to submit. The Austro-Prussian
troops marched through Holstein into Sleswig, and
on the 2nd of February, 1864, struck at the Danes
occupying the Dannewerke. The Prussian troops
in the field consisted of two line-divisions with
a division of the Guard Corps in reserve, the whole
under the command of Prince Frederic Charles.
The venerable Marshal Wrangel was commander-
in-chief of the combined forces until after the fall
of Düppel, when Prince Frederic Charles succeeded

him in that position; but throughout the campaign the control of the dispositions was mainly exercised by the Red Prince.   But neither strategy nor tactics were very strenuously brought into use for the discomfiture of the unfortunate Danes.   Their ruin was wrought partly because of the overwhelmingly superior force of their allied opponents, partly because of their own unpreparedness for war in almost everything save the possession of heroic bravery; but most of all by the fire of the needle-gun and the Prussian advantage in the possession of rifled artillery.   Only part of the Prussian infantry had used the needle-gun in the reduction of the Baden insurrection in 1848; now, however, the whole army was equipped with it.   Ever slow to take new impressions, military Europe did not awake to the full value of the breechloading rifle until it stood forth as the unquestioned leading factor in the phenomenally swift discomfiture of the Austrian armies in 1866; but two years previous to that war the Austrians might have observed how deadly was the new weapon the Prussians carried into action against the Danes.

In their retreat from the Dannewerke into the Düppel position, the Danes suffered severely from the inclemency of the weather, and fought a desperate rear-guard engagement with the Austrians, in which the overwhelming strength of the latter ultimately told, but only after a most stubborn and valiant resistance on the part of the Danes. The Prussians undertook the task of reducing Düppel; the Austrians marched northward into Jutland, and driving back the Danish troops they encountered in their march, sat down before the fortress of Fredericia, and swept the Little Belt with their cannon. The sieges, both of Düppel and of Fredericia, were conducted with extreme inertness, and it was at times difficult to believe that either side was in earnest. But at Düppel the Prussians held the key of the position ever since, in the early part of the siege, they had gained possession of the Broagerland peninsula. There, and on the hill of Rugeböl, they methodically built their batteries, and opened fire on the 17th of March. Under cover of the cannonade, the Prussian infantry moved forward to the attack of the village of Düppel and the heights of Arnbjerg. The defence was as obstinate as the attack was vehement, but the Danes ultimately had to give ground. Again and again the heights of Arnbjerg, like the village of Düppel, were taken and retaken; but the Prussians remained in possession, and the positions they had won gave them important advantages.

Yet the Danes were not beaten. They repulsed

a Prussian assault on the 28th March, and held the ground that remained to them, under an incessant storm of shot and shell from the Prussian batteries, until the 18th of April. On that day, supported by a furious cannonade from their whole line of batteries, the Prussian infantry swarmed up against the shattered Danish lines. The Danes fought with the obstinacy of despair, but were thrust back by superior numbers out of position after position, till at length they were driven clean out of the Düppel works, and across the narrow sound into the island of Alsen. So severe were their losses that certainly less than half the Danish army made good its escape to Alsen, and the proportion of officers placed *hors de combat* was excessive.

An armistice, which lasted till the 26th June, effected nothing in the direction of peace, and three days afterwards a Prussian force, under General Herwath von Bittenfeld, crossed the sound in boats in the morning twilight, landed on the island of Alsen, stormed the Danish batteries in the face of a strong resistance, and drove the Danish forces out of their positions back into the woods. Alsen taken and Fredericia abandoned, nothing remained for Denmark but to yield and sue for peace. The Danish war was terminated by the Treaty of Vienna on the 30th October, 1864, under which the duchies of Sleswig, Holstein, and Lauenburg were handed over to the sovereigns of Austria and Prussia.

King William did not accompany his troops into Sleswig, contenting himself with devoting his whole time and attention to the details of equipment and supply in conjunction with the War Minister. In February he saw brought into Berlin a number of cannon which had been left behind by the Danes when they evacuated the Dannewerke. It had been intended in the Prussian camp to make the assault on the inner line of the Düppel works on March 22nd, the King's birthday; but when William heard of this he ordered the postponement of the enterprise, as he did not desire that his natal day should be associated with the sorrow of the relatives of those who must fall. As it happened, this command saved his birthday from being the anniversary of a reverse, for the attempt made six days later was repulsed. The tidings of the successful storm of Düppel came to him on his way back from having reviewed a battalion of foot guards, and he immediately rode back to the field and announced the good news to his soldiers. Two days after the storm he suddenly quitted Berlin for the army, accompanied only by Generals Roon and Manteuffel. Reaching the Prussian head-quarters at Flensburg next day, he found there

Wrangel, Prince Frederic Charles, and the Crown Prince, who was making the campaign as lieutenant-general in command of the Guard division. Accompanied by those officers and Marshal von Gablenz, the Austrian commander, the King reviewed the troops who had done the fighting three days before, then visited the trenches, where he decorated General Manstein, and as he passed through the field hospital, gave the order "*pour le mérite*" to the dying Raven, the first Prussian general officer that had been mortally wounded since the campaign of 1815. William had not long returned to Berlin when there was for him the grateful duty of leading down the Linden from the Brandenburg Gate the long procession of 118 guns taken from the Danes when Düppel had to be abandoned. The medal struck for the Sleswig campaign he himself wore, considering himself entitled to it by having been inside the enemy's country while the war was in progress.

Out of the Danish war of 1864 grew almost inevitably the war of 1866, between Prussia and Austria. The wolves quite naturally wrangled over the carcase, and the astuter wolf had so much the better of the wrangle that the duller one, unless he chose to be partly bullied, partly tricked out of his share, had no alternative but to fight for

it, with the result that he clean lost that and a
great deal more besides.

The future of the Elbe Duchies was played at
pitch and toss with between Prussia and Austria
for the best part of a year; the details of the
game were too intricate to be followed here. The
condominium of the two Powers in the duchies
produced constant friction, which was probably
Bismarck's intention, especially as Prussia had
taken care to keep stationed in them twice as
many troops as Austria had left there. Relations
were becoming very strained when in August, 1865,
the Emperor Francis Joseph and King William
met at the little watering-place of Gastein, and
from their interview originated the short-lived
arrangement known as the Convention of Gastein.
By that compact, while the two Powers preserved
the common sovereignty over the duchies, Austria
accepted the administration of Holstein, Prussia
undertaking that of Sleswig. Prussia was to have
rights of way through Holstein to Sleswig, was
given over the right of construction of a North Sea
and Baltic Canal; and while Kiel was constituted a
Federal harbour, Prussia was authorised to construct
there the requisite fortifications and marine estab-
lishments, and to maintain an adequate force for
the protection of these. Assuming the arrangement

to be provisional, as on all hands it was regarded, Prussia clearly had the advantage under it. If it should be violently ruptured, Prussia, the possession of Kiel apart, would have the Austrians in Holstein under two fires; and as a fact, when the rupture did come in the course of a few months, the position of the Austrian garrison of Holstein was so untenable that it evacuated the duchy without firing a shot. But the Gastein Convention contained another provision — that Austria should sell to Prussia all her rights in the duchy of Lauenburg (an outlying appanage of Holstein) for the sum of 2,500,000 thalers; thus making market of rights of which she was but a trustee for the German Confederation. The Convention of Gastein pleased nobody, but that mattered little to Bismarck. The Confederation was offended by the trafficking in the Lauenburg duchy, and the Prussian Parliament denounced the transaction for which it assumed Prussia would have to find the cash. But King William drew this sting from his refractory Commons; he paid Austria for Lauenburg out of his own private purse.

Bickerings recommenced before the year 1865 was out, and early in 1866 Austria began to arm. Would the armament of Austria, by whose side the other states of the German Confederation were sure

to range themselves against this truculent and shifty
Prussia, enforce on that power the policy of chang-
ing her tactics of self-aggrandisement?　Or would
Prussia daringly confront fate, and hold herself a
match in war, should war be the issue, for all the
rest of Germany ranged against her single self?
Prussia, or rather Bismarck—for indeed the
Prussian nation looked askance at his strange
mysterious statecraft—was ready to fight, but was
not above looking around Europe for an ally.
France would be neutral; Bismarck had arranged
that much, and would ask of her no more.　But
Italy, with her inveterate hatred of Austria, burning to finish the work of 1859—Italy, with her
strategic position on Austria's reverse flank, was
just the ally for Prussia; so in March, 1866, a
secret treaty was formed between Italy and
Prussia, by which they pledged themselves to
joint and simultaneous action in case of hostility
with Austria.

The spring was spent in abortive negotiations
between Prussia and Austria, having for their professed object the preservation of peace while both
nations were engaged in preparing for war.　The
Prussian army was mobilised in May, with a smooth
methodical rapidity; half a million of men stood
ready equipped in all respects for a campaign

within fourteen days of the issue of the mobilisation order. That proved with what sedulous care Prussia must have been long engaging her energies in the consummation of her military preparedness. Her forces by the end of May were so disposed on her frontier that she might have struck at Austria at once, and this with great advantage, since the Austrian military preparations were still in a very backward state. That she then refrained from immediate action has been adduced as an argument in favour of her anxiety to keep the peace. But there certainly were other causes for Prussia's self-restraint. Her army was ready, and might have attacked Austria, but the communications of an invading force would have remained exposed to molestation from the troops of the minor German states, and until Prussia was in a position to take measures with the latter, she acted discreetly in refraining from the offensive against Austria.

A proposed conference of the great Powers in the interests of peace proved abortive. Prussia threw the Convention of Gastein to the winds by civilly but masterfully turning the Austrian brigade of occupation out of Holstein. Then Austria in the Federal Diet, complaining that by this act Prussia had disturbed the peace of the German Confederation, moved for a decree of Federal execution against that state, to be enforced by the Confederation's armed strength. On the 14th June, Austria's motion was carried by the Diet, its last act; for Prussia next day wrecked the flimsy organisation of the German Confederation, by declaring war against three of its component members, Hanover, Hesse, and Saxony. There was no formal declaration of war between Austria and Prussia, only a notification of intended hostile action sent by the Prussian commanders to the Austrian foreposts. On the 17th the Emperor Francis Joseph published his war manifesto; King William on the 18th emitted his to " My People ; " on the 20th, Italy declared war against Austria and Bavaria. The great game had begun.

CHAPTER IX.

THE SEVEN WEEKS' WAR.

IT was under strange conditions that the kingdom which William ruled entered upon the war of 1866. Austria was Prussia's principal antagonist, but Prussia was so hemmed in by minor enemies that it was only away down in Silesia, that long south-eastern salient which she owes to Frederic the Great, where her frontier marched with the frontier of Austria. Along her western border from the Elbe to the Thuringian forest, stood enemies; on her southern she had to deal with hostile Baden, Würtemberg, Bavaria, and Saxony, which latter kingdom stood right between her and Bohemia, the country that was to be the cockpit of her struggle with Austria.

Before she should get to close grips with Austria, it behoved her to make for herself elbow-room about her own confines. Hanover, for instance, and Hesse Cassel, had to be promptly muzzled. Then Bavaria, Würtemberg, and the minor states of the German Confederation had to

be deterred from molesting her while she was fighting out the greater fight with Austria.   In a week
after the declaration of war, the kingdom of Hanover
was under quiet Prussian administration.   Its army,
on the evening of that declaration, had made a rush
to the southward, with intent to reach Bavaria,
and unite with its army.   It had to halt at Got-
tingen, and when it recommenced its southern progress through the Thuringian forest, its progress
was slow and undecided.   Hemmed in by three
Prussian divisions, it fought at Langensalza a fight
worthy of the military renown of Hanoverian
soldiers, and then there remained for it no alternative but to accept an honourable capitulation.   The
Hanoverian army no longer constituted an element
of flanking danger to Prussia after it had moved
southward on the 15th June ; on the 28th by its
capitulation it passed out of existence.   As for
Hesse Cassel, a Prussian force had overrun that
Electorate within a week after the declaration of
war ; its prince was a state prisoner of Prussia,
and his troops, driven from their own territory, had
joined the Federal army gathering at Frankfort.
Thus summarily had Prussia swept clear of possible
molestation her western flank.

   She had still to deal with the Bavarian army,
and the composite assembly of regiments which

was termed the Eighth Federal Corps—the Bavarians were the Seventh. Neither of these bodies was aggressive. The Bavarian army was covering its own northern frontier along the Maine. The composite Eighth Corps lay about Frankfort. To these two bodies Prussia opposed the force, three divisions strong, known as " the Army of the Maine," commanded first by Vogel von Falckenstein, and afterwards by Manteuffel. The former, with a considerable amount of hard fighting, drove his adversaries to the south side of the Maine during the first fortnight of July, and occupied Frankfort. Subsequently Manteuffel gained several successes over his Federal antagonists, and when the armistice was announced on 26th July, had them jammed in a very precarious position in an elbow of the Maine, all but cut off from the territories they were attempting to defend.

Thus did Prussia by a prompt and vigorous offensive, sweep away or hold at bay the enemies who threatened to hamper her feet in her great contest with Austria. There remained but Saxony, and that state lay right in Prussia's path to the Bohemian frontier. It was a military necessity that Saxony should be occupied. War was declared on the 15th, and on the 20th of June the whole of Saxony was in the undisturbed possession

L

of Prussian troops, and the Saxon army had crossed the frontier into Bohemia and joined the Austrians.

This occupation accomplished, and the dispositions following on it perfected, no obstacle now intervened between Prussia and the invasion of Bohemia. The aphorism that "Everything comes to him who can wait," has a fine speciousness, but whatever may have once been the case, it is not now true of a nation which has engaged in a great war. A nation with that species of undertaking on its hands gets no opportunity to play the waiting game. It must strike, or it is lost. The history of Prussia during the years of William's reign proves conclusively how a nation can profit by placing its practical faith in another aphorism, " If you wish for peace, be prepared for war." His reign began in 1861. Of its long duration Prussia spent in war, all told, not more than fifteen months, enjoying peace during all the rest of its years; but look what she accomplished, what she gained, in her three short bouts of warfare! Her career of victory all but unchequered; her position among the nations so raised that Berlin may be said to dominate Continental Europe; her treasury recruited by what for the most part depletes national treasuries; her area and her population doubled.

All these things came to her because of success
in three short campaigns. And that success was
not achieved by brilliancy of military genius displayed by any soldier of Prussia. No Teutonic
Napoleon it was who gained for her those swift
triumphs. She won them, and gained all they
brought her, simply because her men responsible
for her military condition knew and acted on the
knowledge, how all important it is for a nation
to live ready for war; and who knew, too,
how best to improve the advantage accruing
from that attitude of preparedness. The lesson is
written so clear that he who runs may read; but
there are nations which studiously look the other
way, in the apparent belief that the millennium is
nigh at hand. They would have their millennium
on the cheap—an aspiration of the folly of which
time will sternly convince them; Prussia asks
nothing for nothing, and honestly fights out her
own millennium.

The millennium, whether for Prussia or as a
general thing, was rather at a discount in Bohemia
in the summer of 1866. That dependency of the
Austrian Empire, whose hills and valleys had echoed
to the din of the Seven Years' War, and had been
trodden by the conquering legions of the First
Napoleon, was now to be the scene of a short but

bloody conflict. The northern and north-eastern frontier of this great bastion of Austria is protected by the chain of the Reisen-Gebirge, inside of which bulwark is the basin of the Upper Elbe and its tributaries. In that basin lay the Austrian army commanded by Benedek. It had lost the power of initiative through unpreparedness, and now, disposed around the central point of the fortress of Josephstadt, its *rôle* had to be that of the defensive. Because of Prussia's preparedness, the privilege of the offensive vested in her armies. Of these on the 23rd of June the First Army, commanded by Prince Frederic Charles, stood on Saxon soil, ranged along a section of the northern frontier of Bohemia. Nominally this force, made up of four-and-a-half army corps and a proportionate complement of cavalry, consisted of two armies, the "First Army," commanded by Prince Frederic Charles, composed of three corps, and the "Army of the Elbe," composed of one-and-a-half corps, commanded by General Herwath von Bittenfeld; but since a few days after the invasion both armies were placed under the supreme command of the Red Prince, it is unnecessary here to maintain the distinction between them. On the north-eastern frontier of Bohemia, on Silesian soil, lay the "Second Army." Its chief was the Crown

Prince of Prussia, and it was composed of four army corps, with proportionate cavalry.

The task in the first instance assigned to both armies was to penetrate through the mountain passes of the Bohemian frontier, operating separately; and this accomplished, to form a junction somewhere about Gitschin, in the Upper Elbe basin, and deal in conjunct action with the Austrian forces which might be expected thereabouts to stand in the path. Great discretionary freedom of action, as is the Prussian custom, was left to both commanders, within the limit of keeping in view the need for concentration " for the principal decision," and they were to afford each other what mutual support might be possible.

The First Army crossed the frontier earliest, partly because it had to travel the greater distance, partly because its movement in advance might in some measure relieve the Second Army, whose march, although the shorter, had to be made through four separate mountain passes, and was infinitely the more arduous, from the pressure of Austrian opposition. The combined operation had its manifest dangers, since Benedek had the possession of the interior lines, and might concentrate his whole force against either army. On the morning of the 23rd, Prince Frederic

Charles entered Bohemia near Reichenberg. On the night of the 29th he had his headquarters in Gitschin. He had fought hard for almost every step of his progress, at Liebenau, at Hühner-wasser, at Podoll, at Münchengrätz, and for the right to enter Gitschin, having been opposed by about 60,000 Austrians and Saxons under the command of Count Clam Gallas. In a campaign on a smaller scale, some of the actions fought between Reichenberg and Gitschin would have been regarded as great battles. In the fighting, for instance, that resulted in the Prussian occupation of the latter place, the Austrians lost 10,000 men in killed, wounded, and prisoners.

The Second Army, for its part, quitted Silesian soil, and plunged into the ravines of the Reisen-Gebirge, on the morning of June 27. It used four passes, and had to fight its way through two. At Trautenau one of the columns experienced a reverse which was retrieved on the following day: Nachod, Skalitz, Soor, Königinhof, and Schwein-schädel, were all Prussian successes; and on the fourth day from his crossing the frontier, the Crown Prince had conquered the mountains, driven back the Austrians, reunited his divided columns of march, stood possessed of the line of the Elbe as far south almost as Josephstadt, and had his communications established with Prince Frederic Charles at Gitschin. Thus far the Prussian programme had " come off." Benedek had thrown away the advantage of the interior lines. Of his divided opponents he had crushed neither, and now they were no longer divided. By opposing three corps to the Crown Prince, instead of the six at his disposal, he had merely got the three mauled, without having hindered the Prussian convergence. And presently, having, when it was open to him, failed to reap the advantage of the " interior lines," he was to find himself in a situation where their advantage was to change into mischief. An army attacked in front and in flank in the battle-field stands, it is true, on an inner line of operations, but the strategical advantage is eliminated by the tactical disadvantage, as Benedek found at Königgrätz. But before Königgrätz his position had clearly become seriously compromised. Of his eight corps five had been decidedly beaten, and had suffered heavily in men and morale. He had no hope of reinforcements. Prince Frederic Charles in Gitschin threatened his left flank; the Crown Prince on the Elbe his front. He was in that plight that he could not take the offensive, at all events until he had fought and won a great battle in a defensive position. On the arbitrament of such a contest he elected to stand or fall; and on the 30th June issued orders that his army should withdraw to the vicinity of Königgrätz.

While the armies of Prussia were gathering and marching, the anxieties of the situation bore hard on King William. He was a simple man of a kindly nature, and while he did not refuse his sanction to the projects of his great Minister, or to the somewhat tortuous methods by which those projects were furthered, he found the path along which he was being led rough and thorny. He had been glad to recognise the Convention of Gastein, as constituting the firm establishment of friendly relations between Prussia and Austria, and was disappointed when he found the ground that he had thought so solid, hollow and precarious. War with Austria was distasteful to him, and if genuinely convinced of its expediency, if not of its necessity, he was convinced against his will. It was no secret that to his son the quarrel was repugnant, and that before duty called him into the field of action, the Crown Prince had warmly exerted his influence in favour of the maintenance of peace. A powerful section of the Court party, supported by the influence of the Dowager Queen Elizabeth, threw its weight into the scale against war with Austria. The Liberals were vehement against it, and the

nation's dislike to it was unmistakably manifested.
Demonstrations against the war were made by
corporations, by mercantile communities, and in
more than one instance by the Landwehr troops
summoned to fight against an Empire of German
affinities and German relations. Private sorrow
swelled the burden of public anxiety, for in the
middle of June, William had to mourn the death
of a little grandson. Racked by solicitude, he was
sedulous in the discharge of his military duties.
His time was spent in holding farewell reviews of
regiments before they marched away to the frontier,
in superintending the orderly despatch of troops,
and in assiduous superintendence of the preparations
for the campaign. While Bismarck, with stern
resolve and teeth hard set, worked out his schemes
in the Foreign Office, and while Moltke, seated
before his maps, telegraphed strategic instructions
to the leaders in the field, the King was bidding
adieu to old comrades going down into the battle, and
inspiring enthusiasm in his departing soldiery by
his presence and his exhortations.

The sun began to break through the gloom of
his dull horizon when, on the 27th June—the day
appointed by him for general prayer throughout
the Kingdom — intelligence reached Berlin by
telegraph of the threshold successes at Podoll and

Nachod. The tide of popular feeling was on the turn. Two days later universal enthusiasm was flowing in a great rushing stream, for the news had come of the more important victories of Skalitz and Münchengrätz, and of the capitulation of the Hanoverian army at Langensalza. As if by enchantment, all Berlin was suddenly dressed with banners of the national colours; every street resounded with the chant "*Ich bin ein Preusse; Kennt ihr meine Farben?*" The multitudes flocked to the Palace, where the King stood greeting his people from the accustomed window, while from the balcony an officer read the news of the victories. Bismarck shared in the enthusiastic greetings of the populace; on that day Prussia rejoiced to put her stubborn neck under the great minister's foot.

Before the good news came, it had been already decided that the King and his military and political advisers should without delay join the armies in the field. When the tidings arrived, William was in his cabinet, engaged in a strange task. His childhood had taught him how sudden and swift may be the reverses of royalty, and how wise it was to take precautions against untoward contingencies. Before leaving for the field, he was selecting and packing up the more important of his private papers. What had happened after Jena

might happen again; if the impending struggle
should be overwhelmingly adverse to Prussia, he
knew by experience what confusion might ensue.
In case of accident, he would get his private papers
packed ready for transport. He hoped to march
on Vienna; but in the meantime it was wise to
secure the safe retreat from Berlin. It was while
thus hedging against disastrous eventualities that
there came to him almost simultaneous messages
announcing three important successes. He finished
his packing all the same; and then from his window
he beckoned to him a passer-by whom he recognised,
and shouted to him : " My son has gained a victory.
News of victory on all sides ! I will have the
good tidings published immediately—but meanwhile tell everybody you meet." Of a cordial
nature, he could not rest till he had visited old
Prince Charles, and congratulated him on the success achieved by that senior's son, Prince Frederic
Charles, whose birthday it was; and he went also
to tell his daughter-in-law—our English Princess
Royal—how her gallant husband was proving himself not less an able commander than a fine soldier.
In the evening, from his palace window, after the
densely-massed Berliners on the Linden had sung
" *Ein feste Burg,*" he spoke to them words of
thankfulness and farewell; and next morning he

left his capital for the seat of war. After he had
closed his window on the populace, he had kept
long lonely vigil; the sentries saw him walking up
and down his room till three in the morning.

Five trains were needed for the conveyance of
the royal entourage, for there accompanied William
on campaign not only the headquarter staff and his
own personal suite, but also the whole of the civil
and military cabinets. Austria was to be fought
in the field : Prussia was to be governed from the
field. Bismarck, of course, went into Bohemia
with his royal master. The King had prepared a
short stirring address to his army, which was issued
on the day he left Berlin. "To-day," it ran, "I
am coming to join you, my brave soldiers in the
field, and to give you my royal greeting. Within
the space of a few days your bravery and devotion
have achieved results that may worthily rank by
the side of the great deeds of our forefathers. I
regard all branches of my faithful army with pride,
and look forward to the future of the campaign
with full confidence. Soldiers! Great hosts are
in the field against us. Let us, however, put our
trust in God, who is the God of battles, and in
the justice of our cause. He will direct Prussia's
oft victorious banners to fresh victories through
your bravery and perseverance."

The destination for the night was Reichenberg, a day's march inside Bohemia. Count Clam
Gallas was not at home, from unavoidable causes:
he was in command of the Austrian troops that had
tried to oppose Prince Frederic Charles's advance,
and had been swept away back before the torrent of
Prussian soldiers; but King William was his guest
in the château of Reichenberg. In the evening
there went out to salute him a civic deputation
from the town of Reichenberg, to whom he said:
" It was one of the saddest moments of my life
when I crossed the boundary of your country as
an enemy. I believe I am right: your emperor
believes he is right. Would that the question had
been left for settlement between us two, but others
have involved themselves in it, and it has now become
very complicated." At Reichenberg the King was
hardly safe from the enemy, who were known to
have some cavalry up among the hills about Leiter-
metz, and the chain of sentries round the headquarters was exceptionally strong. But the Austrians had little enterprise and worse intelligence;
and on the following day the royal headquarters
moved forward to Sichrow, where the King occupied
the fine castle of the princely Rohans. He made
the journey by carriage, the railroad having been
broken up; and on the way everywhere were passed

Austrian prisoners tramping to the rear. From Sichrow, on 2nd July, the King moved on into Gitschin, where his quarters were in the Golden Lion. He had been met on the battle-field of the 29th by his nephew Prince Frederic Charles, who, as they drove into Gitschin together, put his Majesty in full possession of the military situation so far as it had then developed itself. The King spent the afternoon in going about among the wounded; and here, too, he had something to say to the local civic deputation. "I must tell you," said the King, "that I am not making war against your nation, but only against the armies which oppose me. If, however, the civilian inhabitants commit acts of causeless hostility against my troops, I shall be forced to make reprisals. My troops are not savage hordes, and only claim the supplies necessary for subsistence. It must be your care that they have no cause for just complaint. Tell the inhabitants that I have not come to make war upon peaceable citizens, but to defend the honour of Prussia."

There was no expectation of severe fighting on the 3rd July. At the council of war held in Gitschin on the morning of the 2nd, reconnaissances were prescribed for that day to discover Benedek's whereabouts, otherwise the Prussian armies were to stand firm. Prince Frederic Charles's reconnoitring officers rode far and fast; and when, returning from Gitschin, he reached his farther-forward quarters in Kamenitz, there were tidings waiting him that changed the whole complexion of affairs.

Benedek had not retreated far. He had brought all his force to the right bank of the Elbe, and now stood with his back to that river, occupying the space between it and its tributary the Bistritz, with a front on the latter stream extending from Benatek on the right, to Nechanitz on the left. Prince Frederic Charles drew the inference from this disposition that it was Benedek's intention to advance next day from the line of the Bistritz, with the object of attacking the First Army with superior force, before the junction between it and the Crown Prince's army should be practically effected. Prince Frederic Charles at once saw his double opportunity. It was for him to concentrate and move forward against the Bistritz line. If Benedek meant the offensive, then the Red Prince would meet him and fight him, straining every nerve to thwart the success of that offensive till the Crown Prince should come up and strike the Austrian's right flank. If, again, Benedek did not intend the offensive, but preferred to stand fast on the Bistritz and offer battle to Prince Frederic Charles, then that commander would accept the challenge, and put forth his whole strength to "hold" the Austrian there until the Crown Prince should come up and assail with crushing effect his right flank. Benedek's attitude, whatever might have been his intention, is explicable only on the hypothesis that he believed the two Prussian armies had already effected their junction, that the mass of both was in front of him as he lay on the Bistritz, and that the Prussian commanders designed an attempt to strike at his left, and so cut him off from his communications with Vienna. The scouting of the Austrians throughout the campaign was very badly done, and their intelligence extremely defective.

Prince Frederic Charles was a man of prompt action, and there was no time to lose. It was already 9 p.m. when the gallopers dashed out from his headquarters in Kamenitz, carrying his detailed orders to the various corps of his army for their immediate concentration to the front. An hour later an officer started on the long dangerous ride to Königinhof, with a letter to the Crown Prince requesting him to co-operate by sending one of his army corps to strike at the right flank of the Austrians, while the First Army was *aux prises* with their front. So well did Von Normand ride, that he rejoined Prince Frederic Charles at 4 o'clock on the morning of the 3rd, with assurances of the Crown Prince's co-operation.

In his quarters at Gitschin the King had been sitting at his writing-table all the evening, and was preparing to lie down for the night on his camp-bed, when there entered to him General Voights-Rhetz, the chief of Prince Frederic Charles's staff, who had been sent back in haste from Kamenitz to inform his Majesty of the altered dispositions for the morrow, and to desire his approval of them. A practised soldier, William found it hard to believe that Benedek could have projected himself into a position so radically vicious. But he knew how safe a man was his nephew, and even were he mistaken, no harm could arise out of the dispositions he had ordered. Moltke joined Voights-Rhetz in the King's bed-room, and one amendment on Prince Frederic Charles's arrangements was resolved on. If he were right, Benedek's position was such that it was worth to " mak' siccar " of the Austrian's utter discomfiture, by bringing to bear upon it the whole strength of both the Prussian armies. So at midnight two messengers, lest one should fail, were sent to the Crown Prince, bidding him advance not with one corps, but with his whole army, against the Austrian right flank, make all

M

speed, and commence his attack as early as possible.

In the darkness of a stormy night, Prince Frederic Charles's army was gathered in the long hollow behind the ridge of Dub, ready to issue from its ambush and attack the Austrians if they should advance. But the Austrian army came not. As the morning wind blew aside the mists, the Austrian position on the face of the slope rising from the further bank of the Bistritz could be accurately discerned. Benedek's centre was in front of Chlum, whose church-tower crowned the slope. He held the Bistritz line from Benatek on his right, and the hill of Horenowes behind it, through the villages of Sadowa, Dohalitz, Dohalicka, Mokrovous, Popowitz, and Lubno, to Nechanitz, where his left rested supported by the villages of Problus and Prim further back. So stood the Austrian line which confronted Prince Frederic Charles's army. Benedek had intended that his position should have a semi-circular front, with the right extending backward from the Bistritz towards the Elbe, but his projected arrangements had not been carried out, and the Austrian line of battle actually formed a very gentle curve, the length of which from Prim to Horenowes was about six and three-quarter miles, and on which stood four and three-quarter army corps, the rest of his force, which in all was about 206,000 strong, being in reserve. The Prussian frontal attack was delivered by Prince Frederick Charles with 124,000 men. The Crown Prince came down on the Austrian flank with 97,000 more; so that in all the Prussian force on the field numbered 221,000 men. On both sides a considerable proportion did not come into action.

The first shot was fired before seven, but the atmosphere continued thick with fog and rain, and the cannonade did not become general along the Bistritz till after eight. The Prussian infantry presently approached the Bistritz; and since it was the task of the First Army to pin the Austrians to their position there until the Second Army should come up, it was necessary to occupy them along their front. To this end the Bistritz had to be crossed, and immediately the battle waxed fierce. Fransecky on the Prussian left dashed on Benatek, and came at once to hand-to-hand fighting. Horne promptly flung his Brandenburgers against Sadowa; Herwath's Pomeranians battled their way into the blazing Dohalitz; and Werder led the Third Division through the Austrian cannon fire upon Mokrovous. An hour's hard infantry-fighting sufficed for the Prussians to clear the Austrians out of the villages along the Bistritz; and about eleven

o'clock they began the attempt to press up the
wooded slope beyond. But in vain. Not only
could the First Army, spite of all its efforts, and
they were many and strenuous, gain no more ground
in the face of the stubborn resistance offered by
the Austrians, but it was hard put to it to retain what advantage it had gained.

For neither Prussian king nor Prussian private
soldier had there been a reasonable amount of sleep
on the night before Königgrätz. It had been past
midnight ere William, lying on his camp bed in
the "Golden Lion" of Gitschin, had been left by
Moltke and Voights-Rhetz, and by five o'clock,
seated in an open carriage with his mantle about
him to fend off the drizzling rain, he was on his
way to the battle-field, to witness a combat to
which the Bar-sur-Aube of his youth had been
child's-play. He was still hesitating to accept
the conviction that Benedek had committed the
strategical error on a belief in which Prince
Frederic Charles's dispositions were based; and he
expressed his apprehension to Count Lehndorf, his
carriage companion, that the Prussian concentration
which had been ordered would turn out to be "a
stroke at empty air." At the village of Klenitz
his saddle horses were waiting him, but before
mounting he went into the inn to accoutre himself

for horseback. A Prussian chronicler gives the
details of his costume with innocently minute
particularity. It seems that he got into his greatcoat, and put on goloshes over his boots. A wrong
pair of spurs had been brought from Gitschin and
would not fit. It may be permissible for a king
close on seventy to ride down into the battle in
goloshes, but goloshes even on a king will not
excuse spurless heels. A groom whipped his off
and strapped them on over the royal goloshes ;
the King mounted the good mare " Fenella "—
from that day thenceforth to be called " Sadowa "—
and rode forth with glass hung round his neck by
a " long strap." The thunder of the cannon had
been audible for some time, and on the knoll
beyond Klenitz Prince Frederic was found, who
told the King from his own personal inspection
that von Ungar had brought back correct intelligence, and that the whole Austrian Army was
down there behind the Bistritz.

Riding still forward and leftward, amid the
vociferous cheering of his troops, William rode
on to a hillock over against Sadowa, where stood
General Horne superintending the deployment
of his division, which was presently to assail that
village. The spot was within range of the Austrian
cannon, and the King was followed by a suite that

loomed on the sky-line like a regiment, and that was sure to draw fire if the Austrian gunners knew their business. Horne urged his Majesty to retire; the advice, however, was not palatable and was not taken. A moment later a shell fell close to the King, and its fragments brought down a shower of leaves and twigs from the tree alongside of which he was standing. Another went whizzing over King and suite and burst somewhere in the rear. The King quietly remarked to Lehndorf that the close group about him was provoking the fire, and Lehndorf gave the word for the suite to disperse. Riding still forward, his Majesty met the first of the many wounded he was to see that day; and mounted the Roskoberg, from the crest of which a view was commanded of the whole Bistritz line. The cannon smoke, indeed, kept down by the weight of the damp atmosphere, hung low in the valley, and obscured the troops down in its trough, but the whole range of the Austrian batteries was visible on the long slope on the further side.

Prince Frederic Charles gave him the word that the moment was ripe, and shortly before ten his Majesty gave the order for his infantry to assail the villages and so force the passage of the Bistritz. Up there on the Roskoberg the King watched with engrossed intensity the long, fierce struggle of his soldiers. From out the heart of it the débris of the fight drifted to the rear, the men tried beyond endurance. One mass of troops came surging in disorder along the chaussée. William rode down from the height, and asked an officer "whence they came and whither they were going?" The officer replied that the loss in the front had been so heavy that disorganisation had resulted, and that the order to join the reserves had been given. Meanwhile the soldiers continued their hurried retirement. That is a very infectious movement in the crisis of battle; and the King stopped it with the loud imperious order, "Halt! Front!" The soldiers at first obeyed mechanically; then recognising their sovereign, fell into some semblance of line facing him and with their backs on Sadowa. "In the battle," asked William, "where is the front?" and the soldiers replied to the question by facing about. Dismounting, his Majesty set about reorganising the dishevelled companies, and order had just been re-established when an officer galloped up with the urgent command that every available man was to return to the front. The King himself gave the detachment the word to march, and as it passed him—they were men of the Second Army Corps —he called out, "Now, remember you are Pomeranians!"

It was past noon. The army of Prince Frederic Charles was engaged up to the hilt, and could gain no ground from the stubborn Austrians. The Prussians had fought their way about half way up the slope through the woods and copses, but could get no further, and had indeed to strain every nerve to hold the positions they had won. Anxious eyes watched from the Roskoberg for signs of the approach of the Crown Prince. He was overdue, there, on Benedek's right flank, but there was no indication to the eager watchers that he had begun to make his presence felt. The Austrian cannon still had their muzzles turned toward the Bistritz; Fransecky in Benatek was being punished worse than ever; no commotion in the Austrian right wing gave token of an impending diversion.

But all the same, the Crown Prince had kept tryst, and had been striking at the Austrian flank since before noon. There stood in his path between the hill of Horenowes and the Trotinka only one weak corps of the Austrian. That he had brushed aside to his own left, away in the direction of the Elbe. By one o'clock he had carried the height of Horenowes, in rear of Benatek, where the fight was still raging furiously. Then without hesitation he led his Guards to where, through the smoke drifting up from the battle-field, was visible the church steeple of the village of Chlum, right in rear of the centre of the Austrian position on the Bistritz. It was an astounding evolution, yet it was successful, and, strange to tell, entailed in its execution no serious loss. The Austrians were intent on their Bistritz front, and the Crown Prince, almost without molestation, marched a division of the Guards some two thousand paces along the rear of the Austrian fighting line. The Prussian Guards were in Chlum before three in the afternoon.

Benedek was near the place, and could not believe the tidings brought him that it was no longer his. As he rode towards it, a volley from Prussian needleguns met him, which told with severe effect on his staff, and convinced him of the misfortune that had befallen him. The Austrian reserves were hurled on Chlum with intent to re-take it, and a desperate combat ensued. It was but one division of the Prussian Guards that held Chlum, and they had to struggle hard to retain the all-important position. But succour was near; the other, the Second Guard Division, was at hand. Two more corps of the Crown Prince's army, eager for the fray, came surging up out of the Trotinka hollow on the Austrian rear. With the entry of the Prussian Guards into Chlum, the battle of König-grätz had been lost and won.

But, strangely, this result had been attained entirely without the cognisance of any part of Prince Frederic Charles's army, held stationary there on the Bistritz front and hard pressed still to hold its own. The leading Prussian division that penetrated to Chlum had moved along the reverse face of the ridge, invisible alike to the Prussians and the Austrians locked in mortal strife along the line of the Bistritz. Chlum was occupied and the battle won before the second Prussian Guard Division advancing toward that village, not along the reverse but the hither slope of the ridge, was seen by the anxious watchers on the Roskoberg, and it was a welcome sight that spoke volumes. Bismarck, in his Landwehr uniform, was up there with the King. By them stood Roon, Moltke, Lehndorf, and others, all intent on the direction whence the Crown Prince was expected. Suddenly Bismarck lowered his field-glass, and drew the attention of his neighbours to certain lines in the far distance. All telescopes were pointed thitherward, but the lines were pronounced to be ploughed ridges. There was a deep, anxious silence; then Bismarck brought down his glasses abruptly, and exclaimed in a tone of decision, "Those are not plough furrows; the spaces are not equal; they are marching lines!" Bismarck had been the first to discern the advance of the Second Army.

As the Prussian Guards dashed at the Lipa batteries, the First Army sprang forward, and with loud cheers and drums beating, went straight up the hill face. The Sadowa road was cleared as if by magic, the Austrian batteries carried with a rush, and the guns in position captured. There was still desperate fighting to be done, as the Austrians vehemently revolting with cannon and cavalry against the steady, relentless pressure with which the Prussians pushed them back out of position after position, till the bridges across the Elbe were reached, covered by the fortress guns of Königgrätz. The Austrians could not help but retreat; the day had wrought them terrible disaster; but so staunch were their infantry, so well handled and well-served their field artillery, so recklessly self-sacrificing their cavalry, that the retreat never degenerated into a rout. Yet never was victory more decisive than that won by the Prussians on the field of Königgrätz.

As soon as Horne had made good his advance up the slope from Sadowa on Lipa, King William galloped down the Roskoberg, rode through the blood and slaughter of Sadowa, and followed the chaussée on to the ridge near Langenhof, where he first found troops belonging to the Crown Prince's army. Flushed with the fight and the victory, they gave him a reception which he described in a letter to Queen Augusta: "You cannot conceive the enthusiasm which broke out when I came among them. The officers rushed to kiss my hand, which I was forced to allow for this once; the men greeted me with endless hurrahs right in the midst of the still enduring cannon-fire." Dying officers raised themselves as he rode by, eager for a word or a glance ; the King bent from the saddle and shook the hands soon to be cold in death. Following the tide of battle, he had a narrow escape from being ridden down by a headlong rush of Austrian cavalry flying from a mêlée with Prussian horsemen. He had been searching everywhere for his gallant son, and found him at last, up in the front, of course, near the village of Rosnitz, urging on the Prussian cavalry. Both father and son were greatly moved. The King took from his breast his own order *pour le mérite,* and gave it to the Crown Prince. He had before leaving Berlin conferred on him the decoration by telegraph in recognition of the Prince's success at Skalitz, but the message had never reached his Royal Highness. Rosnitz was still the centre of hard fighting, and the King was not to be restrained from exposing himself to the perils which

his troops were confronting. Bismarck, in his
capacity as Minister-President, ventured to entreat
him to desist from incurring needless danger, especially now that the victory was assured. William's
answer was worthy of a soldier-monarch : " My
troops and I are here on the battle-field : would you
have me ride away out of the shell-fire, while they
remain under it ? "   " It was well," wrote Bismarck to his wife, " that I was with him, for all the
warnings of others were in vain, and no one else
would have spoken to him as I finally did, when
I did produce some effect, after a knot of ten
soldiers and fifteen horses of the 6th Cuirassier
regiment were rolling around in their blood, and
shells were flying in very unpleasant proximity to
our sovereign. Yet I would rather have it so,
than that he should be over-prudent. He was full
of enthusiasm at his troops, so that he never heeded
the turmoil and fighting around him, and rode
about quite quietly and comfortably, as on home
parade, continually coming across battalions whom
he had to thank and say ' good-night ' to." The
old Warrior-King kept in the field till after
dark, engaged in tasks which became him. He
comforted his own wounded with words of praise
and hope. He bade his own surgeon see to the
wounds of an Austrian officer who lay in danger of

bleeding to death. He gave strict injunctions that the prisoners should be well treated, and receive share and share alike of rations with his own troops. He would have been glad at the moment of a ration, however meagre, for himself. He had swallowed a morsel of breakfast at the Klenitz inn, while they were settling the little trouble about his spurs, but while they waited on the Roskoberg for the Crown Prince to strike, his Majesty got extremely hungry. Nobody about him seemed to have had the Dugald Dalgetty virtue of looking after the provant, and not so much as a sandwich was forthcoming. A field-gendarme pulled out of his wallet a dry crust of black bread; as there seemed nothing else, perhaps his Majesty would deign to eat this humble contribution. His Majesty deigned with the keenest zest; and then a sergeant, emboldened by the royal condescension, tendered his drinking-keg, which contained a driblet of the sour wine of the country. With the sergeant's rinsings the King washed down the gendarme's crust.

Far across the ghastly battle-field, through darkness lit up by blazing villages, the King rode back from the fighting line to the village of Sadowa, where his carriage awaited him. It was a long drive back to Gitschin, and Prince Frederic Charles suggested that his Majesty should occupy

the quarters that had been taken up for himself in
the petty village of Horitz. The King was tired;
Horitz was nearer the field than Gitschin, and he
accepted the offer. The Red Prince was a man
who cared little for luxurious comfort on campaign,
and he told his uncle not to expect great things.
But the King found all he wanted—food and rest.
He ate the supper that had been got ready for his
nephew, and we are told he drank a cup of tea.
But there was no bed; the furniture of the room
consisted of a table, two chairs, and a remorselessly
hard sofa. The cushions were brought in from the
carriage, and spread on the hard sofa; the King
lay down, with his writing-case for a pillow and
his mantle for a blanket, and was sound asleep
long before Prince Frederic Charles came in from
arranging the bivouacs of his army.

No time was to be lost in reaping the fruits of
the victory of Königgrätz. News had reached the
Prussian headquarters of the approach of Benedetti,
the French Ambassador to the Court of Berlin;
and the inference was drawn that the French Emperor, jealous of the Prussian successes, was anxious
for the prestige of being a successful mediator in
the quarrel. Every step forward into Austrian
territory was a political as well as a military gain
to Prussia; and the advance on Vienna was begun

on the morning after the battle.   Benedek, sending
his most shattered division direct to Vienna, was
falling back on Moravia, the mass of his army
under orders to move on the entrenched camp of
Olmütz.   King William remained in Horitz till
the afternoon of the 5th, when royal headquarters
were advanced to Pardubitz.   Early in the morning
of the 4th his baggage had been brought on from
Gitschin to Horitz, and his servants wished him to
quit the sofa and get into his camp bed.   But his
Majesty found the sofa so comfortable that he
declined to leave it, and continued to sleep on it
till seven A.M.   He would not have the names of
the fallen sent home in the first bulletin.   "First,"
he ordered, " let the good news of victory spread;
the sad, inevitable list of losses will appear later,
and then too soon.   In the afternoon, as he was
riding over the battle-field of the previous day, he
met the Austrian Field-Marshal von Gablenz, whom
he knew well personally.   The Marshal had come
from Benedek to treat for a suspension of hostilities,
and at the foreposts he had been blindfolded by a
bandage over his eyes.   The King imagined he had
been wounded, and alighted from the carriage to
offer him condolences.   When he was informed of
the Marshal's mission, he had the bandage removed,
and sent him to Horitz to discuss his errand with

Moltke. The King himself went on to Sadowa to be present at the interment of his soldiers who had fallen there; and afterwards at Chlum took part in the funeral services over the bodies of General von Hiller and Colonel von Helldorff, both officers of the Guards who had been personally known to him. The truce which Gablenz had been sent to ask was refused, as Prussia and Italy were mutually bound to accept no suspension of hostilities save in common concert. Next day there was received a communication from the French Emperor counselling that Austria should be allowed terms. On his way to Pardubitz in the afternoon, the King rode close to the fortress of Königgrätz, and saw what a mass of war material the Austrians had abandoned under the guns of the fortress. In the Castle of Pardubitz he found 800 wounded Austrian soldiers lying entirely without surgical attendance, and immediately ordered to their assistance all available Prussian surgeons. He was laid up in Pardubitz for three days with acute sciatica, but continued to transact civil and military business in his room. On the 8th Marshal Gablenz came on a second mission, this time commissioned by the Austrian Government to treat for an armistice. His proposals were not accepted, as the conviction in the Prussian headquarter was that Austria was not

N

eager to conclude a definite peace, but wished to gain time to bring up her army of the South from Italy. On the 10th his Majesty, still ailing, crossed the frontier into Moravia, amid a great assemblage of local priests and inhabitants, and was quartered for the night in Zwittau, a Moravian town. While the royal headquarters remained in Zwittau, Benedetti arrived, and was received by the King on the morning of the 12th. After his audience of William, Bismarck took the Frenchman in hand.

Meanwhile the Prussian armies were marching steadily southward on a broad front, their faces set towards the Danube. Prince Frederic Charles moved direct on Brünn, which he entered on the 12th, having encountered but trivial opposition on his march. The Crown Prince, moving on his cousin's left, had inclined towards Olmütz, with the object of watching and masking Benedek's force gathered into the entrenched camp there. But it was not intended that the Austrian army of the North should remain in Olmütz. Before he was superseded in the supreme military command by the Archduke Albert, Benedek had sent away three of his corps by rail in the direction of Vienna. A part of the remainder of his force was on the march by road—the railway having been cut by the Prussians—when it was attacked at Tobitschau on the

15th by one of the Crown Prince's corps, and
defeated with the loss of 1,200 men and eighteen
guns.   The Crown Prince found that one corps
would suffice to watch Olmütz, and with the rest
of the army he followed in the track of Prince
Frederic Charles, passing through Brünn on the
19th.   By the 21st the Prussian hosts had come up
into line, and stood concentrated on the historic
Marchfeld, within thirty miles of the Austrian
capital.   From the forepost line the gleaming
pinnacles of the lofty spire of St. Stephen's Cathedral could be dimly seen through the heat-haze.
But between the Prussians and Vienna lay the
heavily-armed lines of Florisdorf, the redoubt-
crowned Bisamberg, and all the Austrian troops
which the Archduke Albert had been able to gather
together.

Whether those defences would have sufficed to
hinder the Prussian officers from drinking Voslauer
in the "Herzog Karl," and the Prussian soldiers
from being defrauded with sham meerschaums in
the Graben and the Kärnther-Strasse, was a problem
that happily was not to be solved.   The King had
reached Brünn on the afternoon of the 13th, received ceremoniously by the bishop and the burgo-
master, at the head of a deputation of clergy and
citizens.   In the midst of war—for a whole army

N 2

stood halted for the day in Brünn—the air seemed
to savour of peace.   Benedetti's secretary had gone
into Vienna with the conditions on which the King
would consent to an armistice.   He returned to
Brünn on the morning of the 14th with counter-
proposals, which William and his advisers regarded
as inadmissible.   So the negotiations were broken
off, and the march of the Prussian armies was resumed on the following morning.

But peace in the abstract was a general de-
sideratum.   The Austrians had encountered experiences scarcely calculated to make them sanguine
as to the issue of prolonged hostilities.   William
was privately shuddering at the idea of entering
Vienna by force, and driving his brother monarch
Francis Joseph out of the Burg-hof.   Napoleon III.
was bent on attitudinising before Europe in the
attitude of a puissantly successful mediator.   As
for Bismarck, he was the genial cynic of the piece,
and, for that matter, of the peace.   He had no
personal or professional ill-will to anybody—only
he meant to have just what he wanted.   If Austria
would give him his terms, he would much rather not
exacerbate the situation by going into Vienna; if
she would not, then her blood be upon her own
head.   If he got his terms, he did not in the least
mind that Napoleon, if he had the fancy that way,

should figure as the *Deus ex machina*.   And indeed,
if Napoleon chose to nourish the notion that he
was to make a profit out of the function of umpire,
was it his place rudely to shiver the illusion ? Was
it not politic rather to let the assumption pass with
that absence of direct negative which might be
construed into an indefinite affirmative, and let the
future arrange itself ?

Benedetti was cheerfully fussy in the business
of mediation.   He went into Vienna on the 15th
with the news of the Prussian refusal of the
Austrian proposals, and spent a couple of days in
the Austrian capital, where he had free and quick
telegraphic communication with Paris.   On the
evening of the 17th, the King, in the midst of a
general illumination, reached Nikolsburg, and took
up his residence in the magnificent castle of the
Dietrichstein Princes, from whom it had passed to
Count Mensdorff, the Austrian Foreign Minister
and the political antagonist of Bismarck.   In the
Castle of Nikolsburg, Napoleon the Great had
resided in the interval between Austerlitz and his
entry into Vienna, and King William slept in the
room that had been occupied by the man who had
driven his parents out of Berlin.

To Nikolsburg came Benedetti on the following
day, bringing amended proposals from Vienna, and

on the 22nd an armistice to last for five days—till
mid-day on the 27th—was agreed upon. The line
of demarcation was defined, and each within its own
bounds both armies worked hard to be ready for
the alternative of renewed hostilities, should the
peace negotiations miscarry that were being wrestled
out in Bismarck's cabinet at Nikolsburg. But the
great Prussian lion couchant on the Rossbach was
not to spring. On the evening of the 26th the
preliminaries of peace were agreed on, and the
Seven Weeks' War was at an end. Its results to
Prussia were momentous. Austria accepted her
utter exile from Germany, recognised the dissolution
of the old Germanic Confederation, and consented
to non-participation in the reorganised Confederation of which Prussia was to have the unquestioned military and diplomatic leadership. Saxony
had to enter the new Confederation bodily, and
Hesse-Darmstadt as regarded her territories north
of the Maine. To Prussia were annexed Hanover,
Electoral Hesse, Nassau, Sleswig and Holstein,
the City of Frankfort-on-the-Maine, and pieces of
Hesse-Darmstadt and Bavaria. Prussia's total
acquisitions amounted to over 6,500 square miles
of territory, with a population exceeding 4,000,000.
The States with which she had been at war paid
her by way of indemnity for the charges she had

been put to in worsting them, sums amounting in all to nearly £10,000,000 sterling. In a material sense, it had not been a bad seven weeks' work for Prussia; in a sense other than material, she had profited incalculably more. Henceforth Germany and Prussia were virtually synonymous terms.

On the 31st of July his Majesty reviewed the army of Prince Frederic Charles, drawn up on the Marchfeld within fifteen miles of Vienna. In long array there defiled past him the victors of Podoll, of Münchengrätz, of Gitschin, of Königgrätz—a great host in grand condition and in the finest discipline. At Brünn, on the 2nd August, on his way back to Berlin, he reviewed the Crown Prince's army, when with drawn sword he rode past the saluting point at the head of his own regiment of West Prussian Grenadiers. Travelling through Prague he arrived in Berlin on the 4th, and next day went to the Cathedral to return thanks for his safe return, spending the rest of the day in visiting the hospitals. By the 18th of September there was not a spiked helmet or a needle-gun on Austrian soil; and Berlin on the 20th and 21st was the scene of magnificent *fêtes* to celebrate the return of the army. The triumphal entry of the King and his victorious troops took place on the former day;

on the evening of the latter the King entertained
at dinner, in the Palace, twelve hundred generals
and principal officers who had served in the campaign, and all Berlin sparkled and glowed in a
universal illumination.

CHAPTER X.

THE GATHERING OF THE GREAT STORM.

REALISING from the commencement of his reign that his hold on France was precarious, Napoleon III. was ever restlessly eager to strengthen his position by pandering to the national hunger for the prestige of successful military operations and the acquisition of territory. The earlier years of his reign had been fairly fortunate both in war and in annexation; but his Mexican enterprise was going badly; and the Gastein Convention, which seemed to establish amity between two Powers whom he would rather have seen at variance, gave him disquietude. Its rupture brought him new hopes, and, on the eve of the war of 1866, he made Prussia the offer of active co-operation in return for what Dominie Sampson called a "consideration." Austria defeated by the conjunct arms of France, Prussia, and Italy, the face of Europe was to undergo material alteration. Prussia was to have

all North Germany, Venetia was to be allotted to
Italy, and Prussia in return for France's co-operation
was to compliment her with the territory lying
between the Moselle and the Rhine.

Prussia declined the proposition, but Bismarck
was wily enough to secure by vague non-committing
half-promises the neutrality of France during the
weeks while Prussia was crushing Austria in
Bohemia.   But Königgrätz startled Napoleon, and
set France in ferment.   Austria tempted him with
the cession of Venetia to strike in for her, but the
gravity of the possible issues caused him to hesitate.
Prestige, and something perhaps more substantial,
might be gained by his assumption of the *rôle* of
a weighty and powerful mediator.   He was not,
indeed, strong enough to get all for himself he
asked, for Prussia point blank refused his demand
for the fortress of Mayence, made though that
demand was under threat of war.   But Prussia
had to confront the alternative of making certain
concessions to the importunate mediator, or of
going to war with him.   Bismarck was wise and
could wait. " I thought it my duty," said he, later,
" to advise his Majesty to sanction the terms submitted as they stood, rather than jeopardise our
previous success and gamble for more."   The cards
were being made up in case the gamble had been

ventured on. While the negotiations were in
progress, Roon had been making his preparations
for the contingency of war with France. Half a
million of Prussian soldiers were already in the
field, but their hands were full; Roon had warned
for immediate mobilisation 350,000 more.

Napoleon had thought to raise in Germany a
counter-buttress against Prussia's supremacy by
enforcing the stipulation that the South German
States should be at liberty to form themselves
into a South German Confederacy It was thus
hoped to avert the ultimate fusion of Germany into
a Federal whole, and to establish a power which
the smart of defeat and jealousy of the conqueror
might in a future war range on the side of Prussia's
enemies. But Bismarck was a better diplomatist
than Napoleon. Confident in the hindrances to
the formation of a Southern Bund, Bismarck did
not refuse assent to the Austro-French stipulation; but he formed and knit together the North
German Confederation in which Prussia was
dominant, and quietly negotiated an alliance offensive and defensive with each of the Southern
States separately. No Southern Bund was ever
formed, and when the Franco-German war broke
out, Napoleon saw the shipwreck of his abortive
devices in the spectacle of the troops of Bavaria .

and Würtemberg marching on the Rhine in line with the battalions of Prussia.

Königgrätz stuck in the throat of France, and the master-men of Prussia recognised from the hour of the victory that as the outcome of it France would have to be dealt with one or other of two ways. Either Prussia would have to fight France, or make such concession to France as would smooth France's national vanity ruffled by Königgrätz. Concession was scarcely a palatable expedient; and regarding war sooner or later as inevitable, Prussia assiduously addressed herself to the task of preparing for the conflict. The Bohemian campaign, though swift and glorious, had been none the less pregnant of lessons and warnings to William and his military subordinates. " Rest and be thankful " was no motto for the new army which William had called into existence; to it the use of victories was to teach it how to win other victories.

Less purposeful, less resolute, less gifted with the power of concentration, France foresaw war not less clearly than did Prussia. It may be said that while the latter accepted the inevitable, the former it was which created and maintained the inevitability. The French nation and its head acted and reacted on each other in a curious mutually detrimental fashion. Napoleon would probably have preferred a quiet life; he was a phlegmatic man, and while ungifted with energy enough to prepare himself for serious contingencies, had quite acuteness enough to perceive how dangerous it was unprepared to confront or create such contingencies. But if he would pursue an unaggressive policy and let France enjoy quiet, then France proceeded to give him trouble and endanger his position by clamouring for the concession of liberal institutions. That kind of concession he perfectly realised led straight up to an end of him. It was pleasant to be an Emperor, and he did not want to go. But he could only stay—or rather there was for him the only chance of staying — by diverting the nation from hankering after liberty, and concentrating its interest on a brilliant and flashy foreign policy. So he was always, to use a military simile, sapping up towards a great coup in the effort to keep France distracted. But France did not find the engineering process sufficiently interesting to lure her from agitation for internal reforms; and the Emperor had to make concessions in this direction. He slackened the curb on public opinion; then public opinion with its head free bolted with him, and carried him into war, if he were not to lose altogether his rather washball style of seat in the saddle. In the end rider and ridden came an "imperial crowner" over the big German fence.

A fine opportunity for a dazzling coup seemed to offer itself in the beginning of 1867. The King of Holland was also Grand Duke of Luxemburg. That duchy had been a member of the old Germanic Confederation which the war of 1866 had shattered. Its capital had been a very important Federal fortress, one of Germany's great bulwarks against France, and the garrison had consisted of Prussian troops since the Treaty of Vienna in 1815. When the Germanic Confederation broke up, the King of Holland acquired full sovereign rights over Luxemburg. Its inhabitants showed no inclination to enter the new North German Confederation which the war of 1866 created; and the higher classes among them were understood to hold Prussia in aversion. It was against the policy of the new Confederation to have included in it possessions belonging to foreign rulers, and no pressure was exerted to bring Luxemburg within its pale. A Prussian garrison, however, still continued to occupy its fortress; although that fortress had been defederalised. Prussia had insisted on this right, holding that it vested in her altogether apart from the relations that had subsisted between the Grand Duchy and the old Confederation; and the right

was not actively challenged by the King of Holland.
He had no particular fondness for his Luxemburg
possession, detached as it was from the rest of his
dominions, and he was a man to whom money was
always peculiarly acceptable.   He had, then, no
objection to enter into an arrangement with France,
whereby the latter was to acquire by purchase the
Grand Duchy.   On the French side there was a
not unnatural anxiety that the negotiation should
be kept secret from Prussia till the bargain had
been carried through, but the King of Holland did
not see his way to this, and formally notified
Prussia of the transaction in progress.   Prussia
refused her assent, and further refused to withdraw
her garrison from a fortress that had been in her
guardianship for half a century.   The Duchy was
German soil, and the public feeling of Prussia ran
high against its alienation.   On the other hand,
France was in a state of acute excitement.   Its national jealousy of Prussia, louring luridly ever since
Königgrätz, flashed out vehemently against the
idea that an arrangement to which the Emperor of
the French had agreed was to be abandoned, simply
because Prussia thought fit to forbid it.

War seemed imminent, yet the guiding forces
on neither side really desired war. It has been said
that Bismarck had great difficulty in restraining

King William from responding actively to the fervid demands of his people, but this is only gossip. Prussia would fight if need were; she would not yield; but she was not yet quite ready for war with France. On the other hand, Napoleon was not eager for war. The French army was in a state of reconstruction, and was not in case for a great struggle. Both nations were nevertheless arming, when the intervention of the European Powers effected a settlement. By the Treaty of London, ratified on the 31st May, 1867, the Duchy was declared a neutral State under the guarantee of the Powers. The town of Luxemburg ceased to be a fortress, the Prussian garrison was withdrawn, and the fortifications were to be demolished. War, at least for the moment, was averted, and there were sanguine people who believed that an era of lasting peace had dawned on Europe.

The ink of the treaty was scarcely dry when King William, accompanied by his great minister, arrived at Paris on a visit to the Emperor Napoleon. It was the summer of the Great Exhibition, when Napoleon was on the summit of the big soap-bubble he had blown, and was able to vie with his illustrious relative in the possession of a " parterre of princes." The Czar had arrived in advance of William, and was living in the Elysée. The Crown

Prince and Princess were already in Paris before
the King arrived on June 5th.   Bismarck had fired
his salute to France before leaving Berlin, in the
announcement that he had concluded with the
States of Southern Germany a full understanding
as to the relations between them and the North
German Confederation.   At the railway station
his Majesty was received by the Emperor, accompanied by the ministers and marshals of the Empire,
and was escorted to his quarters in the Pavillon Mar-
san, one of the wings of the Tuileries.   After presenting his respects to the Empress his hostess, he
went to the Elysée to call on his nephew the Czar,
who returned the visit next morning, when the
three potentates went out into the private garden
of the Tuileries, and strolled in conversation among
the flower beds of the narrow slip of reserved
garden.   Later in the day Napoleon and his guests
drove to Longchamps to witness on that field a
review of 60,000 French soldiers.   It had not been
the first review William had seen there, nor was it
to be the last.   In 1814 he had witnessed the combined hosts of Prussia, Austria, and Russia march
past the saluting point at which stood a Russian, a
Prussian, and an Austrian monarch.   Russian and
Prussian monarchs were now at the same saluting
point again ; the grandson of Francis was to come

o

later—for the moment he was being crowned King
of Hungary on the Krönungsberg of Pesth.   Five
years later William was to look again on an armed
pageant on the Longchamps sward, when his host
of 1867 was to be his prisoner, and the troops he
was to review the conquerors of France.

William drove out to Longchamps along with
the Empress Eugénie ; the Czar and his two sons
sat in the same carriage with the Emperor.   On
the field each potentate rode at the head of a brilliant staff, while great ladies looked down on the
scene from the imperial tribune.   Bismarck made
himself visible to the Parisians in his Landwehr
cuirassier uniform crowned by the spiked helmet ;
and it is recorded that the Parisians " were getting
reconciled to him on account of his martial bearing
in the field."   Neither the Czar nor the King was
particularly popular in Paris.   Cries of " Vive la
Prusse " were few and far between, and the angry
shouts of " Vive la Pologne " had been yelled at
Alexander ever since he had stepped out of the
Gare du Nord.   But, at all events, nobody tried to
shoot William, whereas Berezouski interfered with
the Czar's ability to boast of the same immunity.
Fête followed fête while the monarchs were the
guests of Napoleon—there was one in the Hôtel de
Ville, when the salons, crammed with 8,000 people,

were illuminated by 18,000 wax candles; another
in the Tuileries, where the dancing was interrupted
at midnight that the guests might witness the
splendid show of fireworks and illuminations in the
garden. There were luncheons at the Trianon and
visits to Versailles and Fontainebleau, till on the
14th the King bade adieu to his host and hostess,
and was back in his own capital next day. His
simplicity of manner was noted by the Parisians
just as the English in 1814 had marked this characteristic of his father. He would not have a
formal reception when he first went to the Exhibition, and in his subsequent visits uniformly strove
to preserve his incognito. He quietly put down
an officious commissioner with the simple remark,
"Pray make no bother on my account, but regard
me but as one more visitor to Paris." His Majesty
took a great deal of interest in diamond cutting,
and spent a good deal of money with the English
jewellery houses, driving, it was reported, rather
close bargains. When the time came for him to
go home, he did not scatter costly souvenirs and
high-sounding orders as the Czar did so lavishly.
During his stay he had continually expressed the
wish that no fuss should be made with him; and
when he went away he simply thanked the Emperor
very warmly for the cordial reception he had met

with, and left 40,000 francs to be distributed among the servants who had attended on him.

Queen Isabella had fled from Spain in September, 1868, but its throne was still vacant in the summer of 1870. There had been some sort of an intrigue in Paris in the previous summer for the promotion of the candidature of Prince Frederic, a younger son of the old Prince of Hohenzollern-Sigmaringen, the house of which King William was head. It was said that the Empress Eugénie favoured the project, and that Prince Frederic might marry a relative of hers. Perhaps such credentials hardly recommended him to the Spaniards, and no offer of the throne was made to Frederic. In the autumn of 1869 it was that Prim's project of inviting the candidature of Frederic's eldest brother, Prince Leopold, was first mooted. The idea was distasteful to the French Court party, at whose instigation Isabella was persuaded to abdicate in favour of her son, Prince Alfonso. But Alfonso's turn was to come later. In the summer of 1870 Prince Leopold signified his readiness to accept the Spanish Crown if the choice of the Cortes should fall upon him.

The news of this acceptance reached Paris from Madrid on July 5th. The political horizon of Europe was then so delusively clear that an English statesman. who certainly had claims to be considered well-informed, affirmed publicly that it was without a cloud. But the storm gathered with a speed which proved how treacherous had been the calm. Paris broke into universal excitement, and the machinations of Bismarck were vehemently denounced. In reply to an interpellation, the Foreign Minister professed a surprise that must have been feigned, spoke significantly of the "balance of power," and affirmed the intention to prevent the election of the Hohenzollern prince, by a line of action in which there should be "neither fear nor hesitation." His words had an unmistakably warlike tone, and they were received with vociferous applause. The minister's statement, which was read, not spoken, had been settled at a council held in the morning, and presided over by the Emperor. The profession of surprise was ridiculous in the face of the fact that Prince Leopold's candidature had been extensively discussed in the press, and that the French Ambassador in Madrid had listened to what Prim said in the Cortes three weeks previously.

France immediately began military preparations. The Paris press, almost with one accord, rushed into menacing and hostile utterances, which inflamed the soreness already existing against Prussia in the popular mind. England offered her good

offices, but without effective results.   The Prussian
Government's reply to the French demand for ex-
planation, although calm and measured, was scarcely
calculated to soothe the irritation into which France
was lashing herself.   Bismarck stated simply that
he knew nothing officially of Prince Leopold's
candidature.   The Prussian Government did not
pretend to interfere with any action the Spanish
nation might choose to take, and were unable to
give any information regarding what negotiations,
if any, might have passed between the provisional
Government of Madrid and the Hohenzollern prince.
A financial convulsion thrilled through Europe,
and in one week there had occurred a depreciation
in stocks common to the Paris and London Ex-
changes representing a sum that could not have
been under fifty millions sterling.

For a few hours the catastrophe of war seemed
averted.   Prince Leopold, as soon as he had realised
what complications his candidature had evoked,
hastened with loyal self-sacrifice to renounce it.
He requested his father to be the medium of
communication to that effect; and on the 12th of
July the Spanish Ambassador in Paris announced
officially to the French Government that Prince
Leopold had signified his renunciation of pretensions
to the throne of Spain.   Upon this announcement

M. Ollivier declared unofficially that the affair was at an end.

But France was not content. She had gained her point, but she thought fit to follow up the success by provocative insolence. She was hurrying troops to the frontier, and was bent on rushing on her fate. On the same day the Prussian minister in Paris was requested to communicate to Bismarck a demand that King William should write a letter of apology to the Emperor. Bismarck's grim reply was that the ambassador must have misunderstood the French ministers, and that he was to desire them to put the demand into writing, and have it presented in the regular form through their ambassador in Berlin.

That ambassador was M. Benedetti, and he was vigorously turned on to William in person. The old King was staying at Ems, taking his annual course of the waters, while angry passions were rising in Berlin and Paris. During his morning walk on July 13th he met Benedetti, and, taking a newspaper out of his pocket, expressed his satisfaction at having learnt from it of Prince Leopold's renunciation, in the wisdom of which he personally quite concurred. To his surprise the Frenchman demanded his assurance that he would never, under any circumstances, give his consent to his kinsman's

candidature.   The King replied that he would give
no such pledge, but must reserve to himself liberty
of action.   At breakfast his Majesty received a
letter from Prince Anton of Hohenzollern, giving
formal intimation of his son's withdrawal; whereupon the King sent his aide-de-camp to Benedetti with the intelligence of this confirmation of
the newspaper report, and with the further communication that he looked upon it as terminating
the incident.

To the aide-de-camp Benedetti communicated
his explicit instructions to demand a fresh audience
of his Majesty, and insist on the King's categorical
consent to Prince Leopold's renunciation, with the
further assurance that the candidature should never
be resumed.   William still kept his temper, and
sent back the answer that he consented to the
renunciation of the prince in the same sense as he
had accepted the candidature—as a matter which
had no concern for him as king, and still less
concerned either Prussia or the North German
Confederation.   There resulted an absolute im-
possibility on his part to give assurance as to the
future on a question with which really he had nothing to do.

But Benedetti, driven by those cogent instructions of his, was still importunate for another

audience personally to push for assurances as to the future. The King's back did at last begin to get up. He sent his aide-de-camp with a final message to Benedetti to the laconic effect that he had nothing more to say to him. The story has been contradicted that Benedetti insisted on accosting his Majesty making his afternoon promenade; and that the King turned from him with the direction to his aide-de-camp—"Inform this person that I have nothing to say to him, and desire no further intercourse with him." But there could be but one motive for the unprecedented importunity with which the French ambassador, acting on commands from Paris, set himself to badger the Prussian monarch unattended as he was by a minister. There was the clear intention to force not on Prussia only, but on its sovereign as an individual, the alternative of putting up with a humiliation or of accepting the quarrel so swaggeringly urged.

CHAPTER XI.

IT has been alleged that neither King William nor M. Benedetti was aware that offence had been given and taken in the final communication between them at Ems on July 13th, until Paris and Berlin informed them that each had been insulted. If this were indeed so, both must have possessed an abnormal obtuseness, in which neither the French nor the German nation in the least degree participated. And if it were so, William would scarcely have so abruptly interrupted his cure, and hurried back to Berlin without allowing a day to intervene.

The whole German nation had suddenly caught fire. The Teuton blood was up from the Baltic to the Lake of Constance, from Treves to Memel. It was to a capital in a white heat of martial enthusiasm that the King returned on the night of July 14th. As he drove from the station to the palace, the Linden was in a blaze of illumination, and

volleys of cheering greeted him as he passed through
the vast excited multitudes.   In front of the palace
so dense was the throng that the mounted gen-
darmes could hardly make a lane through it for the
royal carriage.   Over and over again had the King
to come to his accustomed window, and acknowledge the patriotic fervour of the subjects who would
not let him rest.   The attitude of the French
nation and the French Government made war all
but certain ; and on the 17th the instructions
radiated by wire from Berlin for the immediate
mobilisation of the whole army of the North German Confederation.   The wonderful machinery was
in perfect order, and within a fortnight there stood
massed near the French frontier upwards of half a
million of men, with all the equipment and appli-
ances required for the field service of a host so vast.
William, during the interval that elapsed before
his departure to join the army, resided partly in
Potsdam, partly in Berlin.   It was at the private
station at Potsdam that, on the morning of the
21st, Dr. Russell saw the King receive his venerable
consort, who had travelled from the Rhine to be
with her husband during the last days he should
spend at home. It was in the New Palace of
Potsdam that, on the 23rd, the royal grandfather
and father were present at the christening of the

youngest-born daughter of the Crown Prince, a
ceremony at which were present also most of the
commanders who a few days later were to be direct-
ing the operations of the armies that were already
hurrying to the front.   It was in Berlin, on the
18th, that the King, in his plain, terse, effective
style, replied to the address presented him by the
Town Council of Berlin.   " God knows," said the
old monarch, "I am not answerable for this war.
The demand made on me I could not do other than
reject.   My response to it has gained the approval
of all the towns and provinces, the expression of
which I have received from all parts of Germany,
and even from Germans residing beyond the seas.
Heavy sacrifices will be required from my people.
We have been rendered unaccustomed to them by
the quickly-gained victories which we achieved
during the last two wars.   We shall not get off so
cheaply this time; but I know what I may expect
from my army and from those now hastening to
join its ranks.   The instrument is sharp and finely-
tempered; the issue is in the hands of God.   I
know also what I may expect from those who are
called upon to alleviate the wounds, the pains, and
the sufferings which war inflicts."

His Majesty opened the Session of the North
German Parliament on the 19th, amidst a whirl-

wind of enthusiasm. In his speech he was emphatic
that the candidature of the Hohenzollern Prince
had been seized upon by France as a mere pretext
for a *casus belli*, "put forward in a manner long
since unknown in the annals of diplomatic intercourse, and adhered to after the removal of the
very pretext itself, with that disregard for the
peoples' right to the blessings of peace of which
the history of a former ruler of France affords so
many analogous examples. . . . But," continued
the venerable soldier-king, "the German nation
contains within itself the will and the power to
repel the renewed aggression of France. With a
clear gauge we have measured the responsibility
which, before the judgment seat of God and of man,
must fall upon him who drags two great and peace-
loving peoples into a devastating war." The echo
of the royal words came from the lips of Bismarck,
when on the same day he announced that the
French *chargé d'affaires*—Benedetti had hurried
from Ems to Paris—had delivered him France's
formal declaration of war against Prussia. The
response of Parliament was practical. For session
after session Bismarck had wrestled in vain for the
sanction of the Prussian Parliament to the expenditure required for the reorganisation of the Prussian army now the North German Parliament

enthusiastically voted fifteen millions sterling **to**
furnish the Army of the Confederation with the
sinews of war.

On the same 19th of July the King decreed the
revival of the order of the "Iron Cross," which
had fallen into abeyance after the wars of the early
part of the century, and announced that the decoration "should be conferred, without distinction of
rank or condition, either on the battle-field, or at
home after the war, as a reward for service in the
cause of the honour and independence of the fatherland." On the 21st he issued the command that
Wednesday, the 27th of July, was to be observed
as an "extraordinary and universal day of prayer,
and solemnised by services in the churches, and by
abstention from public business so far as the pressing needs of the time permit." In a proclamation
dated the 23rd, he thanked the nation for its
patriotic devotion. "There have come to me,"
said he, "from every tribe of the German fatherland, from every section of the German nation, even
from beyond the seas, such countless assurances of
devotion and self-sacrifice for the common fatherland, that I hold it no less a pleasure than a duty
publicly to bear testimony to this German unani-
mity; and to add to the expression of my thanks
as the Sovereign, the assurance that I, for my part,

will return fidelity for fidelity, and unalterably
abide by my duty. Love for our common country,
the unanimous uprising of every branch of the
nation, has smoothed every difficulty and reconciled
every contention; and more united now than at
any former period of her history, Germany will find
in her unity no less than in the justice of her
cause, a pledge that the war will be succeeded by a
lasting peace, and that from this bloody seed will
spring a Divine harvest of German unity and
freedom."

The invasion of the Rhine provinces by France,
which all the world in the first instance had
assumed as a certainty, was becoming more and
more unlikely; and the gathering of German
troops in the vicinity of the frontier line was
already well advanced, when King William left his
capital on the evening of the 31st of July, on his
way to take the active command of his armies in
the field. His departure was made the occasion of
a most moving popular demonstration. His Majesty
drove to the station in an open victoria, with the
Queen sitting by his side, and the route was lined
by dense and enthusiastic crowds, who cheered the
royal couple with strong-lunged fervour. The
emotion of the scene and the occasion moved the
Queen to tears, and William's face was quivering

as his hand nervously smoothed his white moustache.   Along the thronged streets, under the
crowded windows, the covered roofs, and the multi-
tudinous banners, the old soldier-monarch went
forth to his last campaign.   At the station were
Bismarck, Moltke, Roon, Podbielski, and the personnel of a great staff.   It was a touching scene
when the King embraced his wife amidst the
sympathetic silence of the vast throng.   Augusta
was sobbing with uncontrollable emotion, and the
tears were running down the King's cheeks, as
amid cheering that vied with the din of the
thunder-storm which was raging, the train rolled
slowly out of the station.   The departing King
had done a graceful act—announced in language that well became a sovereign going out to
head a nation in arms.   " To my people," was the
following proclamation addressed : " On my departure to-day for the army, to fight with it for
Germany's honour and the preservation of our
most precious possessions, I wish to grant an
amnesty for all political crimes and offences, in
recognition of the unanimous uprising of my people
in this crisis.   My people know with me that the
rupture of the peace and the provocation of war
did not come from our side.   But, being challenged,
we are resolved, like our forefathers, placing full

trust in God, to accept the battle for the defence of the Fatherland."

The railways were so engrossed by the transport of troops and material that the King's journey from Berlin to Mayence, where his headquarters—afterwards known throughout the war indifferently as the "Great" and as the "Royal" headquarters—remained established for several days, was rather slow. On his arrival at Mayence, William issued the following proclamation to his army :—"All Germany with one mind stands in arms against a neighbouring State which has surprised us by declaring war against us without any cause. The defence of the threatened Fatherland, of our honour and our hearths, is at stake. To-day I undertake the command of the whole army, and I advance cheerfully to a struggle which in former times our fathers, similarly situated, fought out gloriously. The whole Fatherland, and I, your Sovereign, trust in you with confidence. The Lord God will be with our righteous cause." They were no empty words which William used when he announced that he undertook the command of his army. He was its chief in deed as well as in name. He shared in the conception of the strategy which Moltke instructed. Nothing of importance was done without his cognisance and approval.

P

His personality made itself felt, not alone in every department of the great headquarter-staff that served him directly, but throughout the whole army in the field. All who were conversant with the conduct of the Franco-German War were well aware how little of a " figure-head " commander was this King on campaign. Few foreigners had better opportunities of judging how paramount were William's supervision and authority than had William Howard Russell, who thus bears his testimony :—" So far as I can see, there never was a more *real* commander-in-chief than this aged King. History will no doubt do him justice. At present his glory is swallowed up or eclipsed in the fame of Moltke and Bismarck ; but the King exercises the most active influence and control over the military operations, and is absolutely and entirely paramount in his administration of the army, and in his direction of its personnel. It was he who created this vast host, and it is he who knows how to use it. His eye is as clear and as keen as if he were twenty instead of seventy-three, and he understands the soldier from his boot-heel to the spike on his helmet."

Before the King crossed the frontier, the two great battles of Wörth and of Spicheren had been fought simultaneously on the 6th of August.

Before then, on the 2nd of August, there had been
the promenade of Saarbrück, and on the 4th Douay
had been overwhelmed by numbers at Wissem-
bourg. Everywhere success had irradiated the
German arms, and already the uneasy consciousness
that their enemies were better men than themselves
had begun to sap that confidence which is
perhaps of more value to French soldiers than to
any other fighting men in the world.

It would be to write a history of the war to
describe in detail the various and frequently
changed dispositions of the German armies in the
field. At the outset there were three armies. The
First, commanded by General Steinmetz, consisted
of the 1st (East Prussian), 7th (Westphalian), and
8th (Rhineland) army corps, and the 1st and 3rd
cavalry divisions; it numbered about 80,000 men,
and was gathered on the frontier between Treves
and Saarbrück. The Second Army was commanded by Prince Frederic Charles, nephew of
the King, and was composed of the Prussian
Guard, the 2nd (Pomeranian), 3rd (Brandenburg),
4th (Saxon Province), 9th (Hessian, &c.), 10th
(Hanoverian), and 12th (Royal Saxon) army corps,
with the Guard, 5th, 6th, and 12th cavalry divisions; it numbered little short of 200,000 men,
and its region of concentration inside the German

P 2

frontier was the western section of the Palatinate.
The Third Army, commanded by the Crown Prince
of Prussia, had its route from Speyer by Landau,
to its region of concentration in the eastern portion
of the Palatinate, and was made up of the 5th
(Posen), 6th (Silesian), and 11th (Mediatised Provinces), North German Army Corps, the 1st and
2nd Bavarian Army Corps, the Würtemberg and
Baden divisions, and the 2nd and 4th cavalry divisions; the numerical strength of the Third Army
being in all about 175,000 men.   The Prussian
official account puts the total strength of the
German field army at 462,000 infantry, 56,800
cavalry, and 1,584 guns; and the same authority
states that, including the reserve and garrison
troops, the number of soldiers drawing rations in
August, 1870 (the month when the mobilisation
was virtually completed), amounted to 1,183,000
men.   It should have been said that South Germany had unanimously and enthusiastically thrown
in its fortunes with the North German Confederation, and thus disappointed the expectation, or at
least the hope, of Napoleon.

The King's headquarters reached Saarbrück on
the 8th of August, two days after the battle of
Spicheren had been fought.   His Majesty had
rooms in the Hotel Guepratt, in the suburb of St.

Johann.   He was now in the only German town
the French had set foot in.   Their occupation of
Saarbrück, barely two miles inside the frontier line,
was scarcely a great stride on the road to Berlin ;
but they never were to get further in that direction,
and they had held Saarbrück only for three days.
When the King reached the little frontier town, it
was crammed with the wounded of the Spicheren,
among whom the King went with words of sympathy and encouragement.   Already his Uhlans
were pushing on towards Metz and the Moselle,
and the infantry of both the First and Second
armies were steadily plodding on behind the
advanced fringe of horsemen.   At length, on the
11th August, William in person invaded France.
On the previous day, indeed, he had crossed the
frontier to visit the battle-field of the 6th, where he
had looked down from the edge of the Spicheren
plateau on the steep ascent so gallantly stormed
by his soldiers, and where a peasant pointed out
to him the spot from which on the 2nd, the day of
the "baptism of fire," the Emperor Napoleon and
his son had watched the advance of Bataille's soldiers
on the long low ridge covering Saarbrück, held so
stoutly by Von Pestel's handful.

There was no more railway travelling now for
the old monarch.   From Saarbrück to Paris he was

to drive in his field carriage. That was a plain, solid, strongly-built barouche, seated for four, but the King seldom had more than one of his personal aides-de-camp as travelling companion. Sometimes Moltke or Roon drove with him instead, and occasionally, but not often, Bismarck, whose carriage usually followed close behind the King's. The royal carriage was drawn by a team of four fine dark brown horses. The postilions — there was no coachman—wore braided dark blue jackets, with tall hats economically covered with waterproof. The King's two valets sat on the box-seat. One of these was an old man —to all appearance as old as his master—who had been in the personal service of his Majesty all his life. In front of the royal carriage rode a detachment of the cavalry escort commanded by a lieutenant; there followed it on the march the plain serviceable carriages of the high officers of the staff; behind those the vehicles containing the minor functionaries; and in rear of these again the baggage waggons and a squadron of led horses, the procession being closed by a smaller section of the cavalry escort. The whole cortège was plain, useful, and workmanlike; the baggage was cut down to severe field allowance; and in its sombre Spartan simplicity the campaigning equipage of King William contrasted mightily with

the elaborate and rather gaudy train which followed
Napoleon out of Sedan.

His first night on hostile soil King William
spent in the little town of Saint Avold, occupying
a house which fronted on the market-place. Now
he was indeed " on campaign," although it was not
until a few days later that he was to listen to the
cannon thunder. He was among his soldiers, and
to encourage them was at once his duty and his
pleasure. Hours of the next day he spent standing
in the market-place of Saint Avold, greeting his
children as they strode by him in the steady,
persistent current of the advance. An eye-witness
describes the scene :—" By his side was Moltke,
gaunt, thin, and wiry. Close behind stood Bismarck.
A few general officers stood about, but there was
no regular staff, nor anything like a guard or
escort. Interspersed among the generals were the
street boys of Saint Avold, gazing up with eyes of
wonder at 'le Roi Prussien.' A private soldier in
his shirt-sleeves, carrying a loaf in his hand, all but
floured his Majesty's elbow, and others stood around,
forming a close circle behind the officers. But if
King William was homely in his immediate sur-
roundings, those who stood by him were spectators
with him of a sight that might well flush his
cheek with pride and emotion. For during the

hours while the King stood in this market-place,
there ceased not to stream past him the army of
which he was the chief. Now it was a regiment
of white-coated, steel-breasted curassiers that came
on stately, the ground shaking under the tramp of
the great horses as the air vibrated to the mighty
cheer from the deep-chested men; then a regiment
of infantry three battalions strong, each with its
band playing at its head, the men marching
eight abreast, and already seasoned in the march
and the bivouac, looking fit to do anything and go
anywhere. The cheering swelled into a shout of
proud joy as regiments came by with ranks already
thinned by the desperate storm of Spicheren, and
when the King with a wave of his hands greeted
them with the appreciative ' Morgen, Knappe
Jungens ! '   Hussars, Uhlans, horse - artillery
diversified the dense masses of infantry, all arms
appearing equally serviceable. With all the field
officers the King shook hands and exchanged
a few words, but he seemed best pleased to look
into the enthusiastic faces of his men as they
passed. King as he was, he was none the less
a soldier. It was amusing to hear him reprove a
man for being out of step, and another for
having his needle-gun on the wrong shoulder.
No one would have imagined that the upright

form and square shoulders carried a load of seventy-three years."

On the 13th the king's headquarters moved forward through Faulquemont, a little dung-hill village a couple of marches south-east of Metz, whither not a week before Napoleon had driven out of Metz with Changarnier, to take counsel with poor Bazaine trying to make the best of a bad business; and on a few miles nearer the Moselle to the village of Herny, where his Majesty billeted himself on the priest. Next day old Steinmetz rather rashly tried to take the bull by the horns on his own account, and committed himself to the bloody battle of Courcelles, or Borny, as the French call it, with a fierce recklessness which was by no means approved of in the royal headquarters. Next day the King, with Moltke and Bismarck, rode over the field, approached Metz so nearly that he was fired upon by the French outposts, and, if tales were true, gave the old "lion of Skalitz" rather a bad quarter of an hour. But in after years Germans will acknowledge what a contribution to the success of the great turning movement the issue of which was the cooping up of Bazaine in Metz, was this perhaps over-heavy onslaught by Steinmetz on Bazaine's rear.

The desperate battle of **Mars-la-Tour was**

raging in full fury away there on the great plateau
beyond the Moselle, as the King drove through the
villages and the vineyards from Herny to the old
historic town of Pont-à-Mousson.   Before he slept
on the night of the 16th there came news to him
from Prince Frederic Charles, quartered in Gorze
amidst a gruesome chaos of wounded, that on that
day had been fought the fiercest battle the Prussian
arms had known since Ligny.

Thus far Moltke's strategy had been successful.
Bazaine had tried, perhaps with no great heart in
his work, to obey the orders which bade him "get
on toward Chalons."   Alvensleben had stood in his
path till Prince Frederic Charles had arrived, and
the issue of the day was the frustration of Bazaine's
attempt to move west.   But Bazaine had not been
defeated, he had only been thwarted.   He was still
out in the open, with diverse potentialities open to
him.   The German conviction from the outset had
been that the French army of the Rhine would
exert its utmost effort to retire from the neighbour-
hood of Metz and effect a junction with MacMahon.
"Consequently," in the emphatic words of the
German Staff narrative, "all measures, from those
of the royal headquarters to the commander of an
advanced guard, were directed without remission to
the one end—that of preventing the execution of

the adversary's supposed intention." It was to that end that Alvensleben had confronted the French army with a single army corps; to that end it was that the King, early on the 17th, hurried to the scene of the yesterday's battle, and spent long hours with Prince Frederic Charles, Moltke, and Roon in discussing the dispositions for the immediate future. The French had in a great measure drawn backward from off the Rezonville plateau, although they still held the section of it nearest Gravelotte. The question with the King and those about him, as the group surveyed the scene from the Flavigny height on the morning of the 17th— the King had left Pont-à-Mousson for the previous day's battle-field by daybreak—was, What were Bazaine's intentions? Did he mean to fall back upon Metz? Did he mean to offer another battle in his present position ere he did so? Or was it his intention still to attempt to get out of the trap by a march on the Meuse along the northerly roads leading from Metz?

The dispositions for the morrow promulgated by Moltke were calculated to cope with any of these contingencies. Steinmetz was to stand fast between the Moselle and Gravelotte, to hinder French offensive in that direction, while the army of Prince Frederic Charles was to sweep to the north in a

broad front, when, if Bazaine were marching out
by the northern roads, it would take him in flank
and force him to change front to accept battle. If,
again, Bazaine were standing fast in a position
covering Metz, Prince Charles's army, pivoting its
right on Steinmetz, would make a great wheel to
the right, and confront if not overlap the stationary
Bazaine. Orders issued to this effect, the King
and his staff drove back to Pont-à-Mousson.

Before the sun of Gravelotte rose, William was
on his way back to the scene of the impending
battle. He took his stand on the height above
Flavigny, among the thickest of the ghastly débris
of the battle of the 16th. As the morning waned
toward noon, reconnaisances made it apparent that
Bazaine was awaiting battle in a strong position
west of Metz, his left on the Moselle above Metz,
his right stretching away northward, with a little
westerly inclination, over Amanvillier and St. Privat
to Roncourt, where his right flank stood—somewhat
in the air. This once ascertained, it took time for
Prince Frederic Charles's army to effect its great
wheel, and meanwhile, the task of Steinmetz was
simply to " hold " Bazaine's left and left centre,
pending the development of the attack of the
Second Army. This he did with artillery fire, using
infantry only to clear the French advance-post out

of Gravelotte.   But as the day drew on, Steinmetz's
infantry had come into action, had fought their
way across the deep ravine of the Mance, and with
terrible losses carried the château and garden of
St. Hubert; and were trying to press forward up
the natural glacis stretching down from the crest of
the ridge at Point du Jour, in the teeth of a dreadful hailstorm of artillery, mitrailleuse, and chassepot
fire.   The King and his staff had ridden forward
from their original position at Flavigny, till they
had reached the Rezonville swell.   But this was
not near enough to the heart of the battle for the
keen old soldier.   He still rode on until about
five o'clock he had reached almost to the verge of
the Bois de Genivaux, on the heights on the
further side of which the fight was swaying backwards and forwards, as now one side, now the other,
fed the fire of the battle with fresh fuel.   Sitting
there on horseback on the Gravelotte-Malmaison
road, the whole arena of the Steinmetz attack lay
before him.

Slowly, as he watched, the French cannonade
in front of him abated its virulence.   The chassepot
fire flickered almost out; one might have thought
the personal presence of the old King had assuaged
the fierceness of the strife.   But the comparative
stillness in front of him enabled William to hear

that the fire was becoming intenser to northward of
him—an indication that Prince Frederic Charles
had brought his army to close quarters. That was
the signal that it behoved Steinmetz to co-operate
with his utmost vigour, if the adversary was to be
crushed all along his front. William caught the
moment, and ordered Steinmetz to fall on with his
last man, and so " end the business." The Second
Army Corps, that had been standing in reserve
behind Gravelotte, was ordered to co-operate in the
impending attack.

As it began to develop, the French suddenly
shook off their temporary torpor. The French
batteries renewed their fire vigorously, and poured
on the woods and on the Gravelotte plateau beyond
a tempest of projectiles. The French infantry,
for once relieved from the defensive and restored
to its traditionary *métier* of the attack, dashed forward with the grand old *élan*, and swept the
Germans backward down the slope almost into the
Mance valley.

Under the stroke of that fierce impact, under
the hurricane of missiles that beat upon the troops
unassailed by the French infantry, Steinmetz's army
reeled to its base. It may be said, without exaggera-
tion, that for the moment the whole of that army
was on the run. The old King was carried back-

ward in the surging press, resisting vehemei tly the
while, and expostulating with great fervour of expression with the component parts of the momen-
tary *débâcle*.   It was a spasm of awful crisis.   A
real panic was imminent, and there were the shells
swishing venomously into the recoiling masses,
every explosion intensifying the infectious nervous-
ness.   If the German front had quite broken, if
Gnügge's battery had been swept clean away from
the St. Hubert garden wall—some of his guns
were carried down the current of fugitives—King
William would hardly have slept that night in
Rezonville.

But the front braced itself, and held its own.
The panic died out as fast as it had kindled.
Still the French shell-fire kept crashing into the
huddled masses, however, around the spot where
the King and his rather dishevelled staff were
gathered together again.   The whisper went round
among the personages that this was hardly the place
for his Majesty.   But who would bell the cat?
Bismarck had been rather snubbed at Königgrätz
for that sort of office—or officiousness.   It did not
seem to be Moltke's affair.   At length Roon
greatly dared; as an old personal comrade and
friend of William, he might perhaps venture
on the liberty.   As Roon spoke—desiring simply

to point out that his Majesty was risking his life
very freely, the King took his binocular from his
eyes, looked hard at honest Roon for a moment,
and then with a smile turned his horse's head backward toward Rezonville.

As he went he passed a portion of the 2nd corps,
that was being hurried forward to throw its weight
into the wavering scale.   He halted while the regiments passed him at the double, cheering as they
went, and then rode on to Rezonville, where on the
edge of the village nearest to Gravelotte a seat was
made for him on a ladder, one end of which rested
on a weighing-machine, the other on a dead horse.
Moltke and other officers of the royal headquarter
staff had not gone back with the King, but stood
on the Gravelotte edge of the Mance ravine, to
watch the issue of the 2nd corps' effort.   The sun
had set on the lurid scene.   The strain of the crisis
was sickening as tidings were awaited.   The
King seemed forcing himself to be still.   Bismarck, with an elaborate assumption of indifference
that his restlessness belied, made pretence to be
reading letters.   The roar of the close battle
swelled and deepened till the very ground trembled.
The night came down like a pall, but the blaze of
an adjacent conflagration lit up the anxious group
here by the churchyard wall.   From out the

medley of broken troops littering the plain in front, came suddenly a great shout that grew in volume as it rolled nearer. The hoofs of a galloping horse rattled on the causeway. A moment later, Moltke, his face for once quivering with excitement, sprang from the saddle, and running toward the King, cried out : " It is good for us; we have won the plateau, and the victory is with your Majesty ! " The King sprang to his feet with a " God be thanked ! " Bismarck, with a great sigh of relief, crushed his letters in the hollow of his hand, and a simultaneous hurrah welcomed the glad tidings. A sutler who happened to be hard by improved the occasion in a quaintly practical way; he brought up his wine-barrel, and dispensed its contents. King William took a hearty pull of the thin red wine out of a cracked tumbler, and never made a wry face.

There was neither food nor accommodation in that miserable shattered village; every room, every passage, every shed, every cellar of which were crammed with wounded men, groaning in their agony. The King meant to sleep in his carriage, in the midst of wounded men and dead horses, but at length a room was found for him in a little public-house, and a couple of cutlets were forthcoming for his supper. There was no food for

Q

anybody else. Of how Bismarck fared, General
Phil Sheridan of the American army, who was
with the royal staff as Commissioner from the
United States, tells a comical story. He, an old
campaigner, had marked a likely house, whither
Bismarck and he went. The ground floor was
packed with wounded soldiers, and the old crone
who owned the place protested with vehement
emphasis that her cottage had no upstairs. Sheridan was too polite to call the old lady a liar, but
he mildly asked her, if there were no upstairs,
where, then, did that staircase lead to? Sheridan
had attended a class of practical logic during four
years of unremitting campaigning. At the top of
the staircase there was a little attic-room, with
three beds in it. Sheridan, as the finder of the
prize, claimed the bed with the cleanest sheets;
Bismarck and his cousin slept in the second bed,
and the Grand Duke of Mecklenburg and his aide-
de-camp occupied the third. All, perforce, went
supperless to bed, save Sheridan, who gnawed a
crust of black bread which Prince Albert, the
King's brother, had given him, as a polite attention
to a distinguished foreigner and guest. Next
morning Sheridan was up early prospecting around,
and presently came back with a couple of eggs
which he had coaxed the old woman out of; at

least he said this was how he got them, and he
looked sublimely innocent when Bismarck picked a
stray feather off the sleeve of his coat. Bismarck
went across and borrowed a little coffee from the
King, and he and Sheridan made a feeble pretence
of breakfast off the two eggs and the coffee.
Büsch gives Bismarck's account of the experiences
of this eventful night; Sheridan's recollections
differ in some minor details from those set down
by the great Chancellor's Boswell.

On the morning after Gravelotte, the King,
still quartered in the pothouse at Rezonville among
the dead and wounded, decreed the immediate
investment of Metz, and entrusted Prince Frederic
Charles with the task of neutralising Bazaine and
the army of the Rhine. The morrow saw the
environment virtually accomplished. With the
Prince was left the whole of the First Army, and
part of his own—the Second. But France had
still to be conquered, and to co-operate with the
Crown Prince of Prussia's army in what future
work this undertaking might entail outside the
Metz theatre of war, three army corps—the Prussian Guards, the 4th, and the 12th were taken
from Prince Frederic Charles's command, and constituted into a fourth army, to be called the Army
of the Meuse, the command of which was entrusted

to the Crown Prince of Saxony, an able soldier who had materially helped to win the victory of Gravelotte. This new army, and the Third Army —commanded by the Crown Prince of Prussia— were to sweep onward toward Paris on a broad front, fighting MacMahon if he should offer battle, whether at Châlons or elsewhere in its track, and making all haste to bring about the "psychological moment."

Those arrangements thus promptly decided on, the King and his headquarter staff returned on the 19th to Pont-à-Mousson; but not until William had spent many hours riding about among his victorious troops, and personally attending to arrangements for the care of the vast mass of wounded soldiers. At Pont-à-Mousson on the 20th, the Crown Prince of Prussia visited his venerable father, to congratulate him on the success of the Metz battles, and to receive instructions as to the spirit of the new dispositions, and their influence on the immediate future of his own army, now mostly west of Nancy, with faces set towards Châlons. It was not until the 23rd that the Royal headquarters left Pont-à-Mousson, and crossing the saddle between the valley of the Moselle and the valley of the Meuse, halted in the pretty little town of Commercy. All the region

in which the King now found himself was familiar
ground, although more than half a century had
passed over his head since he had fought and
marched in Champagne.   In Commercy he was
quartered in the same house he had occupied in
1814.   When on the following day he drove
through the little town of Ligny, he recalled to
mind his previous entrance into its market-place,
when the three allied sovereigns rode abreast—
Alexander of Russia in the centre ; and behind
them a huge staff, "a whole regiment of princes,
marshals, dukes, and generals," in which brilliant
cohort he had ridden.   Two nights (24th and 25th)
the King spent in Bar-le-Duc, awaiting develop-
ments that might sensibly affect the German
dispositions.

MacMahon, it had been known, was concentrating and reconstituting an army at Châlons.
Rumours had come that he had evacuated that
vicinity, but whither had he gone?   In lack of
information on this point, the German march westward had been continued.   But late on the 25th
intelligence reached the Royal headquarters which
led to the belief that MacMahon's objective was
the relief of Bazaine by a wide turning movement
to the north, round the right flank of the German
army.   The news was true.   MacMahon had gone

on a forlorn hope; at the bidding of the politicians
in Paris. The idea was not absolutely crazy—
only relatively so. Partial success might have
been attained if the Army of Châlons had been
so equipped and organised as to be swiftly, compactly, and purposefully mobile; but the reverse
was the case. In MacMahon's favour was the
element of surprise. Precious moments he had
indeed lost, yet on the evening of August 25th he
was actually in position with 150,000 men on the
right flank of the German army facing westward,
while the latter had still no sure evidence that its
adversary was not in its front, somewhere between
it and Paris.

The 26th furnished that evidence decisively,
and the German army, with extraordinary alacrity
and deftness, changed front to the right and
marched northward with hasty speed to strike
MacMahon in the act of his exposure of his
strategic flank. The Crown Prince of Saxony
hurried to head him while the great German
wheel, which yet was not so much a wheel as a
rearrangement of front, was in progress. That
operation is one of the most wonderful episodes of
modern war, viewed simply as a tactical evolution,
carried out in conditions where chaos seemed all
but inevitable, dexterously, smartly, without con-

fusion, and with amazing speed. In the closing days of August, MacMahon, who had hoped against hope to steal a march on the Germans, found that they had not only effectually cut him off from his Metz objective, but were actually barring his line of retreat westward; and on the 1st of September the grand catastrophe occurred. In less than a week after the Germans had first detected MacMahon's movement, they had mobbed him in the open, and the army of Châlons had ceased to exist.

To Clermont in Argonne the royal headquarters moved on the afternoon of the 26th among the soldiers of the Meuse army, whose commander, the Crown Prince of Saxony, the King found there. On the 29th the King moved northward through Varennes to Grand Pré, following up his troops, who on their part were following up the French. The latter had evacuated Grand Pré only on the day before the King entered it. They had not been kind to the place, and in default of better quarters, William billeted himself in the modest house of the local apothecary, in the principal street. On the 30th he watched the progress of the battle of Beaumont, in which the Crown Prince of Saxony distinguished himself so greatly by the skilful handling of his troops. It was the Fourth

Army Corps, of his command, and not the Bavarians, as generally believed, that so effectively surprised de Failly by a shower of shell-fire on his unguarded camp while the unsuspicious Frenchmen were cooking and cleaning their arms. The cannonade was already echoing in the distance when his Majesty near noon drove through the little town of Busancy, a few miles beyond which he took horse and rode forward to an elevation which commanded part of the battle-ground, and from which was visible across the valley the high spur of ground outside the village of Stonne, whence the Emperor Napoleon was watching the combat which presaged so ominously for him.

As William stood with the princes and his staff about him, and looked down on the scene from his elevated position on the Sommauthé height, the prospect that lay under his eyes was so lovely that its beauty might well have distracted attention from the bloody work outraging the calm sweetness of Nature. Immediately below him was a broad shallow valley lined with woods of a beautiful deep green. Beyond, an open, gently-rising country, in the slope of which, away to the right, half-nestled among the trees, was the pretty little town of Beaumont with its fine old church. To the left front, among the exuberant foliage, were scattered

villages, lying at the gates of fine country houses.
Beyond the gently-swelling ground behind Beaumont the prospect was closed in by the dark blue
hills of the Ardennes, seen dimly in the haze of the
heat and the cannon smoke.

All day long the combat raged, watched intently
by the old monarch.   As the dusk began to gather
a fire was kindled, for the Ardennes air is chilly
when the sun goes down, and by it sat the King
on a camp-stool, still watching the battle intently
through his field-glasses.   The German shells
crashed into Beaumont, and the flames from burning
houses rose almost as high as the spire of the old
church.   The French, still fighting desperately,
were slowly driven over the ridge behind it; and
then there was a *sauve qui peut* towards the Meuse.
Some got across by swimming, perhaps more were
drowned, and more still of the broken and driven
men were fain to surrender to the conquerors.   So
sweeping was the German success that the Crown
Prince of Saxony quartered himself for the night
in Beaumont.   The King drove back as far as
Busancy, whither, as he watched the battle, his
quarters had been removed from Grand Pré.   It
was late and very dark when he reached the humble
billet which was all the little place could afford, for
the first part of the road had been cumbered by the

wounded, and then there had to be passed great columns of troops still on the march, and long trains of ammunition and provision waggons. But the King took back to Busancy the realisation that the end was now close at hand for MacMahon and his army. It appeared all but certain that further pressure on it must force the army of Châlons against, if not across, the Belgian frontier, and by the King's direction Bismarck had already telegraphed to Brussels his Majesty's expectation that if French troops should enter Belgium they should be immediately disarmed. Specific orders were issued to the German army that if French troops crossed the Belgian frontier and did not immediately undergo disarmament, they were to be promptly followed without regard to Belgium's neutrality. The Germans on campaign take no concern with fine distinctions.

On the evening of the 31st August the two opponents were facing each other, their advanced troops in immediate contact. The boldly conceived but feebly attempted plan of the French for the relief of Metz had failed before the rapid initiative of the German strategists and the extraordinary marching powers of the German soldier. The Army of Châlons stood gathered in a curve round the obsolete fortress of Sedan. Its situation was almost if not altogether hopeless; the only alternatives presenting themselves were a refuge in the Belgian territory, or a desperate attempt to escape westward over Mézières. Its leaders apparently failed adequately to appreciate the desperate character of the situation. The troops were being rested, when it was imperatively necessary that they should be marching fast and far. Only two of several bridges across the Meuse were destroyed. The Emperor and MacMahon seemed to apprehend no impediments to a retirement on Mézières, the former leaning on the broken reed of a road which he believed was unknown to the Germans, but which was marked on their staff maps.

Opposite this cramped and precarious position of the French stood a victorious and superior army of Germans deployed on a broad concave front. On the east and south-east the army of the Crown Prince of Saxony barred the space between the Meuse and the Belgian frontier. On the south the army of the Crown Prince of Prussia held the line of the Meuse, and had its left wing free to swing round and bar the French retreat westward. In effect, MacMahon's army was in a complete trap. And so strong were the Germans that they could afford to keep a whole army corps out of the impending conflict altogether, fresh for any enterprise which the contingencies of the future might demand.

On the morning of the 31st the King left Busancy early, and drove over the scene of the previous day's fighting, through Sommauthé and onward through the pleasant country to Beaumont, where he had a consultation with the Crown Prince of Saxony. Everywhere were soldiers and everywhere wounded, and for all his Majesty had a cheery, kindly word. Büsch relates an anecdote of this day told him by Bismarck. "Near the church (of Beaumont) the King noticed a soldier who was wounded. Although the man looked somewhat dirty from his work of the day before, the King held out his hand, to the great surprise, no doubt, of the French officer who was standing by, and asked the man what was his trade. He answered that he was a doctor of philosophy. 'Well, you must have learned to bear your wounds philosophically,' said the King. 'Yes,' answered the soldier; 'that I had already made up my mind to.'" A mile beyond Beaumont, at a village called Crehanges, the King had arranged a breakfast, at which he entertained Bismarck, his own staff, and the officers of the suite of the Crown Prince of Saxony. Thence he drove onward through Raucourt to Chémery, where his son had established his headquarters, and where a council of war to consider the arrangements for the morrow was held, those present being, besides his Majesty and the Crown Prince, Moltke, Podbielski, and Blumenthal, chief of Staff to the Crown Prince. From Chémery the King drove on a few kilométrés further to the pretty village of Vendresse, where his quarters were for the night in a large handsome château.

There was early stirring in the German headquarters on the morning of the 1st September, the memorable day of Sedan. The Crown Prince had quitted Chémery before daylight, and made for his commanding position on the hill of Donchery. Already by three A.M. the 5th and 11th Army Corps had broken up from their bivouacs in the valley, and were crossing the Meuse at Donchery on the long arduous march prescribed to them, thereby they were to turn the right flank of the French, and giving the hand to the Guard Corps between them and the Belgian frontier, complete the fell cincture of blood and iron. Already by four A.M., in a mist from the water-meadows so dense that no man could see ten yards in front of him, von der Tann's Bavarians were crossing the railway-bridge and moving forward to the awful tragedy of Bazeilles, amid the roar of the cannon

covering the advance. Half an hour later the
Guards were sturdily climbing the slope in front of
Givonne, and the Saxons were pushing over the
broken ground with their faces set for La Moncelle.
By the time the sun drove away the fog, the battle
was in full activity on the eastern and southern
faces of the French position.

About seven o'clock the old King, driving
through Chémery and Chéhery to its foot, and
thence riding to the summit, reached the bare-
flat top of the hill of Frenois, a position chosen
for him as commanding a wide view of the theatre
of operations. The fog had by this time yielded
to the sun and the air which, where untainted
by cannon smoke, was on this day singularly clear.
At the foot of the hill gleamed through the
trees the white Château Bellevue, soon to become historic. To right of it, between Frenois
and Wadelincourt, there were Bavarian batteries in
steady, measured action. The Meuse wound through
the broad fertile valley from right to left. Away
there across the river to the right, a column of
black smoke curling up from out a shallow fold in
the terrain told where the village of Bazeilles was
burning. The roofs and spires of Sedan, on the
face of the gentle slope, showed above the fortifications which were so formidable when Vauban con-

structed them, and now so obsolete. To the west
of the town ran out a long bare plateau, with an
abrupt drop down into the river meadows on the
south and west; the village just at the base of its
bastion-like projection was Floing—whence the
plateau was to take the name that will endure
down the ages. Ear away to the extreme right,
the clouds of white smoke told where the army of
the Crown Prince of Saxony was fighting hard;
and if one scanned closely the undulating country
on the exteme left, one might perchance discern a
fitful gleam of steel that told where the stout
soldiers of the 5th and 11th corps were pressing
on steadfastly in that long arduous turning movement that had been prescribed to them. Already
the German ring, which in a few hours was to be
welded fast and true, was partly defined. Neither
troops nor cannon smoke showed as yet on the
upland in the northern distance, behind which the
dark wooded hills of the Belgian Ardennes closed
in the picture.

It was a remarkable assemblage that had gathered
on the stubbles here on the summit of the hill of
Frenois to watch, as a surgeon might watch a
patient *in extremis*, the death-throes of the army
of Châlons. Out to the front, observant, un-
demonstrative, the intensity of his interest in what

he saw betrayed only by the constant handling of the heavy white moustache, stood the old King in full uniform. Close behind him in a group were Moltke, Roon, and Podbielski, and behind them again, somewhat scattered, stood or sat the personages of the staff and suite. Old Prince Charles the King's brother, the Grand-Dukes of Weimar and Coburg-Gotha, the Hereditary Grand Duke of Mecklenburg, generals, aides-de-camp, marshals of the household. Among the Germans were the military representatives of foreign powers; Kutusoff, the Russian; Colonel Walker, the British military attache; General Sheridan, the military commissioner from the United States. Another little group, of which the centre was Bismarck, occupied ground a little on the left flank; the great Chancellor himself sat on the edge of the stubble field, more engrossed to all appearance in the perusal of documents than in the study of the battle-field. The position was within range of the fortress guns of Sedan, and occasionally, especially in the morning, projectiles fell at no great distance from where the King stood. He would not give up nevertheless the commanding position which afforded so wide a range of view, but he had given directions that the groups behind him should in some measure scatter themselves, so that as much as might be temptation for hostile fire should be diminished.

The hard fighting during the morning was chiefly on the east and south-east of Sedan, at too great a distance for the progress of events to be accurately discerned from the King's position; but news came that after a desperate struggle with Turcos and Zouaves, the Saxons had fought their way through the woods overhanging the hollow of the Givonne valley, and had forced a victorious path into the village of Daigny. The Prussian Guards had carried the village of Givonne after experiencing a fierce resistance, and their right flank was in possession of the hamlet of La Chapelle, further to the northward. Already by noon the hussars of the Guard were pushing forward through the Ardennes forest, feeling for the head of the 5th corps—the other claw of the great crab. Bazeilles —or rather the burnt and blood-stained skeleton of what at sunrise had been Bazeilles—was at length in the hands of the Bavarians, after a long and furious street-fight, envenomed into ruthless bitterness by the passionate folly of its civilian population.

But before noon the great telescope that had been mounted on a tripod in front of where Moltke stood with his maps spread out at his feet,

R

had been slewed round so as to point in a north-
easterly direction. The other limb of the great
impending hug was making itself manifest. The
5th and 11th corps, which had crossed the
Meuse at Donchery in the first hours of the
morning, had marched round the great Iges
bend. The former corps, on the outside of the
great wheel, having made its northing, then headed
almost due east on Fleigneux, to meet the Guards
edging westward to give it the hand, and so fasten
the clasp of the belt of environment. The 11th
corps for its part, having got round the great Iges
bend, marched partly east on St. Menges, partly
inclined more to the south-east, so as to hold the
space between the Meuse and the 5th corps. For
the French there was a dread significance in this
combined movement of these two corps. Until it
developed, the French field, so to speak, was walled
up only on two sides, the east and the south. But
this movement of the 5th and 11th corps, if
accomplished, would close a third side of the field,
the western, and presaged ominously also the completion of the enclosure along the fourth, the
northern side.

But the French were at first entirely unaware of
these menacing preparations in progress to westward
of them. The village of St. Menges was occupied

by the Prussians without a struggle, and so the space between it and the Meuse, traversed by the road on which Napoleon had professed to build his hopes, was blocked fast against the French. Gradually, as the Prussians completed the great wheel, and came up into their positions beyond St. Menges eastward, the French danger developed itself. From Floing, near the river, right round to beyond Illy in the north-east, a hundred and fifty Prussian field guns were raining their fire on the huddled French army, while from the heights of Givonne the artillery of the Guard was contributing its quota of deadly cross-fire. The grip had been all but effected, but not without fierce and reckless opposition on the part of the French. From the Cavalry of Illy, Gallifet, with his brigade of chasseurs d'Afrique, had surged down upon the Prussian batteries in the act of deployment on the plain south-east of St. Menges, only to recoil before the torrent of shrapnel that struck his squadrons fair in the face. Later the gallant Margueritte threw his life away in a dashing attempt to drive back the Prussian infantry, climbing on to the crest of the plateau west of Illy. It was the flower of the French cavalry that he led out from the Bois de Garenne on this enterprise, his own five light regiments, Savaresse's lancer brigade, and several

R 2

cuirassier squadrons of Bonnemain's division.
Prussian shell-fire tore through the French cavalry,
riding chivalrously on their ruin; musketry fire
rained on them its ruthless storm. Margueritte
went down, and Gallifet dashed to the front and
headed the onset. Broken and with sore-thinned
ranks, the French horsemen were not to be denied.
Their charge thundered right home on the detachments of infantrymen that stood in their path.
Gallantly delivered, the furious onset was as
gallantly received. The Prussian linesmen met it
with their fire and with the bayonet, in open order
mostly; only on open ground did the skirmishers
run into rallying groups for self-defence.

Upon the King's hill-top this onslaught was
watched with breathless interest. Every detail of
the hand-to-hand combat lay exposed to the watchers
there, gazing down on it through their field-glasses.
As the French horsemen recoiled from the firm
Prussian front, and rode back under a withering fire
that left half their number on the field, Sheridan,
the American general, himself a cavalry leader of
great experience and accustomed to gauge the
issues of battles, broke the strained silence by
closing his glasses with a snap, and exclaiming:
" It is all over with the French now ! " Men ran
up to him to shake him by the hand for the word,

for they knew it came from the lips of a past master in the art of war.

But it was not yet that the French were to own to the truth of Sheridan's conclusion. The wild confusion in which the struggle now surged backwards and forwards for about the space of half an hour on the western edges and slopes of the plateau, baffled even the methodical compilers of the Prussian Staff record to describe it in detail. It was indeed a lurid, an awful, yet a magnificent spectacle. The cruel ring of German fire ever gathering in more and more closely on that upland whereon stood huddled the Frenchmen as if in the shambles; the storm of shell-fire that tore lanes through the dense masses all exposed there to its pitiless pelting; the impotent yet vehement revolts against the inevitable in the shape of furious sorties; now a wild headlong charge of cuirassiers, thundering in glittering steel-clad splendour down the slope, with a ponderous impetus that seemed resistless till the biting fire of the German infantrymen smote the charging squadrons fair in the face, and rolled riders and horses into swift sudden death; now the frantic gallop to their fate of a regiment of light horsemen on their grey Arab stallions up to the very muzzles of the needle-guns that the German linesmen held with so unwavering steadiness; now a

spurt of red-trousered foot-soldiers darting against
a chance gap in the stern ring of environment,
quelled and crushed too surely by the ruthless
flanking fire. No semblance of order there, no
indication of leadership ; simply an inferno wherein
raged and writhed an indiscriminate mass of brave
men, rebelling against fate with a noble constancy
sublime as hopeless. But a struggle so one-sided
could not long endure. Slowly and reluctantly the
French began to move backward in the direction of
what shelter the nearer vicinity of Sedan might
afford. Repeated efforts of isolated detachments to
break out in a northerly direction were foiled by
the Germans without serious difficulty.

MacMahon had been wounded early in the day,
and after an interval long enough to be productive
of much ill, Wimpffen had succeeded him in the
command. He had been but forty-eight hours
with the army; his ignorance of its condition, and
want of conversance with the situation generally,
told severely against him ; but Wimpffen was a
soldier of character, and would not have it that the
time had yet come to confess to hopelessness. He resolved on an attempt to break through the German
line in a south-easterly direction, designing to
throw the Bavarians back on the Meuse, and so
open a road toward Carignan.

In more favourable conditions such an attempt would have been of the nature of a forlorn hope; but no chief could have been in a worse plight than was Wimpffen that afternoon. He could get no communication with his master the Emperor, who was inside Sedan. He had no staff officers to carry his orders to the corps commanders; and most of the troops with which he purposed making his effort were already broken, and retiring in disorder on Sedan. But nevertheless his effort, made with a marine division, a few battalions of Zouaves, and perhaps about 15,000 line troops, kept the Saxons and Bavarians fighting hard all the afternoon ere it was finally thwarted. All around the circle the French kept up, until about five o'clock, a resistance more or less fitful, notwithstanding that before that hour the white flag was already flying over Sedan. In the confusion it was impossible to disseminate intelligence or orders—if there were any orders—over so wide an area with any speed; and so desperate and reckless were a considerable proportion of the French army, officers as well as soldiers, that intelligence of the humiliation of an armistice that could have but one result was only an incentive to a yet more virulent resistance.

But by five o'clock the white flag had been hoisted. An hour previous it had become apparent

to the King that his artillery commanded the entire
space upon which the French army stood helplessly
pressed together in confused masses.   Reports from
all directions convinced him that he was everywhere in sufficient strength to defeat any attempt
to break through.   Since the French down there
were stubborn, a yet acuter incentive than the
arguments already applied needed, it seemed, to
be administered.   As in old times, in the name of
humanity, people in the last stage of hydrophobia
used to be put out of their agony by being
smothered, so the final death-throe of the French
army was to be artistically quickened up.   To
quote the German official account :—" A powerful
fire of artillery against the enemy's last point of
refuge appeared under the circumstances the most
suitable means for convincing him of the hopelessness of the situation, and for inducing him to
surrender.   With the desire to hasten the capitulation, and thereby spare the German army any
further sacrifices, the King ordered the whole
available artillery to concentrate its fire upon
Sedan."

The artillery fire turned upon Sedan was not
long in producing the anticipated results.   Flames
began to rise in several places from inside the fortifications—the argument of fire was supporting the

argument of blood and iron. Sedan, like most
towns which are surrounded by fortifications, is
very densely built, with narrow streets and few
open spaces. Putting out of view the civilian
population, it was literally crammed with troops
who had crowded into it in the illusive hope
to escape from under the torture of the German
fire. Every shell thrown into the place must
have told, and shells were rained upon it in hundreds. A Bavarian battalion, moving forward on
the suburb of Torcy, pushed on toward one of
the gates of the fortress. Little resistance had
been encountered, and preparations were being made
for the escalade of the palisades, when the white
flag was run up over the local position. The
French officer in command at the same time desired
the Bavarian colonel to desist from any further
prosecution of his attacks, and expressed the desire
that the Germans should enter into negotiations.
The Bavarian colonel reported the situation to
General Maillenger, the commander of the brigade,
who moved up the nearest troops to points just
outside the Torcy gate, and sent an officer up to
the Frenois hill-top to inform the King of the
French proposals to negotiate. While he was
making his report, there broke out a spurt of hard
fighting down in Balan, close under the King's

eye, as if to mock the message which was being delivered.

The King bade the Bavarian officer inform his chief that all proposals in regard to negotiations must be sent direct to the Royal headquarters, and the Bavarian rode down again into the valley. His Majesty entered into a consultation with the Crown Prince, who had just ridden up from his own position on the hill of Donchery, and with Bismarck, Moltke, and Roon—the Dukes of Weimar and Gotha stood near, but were not called into council. As the result of the conference, the King directed Colonel von Bronsart of his staff to take with him Captain von Winterfeld, to proceed to Sedan under a flag of truce, and summon in his Majesty's name the French commander-in-chief to surrender his army and the fortress. The Prussian officers were received at the Torcy gate by the local staff of the fortress; and Bronsart was sent forward into the town, making his way with difficulty through the huddled masses of wearied soldiery. He had announced that the object of his mission was to negotiate on behalf of the King his master with the commander-in-chief of the French army; but he was conducted instead into a room of the sub-prefecture, in which to his surprise he found the Emperor Napoleon, of whose presence in Sedan

the German headquarters had been in ignorance.
Wimpffen, for his part, was in Balan, still fighting
hard there.　An hour before, as he had ridden
back toward Sedan from the direction of Daigny,
he had been met by an order from the Emperor
bidding him open negotiations with the Germans.
He had refrained from complying, believing that he
saw his way to cut through the Bavarians to Carignan, and had diverged to Balan to pursue a local
success which he unquestionably gained.　At his
instigation the rumour was sped through the
French forces in that region of the field that
Bazaine was at Carignan with the army of the
Rhine, and the white flag that had been hoisted
over Sedan was actually hauled down by General
Faure, Wimpffen's chief of staff.

Napoleon laboured under no illusions.　At the
moment when Bronsart was ushered into his
presence, he was engaged in writing a letter to
the Prussian monarch acknowledging the hopelessness of the situation.　He told Bronsart, in answer
to his application for a French officer of rank to be
delegated with full powers to negotiate, that General
Wimpffen held the supreme command in place of
Marshal MacMahon, who had been wounded.　This
answer he requested him to take back to the King,
and intimated further that he would send with

him to the royal headquarters his aide-de-camp, General Count Reille, to deliver a letter to the Prussian monarch.

Meanwhile, on the Frenois hill-top, general congratulations had been exchanged, and men now found time to eat, pending the return of Bronsart. An officer of the staff, who had ridden out to collect information, came back with the intelligence that the German losses, so far as had been ascertained, were not very heavy; moderate among the Guards, somewhat larger with the Saxons, and less in the other corps which had participated in the fighting. Only a few of the French had escaped through the forest toward the Belgian frontier; all the rest had been driven back on Sedan.

" And the Emperor ? " asked the King.

"Nobody knows," answered the officer.

Tidings of the Emperor were on the way. Bronsart, riding out with Reille, had sent Winterfeld on in advance, with the information that Napoleon was in Sedan, and that an emissary from him was coming out. It was now past six o'clock.

When he had listened to Winterfeld's message, the King, turning round to his retinue, and speaking in a loud voice, said, " This, gentlemen, is indeed a great success ! " Then, with a face of pride and love, he turned to the Crown Prince and added, " And I thank thee, who hast helped so well toward it." With the words the old monarch held out his hand to his son, who, bending low, kissed it in much emotion; then he gave his hand to Moltke, who also kissed it. When Bismarck, in his turn, had kissed his master's hand, the King and he drew aside, and talked earnestly.

Their conference was interrupted by Bronsart, who rode on to announce Count Reille's approach. With the Uhlan in front bearing on his lance the flag of truce, and with an escort about him of Prussian cuirassiers, the French general came up the hill at a walking pace. He dismounted a little way off from where the King stood, out to the front of his retinue ; stepped forward, doffing his cap as he came, was presented by Bronsart, and with a silent reverence handed to his Majesty the Emperor's letter. Then he drew back, and stood alone a little way apart, watching in melancholy self-possession the scene before him. Count Reille had been the imperial equerry specially detailed to attend on the King of Prussia when that monarch was the Emperor's guest in the Tuileries in 1867.

The King broke the big red seal, and read the few words which the letter contained. He stood a brief moment in thought—there was much in the situation to give occasion for thought. It was as

if he had to make an effort to preserve his compo-
sure; and it was in rather a broken voice that,
turning to his people, he read to them the few
words that told so much :—

"Sire my Brother,

          "Not having been able to die in the midst
of my troops, there is nothing left me but to
render my sword into the hands of your Majesty.

          "I am, your Majesty's good brother,
                              "NAPOLEON."

The sword of his "good brother" was indeed
something, but it was not by any means all that the
other brother wanted. Indeed, this proffer of personal surrender rather complicated the situation,
while the army of Châlons remained uncapitulated.
The King and Bismarck talked earnestly together,
while the Crown Prince, with that gracious tact
which never deserts him, entered into conversation
with poor forlorn Reille, standing out there among
the stubbles. Presently this conversation was joined
in by Moltke and the Duke of Coburg-Gotha. The
Chancellor had called up his assistant, Count Hatzfeld, and commissioned him to sketch an answer to
the imperial letter in the sense in which the King
had signified. Hatzfeld brought up the draft, and
the King wrote out his reply, sitting on one chair,

and using the seat of another as a desk, held up by Major von Alten, who knelt on one knee, supporting the chair on the other. The reply was as follows:—

"My Brother,

"While regretting the circumstances in which we meet, I accept your Majesty's sword, and request that you will appoint one of your officers and furnish him with the necessary powers to treat for the capitulation of the army which has fought so valiantly under your command. I for my part have appointed General von Moltke to this duty.

"Your loving brother,

"WILLIAM."

With this laconic missive Reille rode back into Sedan. After issuing orders that offensive movements were to be suspended during the night, but that any attempt on the enemy's part to break out was to be repelled by force, the King drove back to his quarters in Vendresse, receiving along the road the most enthusiastic demonstrations on the part of the troops. The great news had spread like wildfire, and the army was in a wild rapture of triumph. Inside Sedan it was a dreadful evening. Wimpffen had resigned in a transport of shame and anger, and only withdrew his resignation at

the earnest and almost piteous entreaty of the
Emperor. The French generals bandied insults
and reproaches in the very presence of their fallen
master.

While William rested in Vendresse the conditions of the capitulation were being debated in
Donchery. Moltke and Bismarck had already
discussed the terms that were to be conceded, and
at the conference to which Wimpffen came so
reluctantly, Moltke demanded, and adhered to the
demand, that the French army should surrender
unconditionally; in the event of refusal, he was
prepared to enforce it next morning by an appeal
to arms. Wimpffen earnestly urged less stern conditions, but in vain. At one A.M. of the 2nd the
conference broke up, no definite result having been
obtained. Wimpffen had not accepted Moltke's
offer that he should, by personal inspection of the
German positions, convince himself of the futility
of further resistance; and Moltke, for his part,
had refused Wimpffen's petition for a twenty-four
hours' armistice, intimating that if his conditions
were not accepted by nine A.M. he would renew
hostilities.

At six o'clock Bismarck, lying asleep in Dr.
Jeanjot's front room in Donchery, was awakened by
his servant, who said that a French general was at

the door and wanted to see him.   It was Count
Reille, with the news that the Emperor was on his
way out of Sedan and desired a conference with the
Chancellor.   Reille went away, and the Chancellor,
dressing and mounting, followed him along the
Sedan road.   When some two kilomètres had been
traversed, there was seen coming in the other
direction a shabby-looking open carriage, the four
persons seated in which wore gold-braided and laced
kepis.   Bismarck, as he came alongside the carriage,
sprang from his horse, letting it go ; and drawing
near on foot, uncovered his head and bowed low.
The man to whom he spoke—the man with the
leaden-coloured face, the lines of which were drawn
and deepened as if by some spasm, the gaunt-eyed
man with the dishevelled moustache and the weary
stoop of the shoulders, was none other than Napoleon the Third and last.   Bismarck remounted
and followed the carriage on its route toward
Donchery, where he had placed at Napoleon's disposal his own quarters.   Scarcely a hundred yards
had been traversed when the Emperor, leaning
back and in obvious pain, told Bismarck he wished
to halt and alight.   On a little bank, a few paces
off the road, stood a weaver's cottage, which the
Emperor wished to occupy.   It was reported a
miserable place, but that, he said, did not matter.

s

Bismarck and he went up to a room in the first
floor, where, and subsequently seated on chairs
outside in front of the house, they had a long
conversation. During it and again to Moltke, who
had been hastily summoned, Napoleon reiterated
his earnest wish for more favourable terms of
capitulation for his army. This purely military
question Bismarck declined to discuss, and Moltke
adhered resolutely to his unconditional stipulation.
When the problem of peace was discussed, the
Emperor had nothing to say. He was a prisoner,
and it was not for him to decide; he referred
Bismarck to the Government in Paris—probably
discerning that a revolution would immediately
follow on the tidings of Sedan. So while Bismarck
rode away to Donchery to dress himself, Moltke
rode toward Vendresse to meet the King and tell
him of the state of the negotiations, and of the
complication brought about by the advent of the
French Emperor in the German lines, while the
French army remained unsurrendered. Meanwhile
Napoleon strolled moodily up and down a path in
the potato plot by the side of the cottage, limping
slightly, and smoking cigarette after cigarette. A
detachment of cuirassiers had ridden up and formed
a cordon of videttes round the cottage.

About ten o'clock Bismarck returned, and led

the way back in the direction of Sedan to the Château Bellevue, a pretty house enclosed in ornamental grounds overhanging the Meuse. The Emperor followed in his carriage, escorted by the cuirassier " guard of honour." The château reached, he alighted wearily and dragged himself up the steps leading to the main door. It must have been a trying morning indeed, with little to alleviate its bitterness for the crushed, stunned man. A colloquy with Bismarck, stern of heart, sharp if courteous of speech, unyielding in resolve, for an hour or more ; then for another hour a listless inaction, while the man who had conquered was to adjudge the future of the vanquished.

Riding toward Vendresse, Moltke met the King on the road near Chéhery. They had a conversation under a tree a little way apart, when William fully approved the proposed conditions of capitulation, and intimated his declinature to see the French Emperor until they had been accepted. Moltke had given poor Wimpffen no rest. Before riding away to meet the King, he had sent into Sedan an officer with the blunt ultimatum that hostilities would be recommenced at 10 A.M. unless by that hour there was a prospect of the capitulation being arranged. Wimpffen still refused to negotiate, urging instructions from the Emperor not to surrender until the latter should have had an interview with the German king. Captain Zingler remarked that his instructions in that case were to give orders, as he rode back, that the German cannon, 475 of which were in position in a ring round Sedan, should immediately open fire. In stress of an argument like that, Wimpffen consented to renew the negotiations. The King had so far modified Moltke's terms, in acknowledgment of the brave defence made by the army of Châlons, as to admit its officers to their parole, allowing them to retain their swords and personal property on condition of giving their word of honour not to fight against Germany during the war. The negotiations were concluded in the Château Bellevue, and soon after eleven the capitulation was signed.

The tidings were sent to the King, who was awaiting them in his yesterday's position above Frenois, surrounded by the German princes and a great and illustrious retinue. It was a memorable moment for him and for the country which he ruled. It was under the influence of strong emotion that his Majesty addressed to those around him heartfelt words of acknowledgment of the valour and conduct of the army he had led to victories so momentous, and avowed the confident hope of a great future for Germany. Then he mounted, he and his suite, and descending the hill, rode his black charger to where, on the gravel sweep in front of the Château Bellevue, the " guard of honour " stood over the captive monarch inside. As William dismounted, Napoleon came down the steps to meet him.   What a greeting !   The German, tall, upright, bluff, square-shouldered, with the sparkle of victory in the keen blue eye under the helmet-peak, and the flush of success on the fresh cheek.   The Frenchman, bent, leaden-faced, his eye drooping, his lip quivering, bareheaded and dishevelled.   As the two clasped hands silently, Napoleon's handkerchief was at his eyes, and William's face was working strangely.   Then the " good and loving brothers " turned, and mounting the steps, entered the château together.   They spoke for a few moments in an outer room, and then withdrew into a little boudoir opening off the library in the central turret.   The Crown Prince stepped to the door and closed it from the outside, and for a quarter of an hour or so the two monarchs remained closeted together.   When they came out the Emperor was visibly affected, and in talking with the Crown Prince said, with much emotion, that the King had treated him with great kindness and generosity.   As he spoke he brushed the tears away from his eyes with the glove he carried in

one hand, and was overcome for several seconds.
William spoke of his emotions in a letter he wrote
to Queen Augusta next day : " We were both much
moved at seeing each other again under such circumstances.   What my feelings were — I had seen
Napoleon only three years before at the summit of
his power—is more than I can describe."   The
Crown Prince gave Dr. Russell the following account
of what passed at the memorable interview, re-
counted to him by his royal father :—" The King
spoke first.   God, he said, had given the victory
to his arms in the war that had been declared
against him.   The Emperor replied that the war
had not been sought by him.   He had not desired
or wished for it, but he had been obliged to declare
war in obedience to the public opinion of France.
The King made answer that he was aware it was
not the Emperor's doing.   He was quite sure of
it. ' Your Majesty made war to meet public opinion,
but it was your ministers who created that public
opinion which forced on the war.'   His Majesty,
after a pause, remarked that the French army had
fought with great bravery. ' Yes,' said the Emperor,
' but, sire, your Majesty's troops possess a discipline
in which my army has been wanting lately.'   The
King remarked that for some years the Prussian
army had been availing itself of all new ideas, and

watching the military experiments of other nations before '66 and subsequently. 'Your artillery, sire, won the battle,' said the Emperor—'the Prussian artillery is the finest in the world.' The King bowed, and repeated that they had been anxious to avail themselves of the experiences of other nations. 'Prince Frederic Charles decided the fate of the day,' remarked the Emperor; 'it was his army which carried our position.' 'Prince Frederic Charles! I don't understand your Majesty. It was my son's army which fought at Sedan.' 'And where, then, is Prince Frederic Charles?' 'He is with seven army corps before Metz.' At these words the Emperor started, and recoiled as if he had been struck; but he soon recovered his self-possession, and the conversation was continued. The King inquired if the Emperor had any conditions to make or to propose. 'None. I have no power. I am a prisoner.' 'And may I ask, then, where is the Government of France with which I can treat?' 'In Paris; the Empress and the Ministers alone have power to treat. I am powerless. I can give no orders, and make no conditions.'"

The interview finished, the King started on a drive through his victorious army, which lasted until near nightfall. He who was left spent that

night in the Château Bellevue, and next morning
went away into captivity at Wilhelmshöhe. The
army of Châlons was marched out from about
Sedan on to the great peninsula formed by the
Iges bend of the Meuse, and gradually was drafted
off in batches by the prisoner-trains into Germany.

CHAPTER XII.

THE GERMAN EMPEROR.

BY the 6th of September the King of Prussia was
in Rheims, the self-constituted guest of the Most
Reverend the Archbishop in that ecclesiastical
dignitary's palace, hard by the historic old cathedral.
There had been but a short stay for the German
hosts on the field where they had gained laurels so
green and yet so bloody. The dark red tint had
hardly died out of the Meuse, the unburied dead
yet festered in the sun-heat, and the ruins of
Bazeilles yet smoked and stank, when the vanguard
of the Crown Prince's army shouldered their packs
and trudged away along the valleys of the Argonne
toward the fertile vineyards of Champagne, with
their faces ever set Paris-ward, and "Nach Paris"
ever on their lips. Royal headquarters made a
long pause in the old cathedral city, while men all
over Europe were asking each other whether the
catastrophe of Sedan had not virtually terminated
the war, and were hoping for the white dove of
peace to alight on the blood-stained battle-field.

But the Revolution had occurred in Paris, and the
leaders of the new Republic were flushed with the
delusion that republican institutions and untrained
hordes of patriots, who at the talismanic name of
" Republic " might be counted on to rush to arms
eager to fight and proud to die for *la Patrie*
emancipated, could cope with the practised general-
ship and the disciplined and victorious arms which
had crushed the regular armies of the Empire with
such methodised swiftness.

When William went out to war in the name of
the German Fatherland, he put forth that he warred
not with the French nation but with its ruler.
That ruler effaced, it remained for him to find, or
try to find, some person or some body as the successor of the captive Emperor in some species of
right to dispose of the destinies of France.   He
could not conclude peace with the French nation in
the gross; that nation must set up, whether for
peace or for war, something tangible to be treated
with by the victor, if it was to be peace; to direct
war, if the nation's fiat was for war.   The Provisional Government assumed the lapsed reins, and
was tacitly accepted by France.   Then the nation,
through this its new mouthpiece, instead of suing
for peace, instead of asking what terms it might
expect if it had the mind to own to the military

superiority of the adversary, cried out for "War, war to the bitter end—war without a thought or dream of terms!" William thus had no alternative but to accept what was virtually a new challenge, and fight on. And with the new challenge there confronted him a new antagonist. He was now to fight, no longer with the power of the man who was his prisoner, but with the French nation, with whom up till then he had proclaimed that he had no quarrel; and he fought with it because it had taken up the quarrel that might have gone with the *déchéance*, and had made that quarrel its own. The German did not quit his first position; France and the French drove him out of it, whether he would or not. There was no alternative for him but to march on defiant Paris.

The German cordon round Paris was effectively completed on the 21st of September, the capital having closed its gates and constituted itself a world to itself two days before. On the 20th the Crown Prince of Prussia had ridden into Versailles and hoisted the Royal standard over its prefecture. The environment of Paris was made by the two armies which had fought and conquered at Sedan. The Crown Prince of Prussia's army held the western and southern section, from the Seine at St. Germain round to the Seine again at Bonneuil,

where the army of the Meuse, commanded by the
Crown Prince of Saxony, took up the line and
carried it along the eastern face and round the
northern to the Seine again at Sartrouville, opposite
the Forest of St. Germain. This disposition remained with little modification until the close of
the siege; what changes of detail occurred from
time to time need not be recorded here.

It was not until the 14th of September that
the royal headquarters left Rheims and moved
forward to Château Thierry. On the following day
they were advanced to Meaux, within thirty miles
of Paris, whence in the afternoon came Mr. (now
Sir Edward) Malet, with a letter from Lord Lyons,
asking whether the King would consent that
Bismarck and Jules Favre should have a conference. Next day Malet returned to Paris with
a letter in which Bismarck informed Jules Favre
that he should be "exceedingly happy to see him,"
and that he was sending forward Prince Biron to
conduct the Frenchman through the German lines.
Alhough the royal headquarters remained in Meaux
until the 19th, the French Minister up till then had
not shown himself. On that day the King, with the
Chancellor and the principal officers of the staff,
went to reside for a time at the Château of Ferrières, about six miles nearer Paris than Meaux.

On the way was heard the distant cannonade accompanying a sharp engagement between troops belonging to the garrison of Paris and the Bavarians on the heights of Châtillon, and M. Jules Favre was met driving from Paris. The first conference between him and the German Chancellor was held in a château near the road; there was another the same night at Ferrières, and a third there on the following morning, after Bismarck had explicitly stated to his Majesty the nature of the French proposals, and taken his instructions as to the final reply to be given to M. Favre. That gentleman's mission was to ascertain whether the Germans were willing to treat for peace on the basis of a money indemnity to be paid by France for the expenses and losses of the war. Bismarck's reply was firmly in the negative. Germany would require something more. It was necessary, once for all, to secure Germany against the inveterate aggressive policy of France, and this was only to be effected by keeping part of the territory the former had now conquered. The new German frontier, Bismarck propounded, must include Alsace and a portion of Lorraine which he explicitly defined. Against this demand M. Favre protested with passionate fervour, exclaiming that France would refuse to cede a foot of her soil. Bismarck professed reluct-

ance to consent to the armistice in favour of which
Favre argued, in order that a National Assembly
might be elected to decide as to the future Government of France; but ultimately consented, on condition that the fortresses of Strasburg, Toul, and
Phalsburg should be placed in the German hands.
The Frenchman abruptly broke off the negotiation
when Bismarck advanced the stipulation that the
garrison of Strasburg should surrender as prisoners
of war; and returned to Paris to inform his countrymen that the Germans had resolved on the reduction
of France to the rank of a second-class power, and
that resistance to the death had become the duty of
every Frenchman. When Favre returned to Paris
the German investment of it had been completed,
Toul capitulated two days later; and he had not
been back a week when Strasburg had followed the
example of Toul, and its garrison were prisoners of
war.

In Rothschild's beautiful residence at Ferrières
the King lived quietly for more than a fortnight,
and was visited there by his son coming from Versailles. At length the investment of Paris had so
consolidated that there was no reason why the
King himself should not move round to Versailles,
and the journey thither was made on the 5th
of October, his Majesty holding a review of the

Bavarian contingent near Villeneuve-le-Roi on his way, his son having come from Versailles to meet him and take part in this duty. The royal head-quarters in Versailles were located in the prefecture, which had been vacated by the Crown Prince a day or two previously.

The entry of his Majesty into Versailles was an imposing ceremonial. The avenue in which the prefecture stands was lined with troops, and a large number of princes, dukes, and generals had gathered in its courtyard. About half-past five the cheers of the troops heralded the approach of the King; and the officers in front of the prefecture ranged themselves in military order. A troop of Lancers galloped up, wheeled, and halted. Then came the King in an open carriage; he was covered with the dust of the journey, but looked well and strong. The Crown Prince sat with him on his left. In the midst of cheering and clangour of trumpets, the lowering of the colours, and other demonstra-tions of loyalty, William alighted from his carriage, and was at once surrounded by his officers, with many of whom he warmly shook hands. After greetings, he and the Crown Prince inspected the colour company forming the guard of honour, drawn up on the left of the prefecture courtyard. The inspection completed, his Majesty ascended the

steps, turned round and saluted the multitude, and
then passed into the entrance hall.   When on this
5th of October the King entered the portals of the
Versailles prefecture, he little anticipated that he was
to be the occupant of that residence for five long
months.   The stubborn resistance of Paris was to
transcend all expectations, and probably surprised
Paris itself most of all.   The most liberal German
reckoning was that the French capital might hold
out till Christmas, and men in the royal suite when
the King reached Versailles, were ready to wager
that their stay there would not exceed three weeks.
Once, it is true, within that space of time there
was a prospect that they might win their bets, but
scarcely in the way that they themselves were
expecting.   On October 21st the garrison of Paris
made a fierce sortie on a large scale in the direction of Versailles, and succeeded by dint of hard
fighting in getting as far as Bougival.   The
French inhabitants of Versailles made sure the
glad day of relief had dawned, and had swarmed
into the streets to speed with jibes those whom
they regarded as the departing guests. The guests
were only going out to fight, or to witness the
fighting, and duly came back again ; but while the
combat was raging, the King's fourgons and the
Crown Prince's waggons had been packed all ready

for the eventuality of an enforced evacuation. It was simply a precautionary measure, an instance of the German preparedness to anticipate a surprise ; but if the French had not been driven back from Bougival that afternoon, it is quite possible the King would not have slept in Versailles that night. On more than one occasion subsequently the royal baggage was packed ready for departure, but neither it nor the King had to quit Versailles until his Majesty was free to return to his own capital, after he had ratified the terms of peace, to which France, shattered and depleted, had no alternative but to assent.

During the winter of 1870-71, while William held his military Court in its prefecture, Versailles was a French town but in name. A German prefect concerned himself with its administration; the local newspaper had a German editor, and was the official journal of the conquerors. German soldiers on municipal duty tramped its streets along with the French guardians of the peace. German dignitaries, German officials, German officers, were billeted in every house. German wounded lay in the halls and corridors of the palace of Louis the Great. The customers who depleted the cellars of the Hotel des Reservoirs and the Vatel were thirsty Germans of the Zweite Staffel—princes and

T

dukes of high degree making the campaign in the
suite of his Majesty or that of his son. But if
German in essentials during that winter, in one
aspect Versailles was curiously cosmopolitan. There
abounded war correspondents of half a dozen
nationalities. Thither from the ends of the earth
came all manner of curious people on a multiplicity
of errands; sightseers pure and simple, adventurers,
inventors, enthusiasts, diplomatists, sanitary ad-
ministrators, intriguers, and volunteer go-betweens.
Paris and Versailles between them focussed the
interest of the world. Only in occasional scraps
men learned how the great capital bore itself in
its tribulation. But from Versailles daily there
radiated to all points of the compass countless
budgets of correspondence, telling how, while life
was gay there, while men dined and drank, and
visited and skated as if war and battles were not,
there was hardly any hour of hardly any day or
night when the sound of the cannon-thunder ceased
to sound in every ear.

The King led a quiet and retired life, engaging
himself with his counsellors on the innumerable
problems which the ever-changing face of events,
both military and civil, constantly presented.
Always an early riser, he had read before breakfast the reports from all quarters that had come in
during the night, and talked them over with Moltke

and Roon. In the forenoon came Bismarck with his budget of matter needing attention. In the afternoon his Majesty generally took a drive, and on two days a week a large party sat down to dinner in the banquet hall of the prefecture. The dinner hour on those occasions was five o'clock. The table decorations, besides plate and flowers, were masterpieces of sugar bakery representing cannon, trophies of captured French eagles, tri-colour flags, and the like; and the plate was the same as that used in his campaigns by Frederic the Great. Dinner did not last very long. After it, tea and coffee were served in the drawing-rooms, and the King came round and talked now with one, now with another of his guests. The whole function was over before eight, and the King immediately went to his cabinet and worked till bed-time. There were few Sundays on which the King did not attend divine service in Louis the XIV.'s chapel in the château of Versailles. The headquarter chaplain preached the sermon on those occasions. His Majesty's place was on a seat placed in front of the altar, the Crown Prince by his side; behind them in serried rows the officers of the two staffs, the members of the two suites, and other officers, the galleries and passages crowded by the German soldiery.

T 2

To record at length the military events of the winter and the details of the Prussian monarch's life during his stay in Versailles, would swell this volume to undue dimensions. No word can be said here concerning the hard fighting in and about the Loire country, in the east of France, or in the wide district between the English Channel and where German armies stood encircling Paris. Till the end came his Majesty never left the vicinity of Versailles, and never even made the circuit of the cordon of the environment of Paris. On October 16th, as he stood in front of the prefecture, he saw march past him the stalwart veterans of the Guard Landwehr, who had come up to the Paris front to strengthen the somewhat slender belt of cincture, and who later were to fight so valiantly and die so freely in the great final sortie at Montretout. On the 21st October he stood for four hours on the Marly aqueduct watching the sortie made from under the cover of Valérien on Bougival by Ducrot at the head of some ten thousand men. There was great perturbation in Versailles on the evening of 30th November, when news arrived how fierce had been the fighting on that day on the east side of the circle, and that nightfall had left the French in possession of Champigny. Until the evening of the 2nd

December, the day on which the French had to
relinquish the advantages they had gained on the
eastern side across the Marne, and were compelled to
fall back into their former positions, the royal headquarters in Versailles remained prepared for withdrawal at an hour's notice. On 22nd December,
at an early hour of a very inclement morning, the
King inspected a detachment of Prussian sailors
on their way to the south to man the gunboats on
the Loire which had been taken from the French.
After church service on New Year's Day, 1871, he
gave a stirring address to a mass of his troops drawn
up on the Place d'Armes of Versailles, and distributed a number of decorations and iron crosses.
During the siege the King frequently resorted to a
point of observation within easy range of the guns
of Mount Valérien—the villa of Baron Stern at
Ville d'Avray, a secluded place to which access
was attained along a narrow lane flanked on each
side by high walls. The look-out place was at a
window opening on the roof from a darkened room,
and the French had no suspicion that here was the
chosen observatory of his Majesty and the principal officers of his staff. It was from this position
that the King watched the commencement of the
southern bombardment on January 5th.

Public opinion in Germany had been ripening

fast in the direction of German unity, under the
influence of German triumphs in the field. The
union of the several German States under a common
Federal Constitution had already been accomplished
in October; and early in December the proposition
came from King Ludwig of Bavaria to King William,
that the possession of the presidential rights of the
Confederacy vested in the Prussian monarch should
be coupled with the imperial title. The King of
Saxony spoke to the same purport; and in one
day a measure providing for the amendment of
the Constitution by the substitution of the words
" Emperor " and " Empire " for " President " and
" Confederation " was passed through the North
German Parliament, which voted also an address
to his Majesty, from which the following is an ex-
tract:—" The North German Parliament, in unison
with the Princes of Germany, approaches with the
prayer that your Majesty will deign to consecrate
the work of unification by accepting the Imperial
Crown of Germany. The Teutonic Crown on the
head of your Majesty will inaugurate, for the re-
established Empire of the German nation, an era
of power, of peace, of well-being, and of liberty
secured under the protection of the laws."

The address of the German Parliament was
presented to the King at Versailles on Sunday, the

18th of December, by its speaker, Herr Simson, who, as speaker of the Frankfort Parliament in 1848, had made the identical proffer to William's brother and predecessor. There had been a solemn divine service in Louis XIV.'s chapel previously, and at two P.M. the deputation was received by King William in the great drawing-room of the prefecture. He stood in front of the great fireplace in full uniform, wearing all his decorations, his son on his right, and on each side the princes of the new Empire and the great officers of his suite and staff. The voice of the old monarch, as he read his reply to the address, trembled with emotion. Many of the veteran generals who stood around his Majesty sobbed with joy, as in faltering tones which he laboured in vain to control, the words of virtual acceptance came from his lips. The formal ratification of assent to the Prussian King's assumption of the imperial dignity had yet to be received from the minor German States; but this was a foregone conclusion, and the unification of Germany really dates from that 18th of December, and from the solemn ceremonial in the prefecture of Versailles. It was understood that in his acceptance of the imperial dignity, William sacrificed his personal feelings to the request of a nation, the arguments of his advisers, and the desires of his relatives; and one great inducement was the gratification of the wish of his son, who was warmly in favour of the imperial project.

Every obstacle cleared away, William was proclaimed the German Emperor on the 18th of January, the memorable and imposing ceremony being held in the Galerie des Glaces of the château of Versailles, the noble apartment in which Queen Victoria was entertained by the Emperor Napoleon. The day chosen was appropriate, for it was the anniversary of the coronation at Königsberg of Frederic I., the first king of the Hohenzollern house. The bad weather had caused to be foregone the projected State procession from the prefecture to the château, and William drove to the great gates of the latter, where he alighted, and passed to the State entrance through a lane of soldiers consisting of detachments from regiments in the field. To those in the Galerie des Glaces the crash of cannon heralded the approach of the monarch. Rich and sonorous rose the massive strains of the chorale chanted by the military choir, as the King, helmet in hand and in full uniform, moved slowly to the daïs, and, bowing to the clergy in front of the temporary altar, halted, and smoothing his heavy white moustache with his disengaged hand, surveyed the scene that lay before him.

Behind him, ranged in a semicircle, were the regimental colours which the detachments marshalled in the courtyard outside had brought with them from their respective regiments.   Just above William as he stood there was a gigantic allegory of the Grand Monarque with the subscription " *Le Roi gouverne par lui même.*"   On his right was the Crown Prince in the uniform of a field marshal; to right and left of father and son stood in a great semicircle, princes and potentates and the leaders of the hosts of united Germany.   Stalwart and square, somewhat apart, on the extreme left of the semicircle of which the monarch was the centre, with a face of deadly pallor, for he had risen from a sick bed, stood Bismarck, the man of all others who might that day most truly say, " Finis coronat opus."   Psalms were sung and prayers were said, and Court Preacher Rogge preached a short impassioned sermon, followed by another chorale in which all joined.   Then his Majesty, in a loud yet broken voice, read a declaration proclaiming that the German Empire was re-established, and that the imperial dignity so revived was vested in him and his descendants for all time to come, in accordance with the unanimous will of the German peoples.   Bismarck then read the proclamation which his master addressed to the German nation.

As his final words rang through the hall, the Grand Duke of Baden, William's son - in - law, stepped forward a couple of paces, raised his helmet in air, and shouted with all his force, "Long live the German Emperor William. Hurrah!" Amidst a tempest of cheering, amidst waving of swords and of helmets, William, King of Prussia, was hailed as German Emperor, and with eyes streaming with tears received the homage of princes, dukes, and lords of the Empire. The first, on bended knee, to kiss his father's hand was his noble and gallant son. A military band outside struck up the Prussian National Anthem. Louder than the music, heard above the clamour of the cheering, sounded the thunder of the French cannon from Mont Valérien, the "Ave Cæsar" from the reluctant lips of worsted France.

But France was gallantly loth to accept the stern fiat of adverse fate. On the day after the great ceremonial in Versailles, as if in remonstrance against it, the garrison of Paris made a desperate sortie, in which 100,000 men took part. The close and fierce engagement raged from Montretout round to St. Cloud from morning until the going down of the sun. The French fought with sustained fury; but all their efforts were in vain, crushed by the steady, relentless fire of the serried German artillery. And the bombardment, which had commenced on the south front on the 5th January against the outlying forts, but which in a few days was at least partially directed upon Paris itself, if endured by the Parisians with a noble fortitude, accentuated the strain of the defeated sortie and of the scarcity of food. The end was approaching; but Paris endured hunger and shell-fire until the morning of January 28th. At 7 P.M. on that day an armistice was signed for twenty-one days. The long duel had ended. On the following day the French troops evacuated Mont Valérien, and the German soldiers marched in and occupied the fortress. The German Emperor paid a visit to that stronghold on the 30th, and looked at "La Grande Josephine," the monster cannon whose shells had ranged as far as the outskirts of Versailles. The process of revictualling Paris began as soon as the armistice was concluded, and England was foremost and most zealous in the holy work of charity.

The armistice was twice extended while Thiers wrestled with his countrymen and with Bismarck. For six long days did the French statesman contest point after point with the unyielding Chancellor. He appealed from Bismarck to Bismarck's master, to plead that Metz should not be torn from France.

The Emperor received him, the Imperial Crown
Prince compassionated him, but they sent him
empty away, relegating him to the tender mercies
of the Chancellor.   It was not until 6 P.M. of
the 26th February that the preliminaries of peace
were signed.   Thiers had been told that a German
force would occupy Paris between the date of the
expiry of the armistice and the ratification of the
treaty by the Bordeaux Assembly,   On this point
he did obtain some modification.   A mere section
of Paris was indeed occupied ; but only pro formâ,
and the occupation endured barely thirty-six hours.

On the 26th the Emperor transmitted a con-
gratulatory circular dispatch to the Sovereign Princes
of Germany, which ran thus :—" With a heart filled
with thankfulness, I announce to you that yesterday afternoon the preliminaries of peace were signed
by which Alsace without Belfort, Lorraine with
Metz, was ceded to Germany.   Five milliards of
francs are to be paid, and portions of France are to
remain occupied until the amount is paid.   Paris
will be partially occupied till the ratification at
Bordeaux follows.   We are now at the end of a
glorious but bloody war which was forced upon
us with frivolity without parallel, and in which your
troops have taken so honourable a part.   May the
greatness of Germany be consolidated in peace ! "

The 1st of March was the day fixed for the entry of the German troops into Paris, and on the morning of that day the German Emperor held a grand review on the Longchamp racecourse in the Bois de Boulogne, of the troops chosen from the Third Army to constitute the force of temporary occupation. The long double line of horse, foot, and artillery was gradually formed, stretching from end to end of the racecourse, with its accurately dressed front looking toward the grand stand. The Bavarians had the centre, the wings consisting of Prussian troops. Out to front, in the clear space before the centre, stood two mounted men, the Imperial Crown Prince, the Commander of the 3rd Army, and General Blumenthal, his chief of staff. There was a pause of expectation; then suddenly a great cheer flashed instantaneously from the face of the long wall-like line. In a clash of music the bands burst into "God save the King." Half a dozen horsemen were galloping across the racecourse, heading straight for the centre of the line. The leader, an upright, broad-shouldered old man, with snow-white hair, half halted his horse with a hand-wave of salutation as he reached the Imperial Crown Prince, then, with the latter behind him, galloped on toward the right flank. The great staff that had been waiting there came prancing up as the old leader turned his horse's head, and began his slow march along the front. Two horsemen preceded him ; an interval, and then the old man alone, the solitary focus of the splendid picture. The white-haired soldier on the noble black horse was the Emperor William. He had been reported unwell ; but this great day for the Empire of which he was the head seemed to have cured him of his ailments. His crest was as erect, his seat as firm, his bridle-hand as light, as those of his gallant son who, following at the head of his staff, seemed so proud of his father. The inspection completed, the cortège, following its leader, turned toward the saluting point in front of the pavilion, and then men noticed that the royal father and son had drawn together—horsehead to horsehead. Potent as is etiquette, it may yield to love, and father and son never loved each other more tenderly than did William and his heir. The proud father laid his hand on the neck of his son's horse, and the suite fell back as the two conversed. The march past began. The troops passing daintily clean in accurate array had been otherwise engaged for the previous six months than in studying the business of drill and dressing. Fighting, bivouacking, earthworking, marching, as they had been, yet their parade accuracy and neatness had no

whit deteriorated. Even in the months of fighting,
marching, and bivouacking, time had been found
in those German ranks for the practice of methodical drill.

As the troops marched past, the heads of the
columns took their way through the glades of the
Bois de Boulogne, leading on toward the western
entrances into Paris. Already the German cavalry
were inside the capital, and a Bavarian hussar
officer had ridden his horse over the guarding
chains, and passed under the Arch of Triumph.
Down the Champs Elysées, with bands playing and
colours flying, poured the German infantry — a
broad stream of armed men on whose bayonets the
sunlight danced. But with the soldiers as they
entered Paris went neither the German Emperor
nor his son. It was decorous at once and politic,
to refrain from the insolence of triumph. William
and the Prince went quietly back to Versailles.

That same day the Bordeaux Assembly ratified
the treaty, and twelve days later the last German
soldier marched out of Versailles, and a French
regiment re-garrisoned the town which for months
had been the residence of the German monarch.
He had left Versailles earlier, on the 7th of March,
sleeping that night in Ferrières, after having reviewed the Army of the Meuse on the plateau of

Villiers, on the field whereon had been fought the desperate battles of the 30th November and 2nd December. On his way to the parade the Emperor passed the great grave in which 800 French dead had been buried ; as the troops marched past him he stood where to right and to left lay thick the mounds under which lay brave men who had died for him and the Fatherland.

It was not until ten days later that the victorious monarch returned to his capital. That was a day that will long be remembered in Berlin. The sun was bright and the sky clear. All the Linden was dressed with banners. One floated from the pedestal of the statue of Frederic the Great, bearing the legend, " Hail, Emperor William, hail to thee and to the brave German host thou leadest back from victory ! Like the clash of distant bells sounds the glad cheering of the conquerors. Old Fritz looks down with proud glance on his descendants, approving their valour." Long before the time fixed for the arrival of the royal train, the platform of the railway station was thronged with notabilities. There were Bismarck in his white cuirassier uniform, and Moltke and Roon, and other principal persons of the great headquarter staff. There was the venerable Marshal Wrangel, yet an older soldier than his venerable sovereign. There, too, were Vogel von Falkenstein, grim and grey; and old Steinmetz, come from his distant Posen governorship. Of ladies and children of the Imperial house the name was legion. In a siding opposite the platform, whether by accident or design, had been shunted an hospital train, from the windows of which pallid faces looked on the brilliant scene. On the carriage roofs clustered convalescents, and a little squad of fellows maimed at Spicheren and Courcelles gave Steinmetz a cheer—old "Immer Vorwärts," as they styled him; and so with gossip and endless kindly greetings the moments of expectancy passed.

At the sound of a distant whistle, from out the waiting-room stalked Bismarck; Wrangel doffed his plumed helmet; a stream of ladies and children followed Bismarck's stalwart form; in two minutes more a near rumble, and the train rolled up to the platform. Then rose a mighty cheer; and there at the carriage window stood the Emperor, looking out on his relatives and servants. A moment later and he was down the steps and kissing the Dowager Queen Elizabeth. It seemed as if the women of his family were mobbing him, as they crowded round him for his kisses, while grandchildren hung about his knees. The old man was brushing his shaggy brows with the back of his hand as he

U

struggled through the womenfolk about him. In
his path stood the venerable Wrangel, a beam from
the setting sun flashing on his snow-white hair.
The soldier-patriarch raised his hand and tried to
lead off a cheer, but his voice failed him, and the
tears rolled down his face. His master, not less
moved, kissed his aged servant on each cheek.
The two old soldier-comrades embraced, and Steinmetz's wounded fellows on the carriage roof cheered
the greeting. Then the Emperor grasped Bismarck
by the hand and kissed him too ; and old Steinmetz
as well ; he kissed his way right through out of
sight into the waiting-room, the Empress following
shedding glad tears. The scene was like an April
day—shower and sunshine, tears and smiles ; all
state and ceremony were swept away in the gush of
homely affection. When his Majesty reached the
palace, the cheers of his people kept him long
lingering on the threshold ; over and over again he
had to come out on to the balcony with the Empress ; and his final appearance was at the accustomed corner window at which he had shown
himself on the declaration of the war. That war
was now finished, and William had come home
from his last campaign.

CHAPTER XIII.

HONOURED OLD AGE.

WHEN United Germany hailed William as its Emperor, the venerable monarch's life had already exceeded the Psalmist's span of threescore years and ten; but he was yet to survive for many years, and so exceptional was the strength of his robust vitality that those years brought little for him of "labour and sorrow." His vigour showed little organic impairment until his long illness in the spring of 1885, and it was only in the preceding year that he ceased to attend reviews on horseback. In its personal aspect his life ceased to be eventful after the close of his last great war, except for the attempts made upon it by assassins to which reference will presently be made.

A few days after his return to Berlin, the first session of the new German Parliament was opened by the Emperor in full state, the place of meeting being the historic "White Hall" of the old palace. His speech from the throne was uttered with great

emotion and received with fervent enthusiasm. Its
expressions breathed patriotism, dignity, and moderation. "The spirit," said William, "which ani-
mates the German people pervades its culture and
morals, and in no less degree marks the constitution
of its empire and its armies, guards Germany in
the midst of its successes against every temptation
to abuse the power acquired by its unity. Germany
willingly pays the respect claimed for its own independence to the independence of all other states
and peoples, the weak as well as the powerful. Our
new Germany, as it has emerged from the fiery
ordeal of the recent war, will be a trustworthy
guarantee of the peace of Europe, because Germany
is sufficiently powerful and self-reliant to preserve
the regulation of its own affairs as an exclusive,
but at the same time sufficient and satisfactory
heritage."

While unfortunate Paris was writhing in the
throes of civil war, Berlin was celebrating German
victories. On the 16th of June, 1871, a grand
military display was held in honour of the successes of the recent war. The troops who had
taken part in it were now back in their native land,
and a representative army, fifty thousand strong,
mustered on the Tempelhofer Field for the triumphal entry into the capital. Before the old Em-

peror, as he passed down the Linden at the head
of the bronzed and stalwart soldiers, rode abreast
"the makers of history"—Bismarck, Moltke, and
Roon; in the staff that followed him close, besides
the soldier-princes of his own house, were thirty
German sovereigns and princes of reigning families,
who had come to swell the triumph of the chosen
head of the German Empire.   The path of the
triumph all down the Linden lay between a double
row of captured French cannon and mitrailleuses,
behind which Berlin *en masse* thronged and cheered
under the waving banners.   For two hours and
more the stream of war veterans flowed on in a
steady, unbroken current—horse, foot, and artillery.
One " combined " battalion, whose ranks were made
up of men of every German nationality, escorted
the eagles, colours, and standards that had once
belonged to the French army.   From under the
statue of Blücher the Emperor looked on as his
troops marched by, and the *défilé* finished, he
crossed the Frederic's Bridge to where, with the
captured French eagles and colours grouped around
it, stood the yet veiled statue of King Frederic
William III., the father-monarch with whom
William had made the campaign of his early youth.
After a solemn religious service the Emperor uncovered the statue amidst the cheering of his people

and the strains of martial music. At night the
capital was one great illumination—the French
Embassy the only dark spot in the general glow
of variegated light.

All Europe's attention was drawn to the meeting of the German and Austrian Emperors at
Gastein in August. Its ostensible cause was trivial,
but nobody believed that the Imperial interlocutors
wasted many words about the Roumanian railway
bonds. The spectre of socialism loomed grim and
large on the European horizon, threatening all fixed
institutions, and pointing a lean finger of warning
to where anarchy was distracting unfortunate
France. The times were pregnant with suggestive-
ness to monarchs that they should take joint
counsel for the hindrance of the spreading of the
dangerous sore. It was understood that the interviews at Gastein and later at Salzburg in September,
resulted in a cordial understanding and the settlement of a common policy ; that Francis Joseph
acquiesced unreservedly in William's supremacy in
Germany, and that the latter engaged to leave
the German provinces of the Austrian Empire
untampered with. It is certain that the seed was
then sown of the Austro-German alliance, which
has now endured so long as almost to be entitled
to be regarded as venerable. Toward the end of

the year the Emperor and the Imperial Crown
Prince joined a big-game hunting party in the
Hanoverian forest of Göhrde. That his Majesty,
old though he was, could distinguish himself not
less as a sportsman than as a soldier, was proved
by the fact that his share of the bag consisted of
twenty-one wild boars. His usual hunting-ground
was Silesia, the manner of life during his annual
visit to which region a writer thus sketches :—" The
Emperor usually arrives with his guests the evening
before the battue, and takes up his quarters in the
hunting castle of Königswusterhausen, where, after
supper, during which the finest horn music from
Berlin is always played, the whole company
assemble at a 'smoking college' in the same hall
where that function used to be held in the time of
Frederic William I. This hall is decorated with
stags' horns and stuffed boars' heads, trophies of
animals killed by the Emperor. It contains the
same peculiar chairs and long oaken table in use
170 years ago. There the merry company relate
hunting stories, drink beer out of old earthenware
mugs, and smoke Turkish tobacco out of long clay
pipes till a late hour, just as in the days of Frederic
William I."

In September, 1872, the Emperors of Russia
and Austria met in Berlin as the guests of the

German Emperor, who had a great desire to see
Austria and Russia on terms of cordial amity, and
was equally anxious for the resuscitation of the old
Triple Alliance. Whatever may have been the
political results—or no results—of William's well-
meant efforts, the Berlin meeting was fertile in
evidences of personal goodwill between the Czar
and Francis Joseph. The Emperors spent a week
in gorgeous festivities and ostentatious mutual
cordiality. There was a state banquet in the
"White Hall," and the Imperial Crown Prince
welcomed his father's guests to a great entertainment in the New Palace at Potsdam. While the
Emperors exchanged courtesies, a similar friendli-
ness seemed to inspire their ministers, who spent
days in intimate consultation with the professed
object of promoting harmony and goodwill. Certain
outcomes of the Imperial reunion were manifest.
The German Empire had obtained the fullest
recognition from its two great rivals; scant hope
remained to France of accomplishing her *révanche*
with the aid of a strong foreign alliance; and the
German Ultramontanes saw themselves forced to
renounce the prospect of finding a champion in the
head of the House of Hapsburg, the "born de-
fender of the Catholic Church."

When his guests had left him, William visited

Marienburg, the capital of West Prussia, to participate in the centennial celebration of the first partition of Poland, when that province was restored to Prussia, of which it had originally formed part; and to lay the foundation-stone of a memorial to Frederic the Great. The 30th September, 1872, was a memorable day for Alsace-Lorraine, the province which the Franco-German War had added to the German empire. At midnight of that day terminated the interval of "optation," and all who had not then effected their exodus were to be regarded as having elected to be German subjects. Fewer had chosen to emigrate than had been expected; only some 45,000 persons preferred to make sacrifices for the sake of remaining French; and Alsatian recruits proffered themselves for service in the German army in greater numbers than could be received. In this year the aristocrats of Prussia made an unavailing stand for their ancestral privileges, in the teeth of an intimation on the part of their sovereign of his desire that they should yield. The feudal peers and landed proprietors were naturally averse to a measure which, under the title of the Districts Administration Bill, proposed to remodel the social system of the kingdom, by conceding representative institutions and self-government to its villages and rural

circles. The peers held that the innovation would
be a step toward republicanism, and that if William
were so ill-advised as to regard it consistent with
the maintenance of the monarchy, it was their
duty to rescue him from the ill consequences of his
own weakness. When the bill came on in the
Upper Chamber, his Majesty intimated his wish
that it should pass, but it was rejected by the
overwhelming majority of 145 to 18. After a short
prorogation the bill, somewhat modified, was carried
through the Lower House and came up again to the
Upper Chamber. To carry it through there necessitated the creation of twenty-five new peers—a step
to which his Majesty was very reluctant, but which
he was brought to sanction in the realisation of
the responsibilities of his widened position. In
December Bismarck resigned the Premiership of the
Prussian Cabinet, assigning as his reason the over-
pressure of duties and responsibilities. Roon proved
a temporary and inadequate successor. Bismarck
remained Chancellor of the Empire and Minister
for Foreign Affairs.

In 1873 the Shah of Persia was the guest of
the German Emperor, and later in September came
Victor Emmanuel of Italy, between whom and his
host sprang up great cordiality and friendship.
There was a good deal in common in the characters

of the two men, and they took to each other instinctively. Two years later, old as he was, William kept the promise he had given the King of Italy, that he would return the latter's visit; and there was a great outburst of enthusiasm in Milan as the two soldierly sovereigns rode along the Piazza del Duomo. In 1873 William paid as well as received visits. In April, long before the snow had melted from the steppes, the hardy old monarch journeyed to St. Petersburg, to be the guest of his nephew the Czar; and in October he went to Vienna, on a visit to the Emperor Francis Joseph. On the anniversary of the victory of Sedan, his Majesty, with great ceremony, unveiled the "Monument of Victory" on the Königsplatz, making a speech in which he said: " This column of Victory is a monument to the generations of what self-sacrifice and perseverance can accomplish. In conjunction with our faithful allies, we strode from victory to victory by the grace of God, until we attained to the unity of Germany in the foundation of a new empire."

It is impossible to trace the troubled course of the virulent conflict which raged so long between the Prussian Government and the Church of Rome, and in which a section of William's Roman Catholic subjects were almost inevitably embroiled. Whether the enforcement of the "May Laws" deserves the name of persecution, or whether those statutes were rendered necessary by priestly pretensions subversive of the peace of the monarchy, is a question far too wide for discussion here. It was remarkable to what extent, when the struggle was at its bitterest, the Papists of Prussia dissociated the sovereign from any personal responsibility for the severities which they regarded as oppression. That William suffered because of the sufferings under which groaned a portion of his people may be taken for granted, for he was a man of a very tender heart, and had a sincere pity for all suffering; that he was driven against his own sense of right into the reluctant fulfilment of his duty as a Constitutional monarch is easily averred, but might be harder to prove. There is no undertone of lack of personal conviction in the justice of the course he sanctioned, in his famous letter to Pope Pius IX., in answer to a personal epistle of remonstrance from that Pontiff. William's reply reads like the letter of a man who is firm on his own ground; and as it summarises the attitude of Prussian legal authority against Papal pretensions, its reproduction is not inappropriate. The Pope's letter had insisted that the measures adopted by the Prussian Government, "all aimed more and more at the destruction of Catholicism." William's reply was as follows :—

"I am glad that your Holiness has, as in former times, done me the honour to write to me. I rejoice the more at this since an opportunity is thereby afforded me of correcting errors, which, as it appears from the letter of your Holiness, must have occurred in the communications you have received relative to German affairs. If the reports made to your Holiness respecting German questions only stated the truth, it would not be possible for your Holiness to entertain the supposition that my Government enters on a path which I do not approve. According to the constitution of my States, such a thing cannot happen, since the laws and Government measures in Prussia require my consent as Sovereign. To my deep sorrow, a portion of my Catholic subjects have organised for the past two years a political party which endeavours to disturb, by intrigues hostile to the State, the religious peace which has existed in Prussia for centuries. Leading Catholic priests have, unfortunately, not only approved this movement, but joined in it to the extent of open revolt against existing laws. It will not have escaped the observation of your Holiness, that similar indications manifest themselves at the present time in several European and some Transatlantic States. It is not my mission to investigate the causes by which the clergy and the faithful of one of the Christian denominations can be induced actively to assist the enemies of all law; but it certainly is my mission to protect internal peace, and preserve the authority of the laws in the States whose Government has been entrusted to me by God. I am conscious that I owe hereafter an account of the accomplishment of this my kingly duty. I shall maintain order and law in my States against all attacks, so long as God gives me the power. I am in duty bound to do this as a Christian monarch, even when to my sorrow I have to fulfil this royal duty against servants of a Church which I suppose

acknowledge, no less than the Evangelical Church, that the com-
mandment of obedience to secular authority is an emanation of
the revealed will of God.   Many of the priests in Prussia subject
to your Holiness disown, to my regret, the Christian doctrine in
this respect, and place my Government under the necessity, supported by the great majority of my loyal Catholic and Evangelical subjects, of extorting obedience to the law by secular means.
I willingly entertain the hope that your Holiness, upon being
informed of the true position of affairs, will use your authority
to put an end to the agitation carried on amidst deplorable
distortion of the truth and abuse of priestly authority.   The
religion of Jesus Christ has, as I attest to your Holiness before
God, nothing to do with these intrigues, any more than has
truth, to whose banner invoked by your Holiness I unreservedly
subscribe.   There is one more expression in the letter of your
Holiness which I cannot pass over without contradiction,
although it is not based on the previous information, but upon
the belief of your Holiness—viz., the expression that every one
who has received baptism belongs to the Pope. The Evangelical
creed, which, as must be known to your Holiness, I, like my
ancestors and the majority of my subjects, profess, does not
permit us to accept in our relations to God any other Mediator
than our Lord Jesus Christ.   The difference of faith does not
prevent me from living in peace with those who do not share
mine, and offering your Holiness the expression of my personal
devotion and esteem."

It was said at the time that no incident since
Sedan had so powerfully stirred the German mind
as did the publication of the letter quoted above.
Addresses poured in thanking the Emperor for his
firmness in resisting Papal pretensions, which were
described as "arrogant," and he was earnestly

entreated to enforce the laws against the Ultramontanes—"those dishonest, ambitious, and irrational
enemies of the German empire." Catholics and
Protestants alike expressed their satisfaction at the
independent attitude asserted by the sovereign.
The close of 1873 found his Majesty seriously
ailing; and his health and spirits alike were affected
by the death of the Dowager Queen Elizabeth, the
widow of Frederic William IV.

In 1875 a measure for the organisation of the
Landsturm became law; helped, no doubt, by the
curiously frank line of argument held by Moltke,
who frankly said Germany had "the respect of all,
but the sympathy of none ; being in fact universally
regarded as a dangerous neighbour." She certainly
was not rendered less dangerous potentially by a
measure which, in effect, increased her military
strength by half a million of men, and raised that
strength to the stupendous total of 2,800,000 men.
There was a certain political significance in the
effusive cordiality which characterised the Czar's
visit to his Imperial uncle in May of this year.
Relations between France and Germany were at
more than their normal tension. France was
engaged in an increase of her armed strength of a
nature which the Germans regarded as threatening
a special purpose. A German newspaper had bluntly

asked, "Is war in sight?" and popular feeling was stirring on the Spree as well as on the Seine. Alexander took great pains to show his respectful friendship for the German Emperor. At the conclusion of a review during which he had ridden at the head of the "Emperor Alexander" regiment of the Prussian Guard, he gave it the order, as a mark of special homage, to present arms to William. Such things were regarded as a confirmation of the Russian Emperor's confidence in Germany's moderation, with the inference that he regarded France as responsible for the clouds on the horizon. Alexander had previously expressed himself to the effect that a cordial understanding between the three Emperors was a guarantee for the maintenance of peace, unless France were obstinately bent on breaking it, and this visit went to heighten that impression. The international irritation was gradually allayed, and it was characteristic that a year later Bismarck cited as an argument for restrictions on the freedom of the press the question quoted above, which it was hinted at the time he had himself inspired.

The first day of 1877—the year of the Russo-Turkish war—was the seventieth anniversary of the commencement of the Emperor's military life, and the few soldierly sentences he spoke to the officers

who assembled to congratulate him were character-
istically modest :—" When I look back on the day
when I entered the army, I cannot but remember
the state of things which then existed; and from
the moment when my father's hand led me into the
army, throughout my life, my first thought has
been to give grateful thanks to the arbiter of our
destinies. My gratitude is due to all those who
have accompanied me in my military career and
joined in my efforts. I have to thank the valour,
devotion, and constancy of the army for the position
which I now offer. From Fehrbellin to the last
glorious war the deeds of the Prussian army are
enrolled imperishably in the world's history. Prussia
has become what she was chiefly through the
army."

The Emperor attained his eightieth year on the
22nd March, 1877, and the day was celebrated as a
great national festival. Over a thousand congratu-
latory telegrams reached the old monarch, who
made a point of opening them all with his own
hands; and all the windows of the palace were
decorated with birthday bouquets, from behind a
fragrant rampart of which he bowed his acknow-
ledgments to the cheering multitudes below. The
first to pay their duty to him were the Imperial
Crown Prince and Princess with their children;

then followed the princes of the blood, the court
functionaries, ambassadors, ministers, generals, and
innumerable deputations from all parts of the
Empire. The receptions lasted till the afternoon,
and when they were at length finished the Emperor
drove to the old palace, where the King of Saxony
presented him, in the name of the reigning princes
of Germany, with Werner's picture of the memorable
ceremony in the château of Versailles. Among
the other presents accepted by his Majesty this day
were an engraving executed by Prince Henry and
a book bound by Prince Waldemar, the two younger
sons of the Imperial Crown Prince. It is among
the domestic customs of the Hohenzollern house
that each scion of it in youth learns some handi-
craft. William himself was a glazier; his son is a
compositor.

His Majesty in the summer of 1877 paid his
first visit to the new German province of Alsace-
Lorraine. In Strasburg he had from the middle
classes a more cordial reception than had been
anticipated, but it was noticed that the upper and
lower classes held aloof from the demonstrations.
Metz was unmistakably sullen. Its municipal
council declined to vote money to be spent in a
civic reception of the conqueror, and the unfortunate
injury to the grand old cathedral by a fire caused

by the German illuminations did not contribute to
cordiality on the part of the Messins. While
on his way to the autumn manœuvres at Düsseldorf, William paid a visit to Herr Krupp at
Essen, where, on the anniversary of Sedan, he
witnessed a siege gun being fashioned by the
great hammer "Fritz," whose weight is $37\frac{1}{2}$ tons.
The manœuvres of this autumn were on an exceptionally extensive scale, and commencing at
Düsseldorf, were continued at Cologne, Baden, and
Darmstadt, lasting throughout the month of September. Alike of field evolutions, parades, festivals,
and receptions, the hale octogenarian monarch was
the central figure, and his activity and endurance
were phenomenal. Five hours' sleep sufficed him;
he was up and in the saddle by 6 A.M., and midnight found him supping on lobster salad, to his
fondness for which some, indeed, have attributed
his able-bodied longevity. Near the end of the
year he followed the funeral procession of a
comrade whose longevity was yet more exceptional
than his own. Old Marshal Wrangel, of whom it
was said that "he had forgotten to die," had at
length, at the age of ninety-four, remembered that
duty; wearing uniform even on his death-bed—
or rather sofa, for he would not go to bed—so as
to be ready for any summons that might reach

him from his sovereign. The summons came at
length from another King than William, and the
tough old Trojan, who the Berlin boys believed
had fought at Fehrbellin to say nothing of Hohen-
freidberg and Waterloo, had to obey. The Emperor
paid the dead soldier an unprecedented mark of
respect by following his coffin on foot to the
railway station, so violating a canon of court
etiquette which prescribes that the reigning
sovereign should participate in the funeral procession only of his predecessor or of a Queen Dowager.

In the early summer of 1878 two attempts were
made to assassinate the venerable monarch. On
May 11th, as he was driving in the Linden, a crazed
mechanic named Hödel fired two pistol shots at
him from the side-walk. William exclaimed, " Is
it possible these shots are intended for me ? " when
a reply, happily ineffective, was made in the shape
of two more shots. None of the four took effect ;
but less harmless was the attempt made on June
3rd by Dr. Charles Edward Nobiling, a man of
birth and education, and an impassioned Socialist.
Nobiling's weapon was a double-barrelled gun
loaded with swanshot, and fired from a second-
floor window of a house on the Linden as the
Emperor alone in his *calèche* was driving toward
the Brandenburg Gate. Both barrels were fired,

and the charges took effect about the head, face, arms, and back of the victim. Fortunately owing to the distance the charges had scattered considerably; but for this their effect would certainly have been fatal. Extraction was set about at once, the Emperor remaining perfectly composed during the protracted operation. In the course of a short interval he was able to concern himself in despatching a message to the Shah of Persia, regretting his inability to keep a dinner engagement for the same evening with that potentate. Over thirty shot were extracted; some he carried in him to the grave. His Majesty nominated his son to be Regent while he himself should remain an invalid, and the Prince was thus acting for his father and sovereign during the sittings of the Berlin Congress from which Lords Beaconsfield and Salisbury brought back "peace with honour." It was not until December that his Majesty resumed the reins, after a visit to Cologne for the inauguration of a monument in the capital of the Rhine provinces to the memory of his father.

CHAPTER XIV.

IMPERIAL MEMORIALS IN STONE AND BRONZE.

In the decade that followed the close of the
Franco-German war, there were erected many
splendid monuments intended to tell Germany to
all time of the great deeds accomplished during
the life of the Emperor. German unity that had
been the dream of all Germany for ages had through
him been completed. German poets had sung
of him as the modern Barbarossa, the new embodiment of the legend that made the old Red Beard
slumber beneath the Kyffhæuser during the long
period of Germany's disunity. Sculptors and
architects now vied with each other in producing
designs of monuments and monumental structures
that should symbolize the splendid deeds of the
past, and teach in stone and bronze, the great
story of a life that had been consecrated to the
re-establishment of the Empire. Scarcely a hamlet in all Germany that had not erected its monument in memory of its soldiers who had fallen in
the war. Berlin had completed hers : the beautiful Column of Victory in the Thiergarten, commemorating Prussia's great work ; but this memo-

rialized not only the victories of 1870 and 1871, but those over Denmark in 1864, and Austria and the South German states in 1866. The column was a gigantic gravestone for over fifty thousand Prussians who had fallen in these three great wars in defence of their dynasty and their country.

Consequently, the ceremonies connected with the inauguration of that monument on the 2d of September, 1873, had been almost exclusively Prussian in character. The Emperor was attended at the magnificent ceremony by all the princes of Prussia, and by the General Staff of the Prussian Army ; but the Princes of the Empire, Prussia's allies in 1870, had not been invited, for the reason that the monument itself represented victories in which some of them had taken part among the defeated. The foundation stone had been laid on the 15th of April, 1865, on the anniversary of the storming of the Dueppler breastworks, and a document was placed in the corner-stone, telling the "deeds of Borussia and her imperial ally in the fight for the Duchies." Then came 1866 and Sadowa, and the scope of the monument had to be enlarged to commemorate Prussia's victories over her former imperial ally and the South German states. Then came 1870, and once more the monument had to tell a greater story, that of the victories in France and the reunification of Germany under Prussian leadership.

Still greater monuments were yet to be completed, in which all the German princes and peoples could take pride in up-building or in finishing. These were the splendid National Monument on the Niederwald; the Arminius Monument on the summit of the Grotenburg, in the Teutoburg Forest, near Detmold, and the completion of the Cologne Cathedral. In September, 1877, two years after the inauguration of the monument of Victory in Berlin, the Emperor went to the river and there laid the foundation-stone of the grand structure to be erected on the banks of the Rhine, opposite Bingen, and which was unveiled with brilliant ceremonies seven years afterward. It had been preceded, however, by the completion and dedication of the Hermann or Arminius Monument, in August, 1875, a monument in which all the people of Germany took enthusiastic interest. It remains to this day one of the most unique of German memorial structures. The colossal figure of Hermann, Prince of the Cheruskeans, with uplifted sword, telling Germany of the glorious deeds of a long gone past, stands on the highest summit of Teutoburg range, overlooking the ground, where in the ninth year after the birth of Christ, the united German tribes defeated, and slew in a three days' battle, in the defiles of the forest, the forces of Varus, the Roman general sent to subjugate the Teutons by Augustus, who, when the news was brought to him in Rome, refused to be comforted, and for days and nights kept exclaiming, " Varus, Varus, give me back my legions."

The monument itself was a triumph of perseverance on the part of the sculptor, Von Bandel, who spent thirty-seven years of his life in building it, and who probably would have died leaving his great work unfinished, had not the victories of 1870–71 called the attention of Germany to the uncompleted structure on the Grotenburg. Eleven hundred years had passed since Charlemagne had destroyed the Irminsul that had been worshipped by the Teutons ever since Hermann's death ; and the new Irminsul had been erected on the same hills, in greater beauty and with added significance. For the modern Irminsul, in 1875, recalled not only the deeds and symbolical figure of the first great hero of German unity, but with its completion was celebrated the renewal of Germany's unity and the completion of her strength under one whom the Germans loved to style a second Armin. Underneath the dome-like structure on which the figure of Hermann stands had been placed a bust, in relief, of the Emperor, made in bronze after a model by Von Bandel from cannon captured at Gravelotte. Underneath were the dates of the Emperor's eventful life, and the following inscription : " He united with firm hand the long divided peoples. He overcame victoriously the might and craft of France. He led home to the Empire the long lost children. He was, like Armin, the Deliverer. *Armin dem Retter ist er gleich!*"

All Germany sent representatives to attend the ceremonies connected with the unveiling of Von Bandel's colossal monument, and to greet the new Armin, in the person of the Emperor. Fifty thousand people had gathered on the summit of the Grotenburg on the memorable August morning in 1875. In the imperial tribune sat the Emperor, and about him the reigning Prince of Lippe-Detmold, the Princesses of Lippe, the Crown Prince of Germany, Prince Carl of Prussia, and princes or representatives of the reigning houses of all the German states, gallant Von der Tann representing King Ludwig of Bavaria. After the ceremonies a touching incident occurred. The Emperor sent his chamberlain to bring the aged sculptor to him. Leaning on the arm of the court official, the gray-haired old man, with uncovered head, walking slowly, ascended the steps leading to the imperial tribune. The Emperor arose and went to meet the old sculptor, and grasping his hands with great warmth, spoke affectionate words to him on the completion of his great work. The fifty thousand people cheered again and again, and the sight will long be remembered by those who witnessed it. The aged monarch through whom German unity had been accomplished, who had been hailed by his people a second Armin, stood grasping the hand of the equally aged sculptor, who had spent the best years of his life in building the noblest monument to the first Armin, the Cheruskean prince who had first brought the German tribes together to meet and defeat the common foe. The Emperor himself was moved to tears. He spoke of the monument as a beautiful one, and of Germany as at last happily united. Pointing to the colossal figure and the sword held aloft in the hands of the Cheruskean, he said that if all Germans did their duty in the future as well as they had done in the past, the Empire need never fear danger from foreign foes.

Significant politically was the celebration of the completion of the Cologne Cathedral, on the 15th day of October, 1880, in the presence of the Emperor, the Empress, and a brilliant concourse. The beautiful gothic structure had always been looked upon as a monumental symbol of the re-establishment of the German Empire; but had remained long uncompleted during the many years that Germany was disunited, and unable to assert herself in the councils of Europe. A German writer said well, " It was a remarkable dispensation of Providence that the same imperial hand was permitted to fit on the capstone of the glorious Cathedral that had previously laid the foundation of the Empire." The Cathedral of Cologne was commenced in the year 1248, and consecrated to Divine Service on the 27th of September, 1522. But it was not completed during centuries. In 1814, ruin threatened it, when the attention of the then Crown Prince of Prussia was called to its condition. Frederick William III. and Frederick William IV. watched the work of restoration with deep interest. In 1842, Frederick William IV., after he had given permission for the raising of funds, through the agency of the Dombau Verein, laid the foundation-stone of the building in its present dimensions. It was then that, surrounded by the princes of the Houses of Prussia, Austria, Bavaria, and those of all the other courts of Germany, holding the hammer in his hand, which was to strike the last corner-stone, he uttered the remarkable words : " Here, where the foundation-stone lies, shall arise the most beautiful portals of the world. Germany is building them. May they become for Germany, by the grace of God, the portals of a new, great, true era. May the great work itself be a prophet to the latest generations of a Germany great and powerful through the unity of rulers and people, a unity which may enforce the peace of the world without bloodshed." He expressed a hope that within those gates would never enter that evil spirit which served disunion among German princes and peoples.

Unfortunately the brilliant ceremonies that took place in Cologne in the October days of 1880, were marred by the fact that the national unity of which King William IV. had spoken, of which the Emperor should have been the representative, was not complete. The Kulturkampf had not yet been ended, and many Catholics had expressed the hope that the solemn and ceremorial completion of the Cathedral should be preceded by a repeal of the May Laws. However, the ceremonies at Cologne may be said to have marked the beginning of the end of the religious struggle and the obnoxious legislation, which was finally to all intents and purposes repealed. Prince Bismarck, the author of the Kulturkampf, was absent from the Cologne festival, showing that he was not in accordance with the spirit that influenced the Emperor, who in fact had grown weary of the religious struggle in the Empire, and was inspired by the wish to see all internal conflicts settled before he should be called to leave his stewardship in the hands of his son. Nevertheless, in his address, he carefully avoided touching on politics, or even German unity. "Before us stands," he said, "the finished Cathedral of Cologne, one of the greatest edifices of all times, a monument of pious intelligence. May these towers that shoot aloft to heaven remind us that without the gracious help of God, nothing on earth succeeds. Let our

thanks ascend to the Royal Architect, to whose
exalted and creative spirit we are indebted for
this work, which gratefully, from century to century, will stand to praise His name. Let us all
acclaim this glorious monument, and may it, by
the grace of the Almighty, bode gentle peace, in
all our regions, to the honour of God, and to our
own well-being."

Still more important, more in spirit with
the Emperor's works and labours, was the unveiling of the National Monument on the Niederwald, on the Rhine, on the 28th of September, 1883, after the conclusion of the annual
manœuvres at Homburg, made so memorable by
King Alfonso's visit to Germany. It was the most
popular of all the monuments erected in Germany
after the war, and symbolized the great idea first
embodied by Schneckenburger, in his poem of the
" Watch on the Rhine." The figure crowning
Prof. Schilling's monument, is that of " Germania,"
on which is typified to some degree, Ferdinand
Freiligrath's poetical picture of the goddess, written by the stalwart '49er at the outbreak of the
Franco-German conflict. A beautiful bronze relief
on the monument, symbolically represents how all
the German peoples gathered round the Emperor
to keep the " Watch on the Rhine." In the centre of the picture the Emperor is seen on horseback, and around him are the figures of all the Ger-

man princes who reigned in 1870, and the men who assisted the Emperor in the accomplishment of the great work,—Bismarck, Moltke, Von Roen, in fact the leaders of all German troops, of all arms. Every soldier, it is said, can discover in the beautifully modelled group, his corps-commander, his own uniform and accoutrements. The entire monument memorialized 156 battles and victories, among them seventeen of great magnitude, fought by the Germans in 180 days ; a campaign in which 350,000 French soldiers were made prisoners, twenty-six fortified places were taken, and 6,700 guns, 120 eagles and banners captured, and which resulted in restoring Alsace and Lorraine to the Empire and the securing to Germany of a war indemnity from France of five millions of francs.

The ceremonies at the unveiling of the monument were the most imposing of the many national demonstrations witnessed by the Emperor. All classes of the population, both civil and military, from all parts of the Fatherland, had gathered on the Niederwald. Below, the Rhine was crowded with gayly-decked steamers and boats of every description, loaded to the water's edge with humanity. Shortly after noon buglers' signals announced the Emperor's approach. First the band and squadron of the Seventh Rhenith Hussars, the King's Own, from Bonn, passed along the road, followed by outriders and an open carriage,

drawn by four black horses. This contained the
Emperor and the Crown Prince, the former in his
general's uniform and the latter wearing his cuiras-
sier doublet, with a plumed helmet, both wearing
the orange ribbon of the Order of the Black Eagle.
The imperial party comprised, besides, the Crown
Princess and the Princess Victoria, Princes Frederick William, Charles Albrecht, Frederick Leopold, and Alexander of Prussia; King Albert of
Saxony, Prince Leopold of Bavaria, representing
King Ludwig, Prince William of Wurtemberg,
the Grand Duke and Duchess of Baden, the Grand
Duke of Hesse, with the two princes, the Grand
Duke of Saxe-Weimar, the Duke of Saxe-Meiningen, the Landgrave of Hesse, the Princes of Wal-
deck, Pyrmont, Schwarzburg, Reuss, Saxe-Weimar,
Saxe-Meiningen and Hohenzollern, Prince George
of Saxony, and other German princes too numerous to mention. A brilliant suite of military officers stood grouped on either side of the imperial
pavilion. Field Marshal Von Moltke was there.
Prince Bismarck, however, was not able to be
present, though the Emperor did not forget his
faithful Chancellor. In Prince Bismarck's retreat
at Friedrichsruh is a large bronze cast of the Niederwald Monument, to which is attached a sheet of
note paper with the following inscription in the
aged Emperor's own hand:

"CHRISTMAS, 1883: The key-stone of your policy, a ceremony which was chiefly dedicated to you, and at which you could not, I am sorry to see, be present.   **W."**

On the Emperor's arrival the imperial standard, with a white cross, black eagles and crowns and yellow ground, was run up on the flag-staff. It was a most brilliant sight when the Emperor had taken up a position in the centre of the pavilion, with the Crown Prince and the King of Saxony on either side, and the German princes and the dignitaries of the Empire grouped around, all in gala uniforms,with the highest decorations,together with the grand stand filled to the last place, and the dense rows of veterans' societies, singers, turners, students, scholars, sculptors, architects, founders and masons, with hundreds of flags and banners, forming the background of this impressive picture, in the centre and above which towered the huge monument of colossal Germania with the uplifted crown. After the members of the committee had been presented, the Emperor was approached by seven maids of honor, dressed in white, with scarfs of the national color, and oak wreaths on their brows. Frl. Marie Heyt, of Wiesbaden, delivered an address written by the poet Emil Ritterhaus, whose daughter, as well as the daughters of Professor Schilling, the sculptor, were among the chosen seven. After the announcement had been made to the Emperor of the completion of the

great work, the entire assemblage, numbering many
thousands, joined in singing the old hymn, "Nun
danket Alle Gott," with the accompaniment
of all the bands, producing a magnificent effect.
Then his majesty, clearly and audibly, made
a reply.

He said : " When Providence desires to signify
His will with regard to mighty events upon the
earth, He selects the time, countries and instruments
to accomplish His purpose. The years 1870 and
1871 were a time when such purpose was indicated.
Our threatened Germany arose in its love for the
Fatherland as one man, and with the princes at
the head, stood in arms as the instrument. The
Almighty conducted these arms, after sanguinary
conflicts, from victory to victory, and united Germany took her place in the history of the world.
Millions of hearts have raised their prayers to God
and given Him humble thanks, praising Him for
esteeming us worthy of accomplishing His will.
Germany, to the remotest time, desires to give constant expression to this feeling of gratitude. In
this sense the monument standing before us was
erected. In the words spoken at the laying of the
foundation stone—words which my late father,
after the wars of Liberation of 1813 to 1815,
bequeathed in iron to posterity—I dedicate this
monument—' To the Fallen, a Memorial; to the
Living, an Acknowledgment; to the Living Gen-

eration, a Source of Emulation. May God vouch-safe it.'"

By some blunder the signal gun was fired before the Emperor had concluded, and instantly the military battery at Bingen, the guns on the steamboats and in the villages up and down the river roared forth salutes, so that although part of the Emperor's address was thereby rendered inaudible, this thunder of artillery was not an unfitting accompaniment to the Emperor's words. At the same moment the great blue silk cloth that hitherto had covered the central relief on the monument, was dropped down and revealed the bronze representation of the Emperor, surrounded by the princes and generals, while the cheers of the thousands upon thousands of people stationed at the foot of the Niederwald and all the favorable points in the vicinity, and even on the other bank of the river, came up from below amid the roaring of royal salutes and the tolling of bells. Then a dramatic and touching incident occurred. The Crown Prince, bending on one knee, seized and kissed the Emperor's hand, whereupon father and son embraced repeatedly and kissed each other amid the tremendous cheering of the assemblage. The spectators and bands joined in the national hymn, "Heil Dir im Siegeskranz," followed by "Die Wacht am Rhein," and at the moment, as an eye-witness says, "the sun broke through the clouds

victoriously and illuminated this historical scene
once more." Preceded by a hussar escort, the
Emperor and the imperial party were driven off to
Rudesheim and proceeded to the Rhine, where the
Emperor stood on a terrace by the river while a
flotilla of thirty great Rhine steamers, decked from
stem to stern with bunting and crowded with pas-
sengers, passed in review before him, dipping their
colors and firing salutes. At night, while the
Emperor himself went to Wiesbaden, the villages
and castles along the historic Rhine were illuminated and bonfires and blue lights flickered and
flamed from every summit, from the Siebengebirge
to the falls of Schaffhausen.

A marvellous pageant, a grand tribute by Germany, her princes and people, to the worth of the
aged Emperor. But even there, while unveiling
the statue of Germania, the monument symbolical
of Germany's strength and unity, the aged Emperor
had stood all day long with death lurking beneath
his feet. Even to the Niederwald the vile con-
spiracy of agitation had tracked him and had
placed a mine of explosives underneath the monument, and only Providence had saved him from
being hurled to death, with scores of German
princes and thousands of people. A rain-storm on
the night preceding the ceremony had fortunately
rendered the mines harmless. Again it seemed as
if the imperial life had been saved by some mysteri-

ous interposition. The German papers at the time recalled the fact that the Emperor's life had been saved when Nobiling shot at him on the Linden in a strange way. Just as he was about leaving the palace for his afternoon drive, he asked an attendant standing in the lobby the reason of the unusual and gayly dressed crowds in the streets. He was informed that it was because they wanted to see the Shah of Persia, who was then in Berlin. "Ah," he replied, "then I must put on gala," and, smiling, took off the military cloth cap which he intended to wear and replaced it with his Prussian helmet. Within a few hours he was brought back to the palace wounded and bleeding. Then it was found that the steel plating of the helmet had warded off several shots from the Emperor's head. Had the unresisting cloth been there instead of the *Pickelhaube* the result might have been very different. But for the rain-storm of the night of the first and second of September, 1883, who knows what the ending of the ceremonies on the Niederwald would have been?

CHAPTER XV.

NEARING THE END.

In comparison with the pre-1870 period the Emperor's life during its last decade was one of great calm. Family festivals came with their accustomed regularity. Every summer, with scarcely an exception, he spent a few weeks at the baths of Ems or Wiesbaden, then visited his daughter the Grand Duchess of Baden on Lake Constance, and ended his annual "cure" by meetings with brother emperors at Ischl or Gastein. Every year he was present at the autumn manœuvres of the army, in different parts of the empire. Every winter he was in Berlin, engaged in conscientious attention to his imperial duties. He took part in the annual court festivities, and gave earnest attention to the course of legislation having for its object Germany's commercial and colonial development, the well-being of German populations and the continued strengthening of the military and naval forces of the Empire.

Very frequently, during the last years of his

life, reports were telegraphed to all parts of the
world that the Emperor would certainly not be
able to last much longer. But the care of his
physicians and his grand constitution always
enabled him to pull through. Many of his most
serious attacks are said to have been brought on
by eating too generously of his favorite dishes,
among which lobster was one of the easily digest-
ible. Occasionally the rumor would get into print
that the famous ghostly White Lady had made her
appearance in the Old Schloss at Berlin, and as
the loyal Berlinese had a lingering belief that her
coming surely portended a death in the Hohenzollern family, they greatly feared that the time
for the Kaiser to be called away was near. It is
a strange superstition this connected with the
ghostly Countess of Orlamunde, and Hohenzollern
chroniclers do certainly manage to adduce some
curious coincidences in connection with her alleged
appearances. Without delving deeply into ancient
history it may be mentioned that in 1840 the
rumor was current in Berlin that the White Lady
had appeared shortly before the death of King
Frederick William III. She was also reported to
have been seen before the death of Prince Carl in
1883. She was further reported in the winter of
1886-7. But the Emperor lived on. In fact, he
himself had a strange faith in the prophecy of an
old gypsy woman made many years ago, that he

would live to reach within a few years of a complete century.

On the 1st of January, 1877, the Emperor celebrated the seventieth anniversary of his entry into Prussia's military service. All the German princes congratulated him, in person or through their personal adjutants, together with all the field-marshals and commanding generals of the German army, the Crown Prince at their head. Among the many presents that he received at the time was one of a most unique character, given by the officers of the first regiment of infantry of the Garde, in which he began his military career. It consisted of a paper-weight built up in the form of a pyramid out of stones collected from every battle-field at which he had been present, with the name of the battle inscribed upon each stone. On the 9th of February in the same year, the Emperor took especial delight in placing his grandson, the first-born of the Crown Prince, in the same regiment in which he himself had first served. Previous to that, on the 27th of January, he had decreed that the Prince, who had hitherto borne the name of Frederick William, should in future be known as Prince William. At the same time he invested him with the ribbon of the Order of the Black Eagle, and made an address to him that is worthy of being placed on record, as showing the vast importance he attached to the most thorough military training for the Prussian princes.

After describing the condition of the Prussian army under his predecessors, how it had grown in strength by organization and discipline and had enabled Prussia to take her present proud position in the world, he said: " The Garde Corps to which you now belong, and with it the regiment in which you take your place, have contributed in eminent measure to Prussia's glorious successes. The symbols that I wear upon my breast are the public expression of my inextinguishable thankfulness and my never-ending recognition for the devotion with which my army has gained victory upon victory. You have had in your father a grand pattern of what a leader of war and of battles should be. In the military service in which you are about to enter you will meet with many things that have the appearance of being insignificant: but you will also learn that in service nothing is small, and that every stone that belongs to the building up of an army must be properly formed if the entire structure is to be successful and firm. So go on and do your duty."

It is worthy of remark that the Emperor usually composed his own speeches, or at least indicated their substance and purport before they were written out. Usually, when he had to make public addresses of a military character, he would jot down the heads of subjects he wished to treat upon and leave the completion to the inspiration of the moment. On military subjects he was wonderfully well-informed. A correspondent, writing in 1887 of the Emperor's personal characteristics, says on this point: " I was interested in looking over the Emperor's library, which adjoins the historical corner room, and found that the old soldier's taste showed itself here as thoroughly as upon the field of battle. There were about a thousand books in the room, and three-fourths of these were military works. Those most thumb-marked were the reports of his own army. These books he loves to ponder over, and containing as they do nothing but the dryest reports and names of unknown lieutenants, would be most tedious reading for the non-martial mind. But not for this old war hero, who still as in his prime loves to know his 'children,' as he calls them, by name, and there are few of them he fails to recall." But his reading was not confined to military matters, and an anecdote was told of him at the same time that reflected the greatest credit upon his manhood and his literary taste.

Troubled with insomnia, the Emperor was accustomed to command his adjutant to read him to sleep, choosing the literature himself. One night the adjutant was surprised to find on the table a volume of Zola, which he had to read.

Only a few pages had been finished, however, when the aged monarch called to him to cease, adding in a trembling voice: " I wished also to know what the modern realistic novel could produce. Now I am convinced that that book is excellently written, but I do not desire to hear more, because for the short time which I have still to live I hope to retain the illusion which I have of men and women, and not to see them in all their ugliness, stripped of all their virtues." Concluding this royal criticism, we are told, he handed his reader a volume of the poet Victor von Scheffel and soon fell asleep over the ideal thoughts between its covers. The Emperor's relations with women have indeed always been marked with the gallantry characteristic of the Hohenzollerns. With the Empress Augusta he celebrated his golden wedding on the 11th of June, 1879. Her he always revered. The memory of his mother, the sainted Queen Louise, he worshipped. She was to him through life a guiding star. In September, 1879, in company with the Empress, the Crown Prince, the Grand Duke of Mecklenburg-Schwerin, Prince Carl of Prussia, and his grandson Prince William, he made a pilgrimage to the little villa in the village of Hufen, near Koenigsberg, made sacred to him by the fact of his mother residing there during her exile from Berlin. Later, when a bust of Queen Louise was unveiled

in the Thiergarten, at Berlin, the Emperor said :
" In my childhood and in my youth I could not
understand what she foreboded ; and yet God in
His grace chose me to carry to completion what
she foresaw, when I myself had scarcely a premo-
nition of what was to happen. It is clear to me
that God selects His instruments to do His will.
And this inspires me with the deepest humility
and the deepest thankfulness."

On the 22nd of February, 1881, the Emperor
rejoiced in the marriage of his favorite grandson,
Prince William, with the Princess Victoria of
Schleswig-Holstein. In March he was deeply
grieved when he heard of the assassination of his
nephew, Czar Alexander of Russia. In September of the same year, after the autumn manoeuvres
he went to Dantzig to meet the new Czar, Alexander III., who came there to greet him on board
the *Hohenzollern*. The presence of the Russian
and German chancellors gave the interview a deep
importance at the time. On the 18th of October
the Emperor, who had taken a deep interest in the
development of the German fleet, appointed his
grandson, the Crown Prince's second son, Prince
Henry—now usually styled Henry the Navigator
—a lieutenant of the navy. On the 20th of September, 1881, he attended the marriage of his
granddaughter, the Princess Victoria of Baden,
with the Crown Prince Gustav of Sweden. In May

of the following year the Emperor was rejoiced to hear of the birth of his first great-grandchild, the son of Prince and Princess William.

Thus it came to pass that there were four generations of Hohenzollerns in existence, and that the successorship to the Prussian and German thrones was trebly secured. The picture of the four Hohenzollerns—the aged Emperor holding the youngest scion, the Crown Prince and Prince William standing on either side—is one of the most popular photographs in Germany. The youngest Hohenzollern was baptized with great ceremony at Potsdam on the 11th of June, 1882, receiving the name Frederick Wilhelm Victor August Ernst, the Emperor himself holding the little one up at the baptismal font. During the summer of 1882 the Emperor was tireless. In August he met the Emperor Franz Josef at Ischl. In the beginning of 1883, the 25th of January, the silver-wedding of the Crown Prince and Princess was to have been celebrated, but had to be postponed on account of the death of Prince Carl of Prussia—the Emperor's brother. The festival took place, however, a few weeks later, and was made memorable by the Emperor appointing the Prince of Wales, who had gone to Berlin to attend the fetes, honorary colonel of the Pomeranian or Blucher's Hussars (No. 5). The appointment was of historical and symbolical significance, recalling

as it did the Anglo-Prussian alliance and victory
of Waterloo, and, as a German writer says: "not
merely the little farm - house *La Belle Alliance*,
where Wellington and Blucher met after Napoleon's defeat, but that beautiful alliance between
Prussia's Crown Prince and England's Royal
Daughter twenty-five years ago."

It would take a volume to treat at length all
the events of the Emperor's life from this time up
to the end. As a matter of fact they can only be
recorded with just appreciation in a complete
political history of the German Empire under
William I.; and the admirable work of Mr. Charles
E. Lowe, the "Life of Prince Bismarck," really
obviates the necessity of making the story of the
Emperor's life more detailed here.   Every year
since 1882, the aged monarch has attended the
military manœuvres, and after them has visited the
German fleet at Kiel, the principal naval station.
One of the last acts of his life, in June, 1887, was to
attend the ceremonies connected with the cutting
of the first sod of the new Baltic Canal, which,
extending from the harbor of Kiel across Holstein
to the mouth of the Elbe, will, when finished, enable the German fleet to pass from the Baltic to the
North Sea and *vice versa* without let or hindrance.
The Emperor has earnestly supported the idea
that, in order that Germany may take her proper
position among the strongest powers of the world,

her navy must be nursed and drilled and developed
in the same way as was done with the Prussian
army. This has become a necessity, not only for
the eventuality of war but for times of peace,
since, under Prince Bismarck's guidance, Germany
has grown to be an extensive Colonial power, is
founding settlements in Africa, taking possession
of valuable islands in the Pacific and extending
her trade to all parts of the world.

In September, 1883, the Emperor was present
at the manœuvres at Homburg, surrounded by a
score of kings and princes, among them the Prince
of Wales, the Crown Prince of Portugal, the Duke
of Cambridge, the Duke of Connaught, King
Milan of Servia and unfortunate King Alfonso of
Spain, not to mention the innumerable princes and
princesses of Germany and the German houses. It
was then that the Spanish King was appointed
honorary colonel of the Schleswig-Holstein Uhlan
Regiment No. 15, succeeding Prince Carl, the
Emperor's brother. The honor was purchased by
King Alfonso, however, at the cost of French popularity and insult by the populace of Paris on his
homeward journey. On the 17th of November of
the same year the Crown Prince representing the
Emperor paid the return visit to King Alfonso,
and on his way back, at the express wish of his
father, visited King Humbert at the Quirinal and
Pope Leo XIII. at the Vatican. The visit to the

Vatican was intended by the Emperor to give expression to his earnest desire to have the Kulturkampf differences settled out of existence before his death. The Emperor, the Crown Prince is reported to have said to the Pope, wished to leave the Empire not only politically united but its people undisturbed by religious differences in the future.

The following year was full of memorable days. The 27th of February was the seventieth anniversary of the Emperor's baptism of fire at Bar-sur-Aube. On March 22 he kept his eighty-seventh birthday. In July he went to Gastein to meet the Emperor of Austria, and in the September following took place the famous meeting of the three Emperors, of Germany, Austria and Russia, at Skierniewice, near Warsaw, and of the three Chancellors, Prince Bismarck, Count Kalnoky, and M. de Giers. In October, 1884, the subject of the Brunswick succession came up by the death of Duke William; and the refusal of the Duke of Cumberland to give up his Hanoverian claims, necessitated the appointment of Prince Albrecht of Prussia as regent of the Duchy.

The year 1885 passed by with its usual routine of events in the imperial life. The Emperor grieved for the loss of many of his old friends, Prince August of Wurtemberg, Prince Karl Anton of Hohenzollern-Sigmaringen, and also General Vogel von

Falkenstein and Field Marshal Baron von Manteuffel, two of the most famous leaders of the 1866
campaign. He had the pleasure of seeing the oldest son of his only daughter, the Hereditary Grand
Duke of Baden, married to the Princess Hilda of
Nassau, daughter of Duke Adolf of Nassau, one of
the depossessed 1866 princes. The raising of the
German flag on the Caroline Islands threatened for
awhile to bring the Imperial Government into conflict with that of Madrid, but the Emperor himself
placed the difficulty for arbitration in the hands of
Pope Leo XIII., who decided in favor of the
ancient claims of Spain to the islands, leaving certain commercial rights to Germany.

On the 1st of April, 1885, the Emperor was
able to congratulate Prince Bismarck upon the
seventieth aniversary of his birthday, which was
celebrated in Berlin with great festivities.

The Emperor visited his famous Chancellor
and thanked him for the great work he had done
in the creation of United Germany. "It was on
this occasion," says Mr. Charles E. Lowe, the biographer of Prince Bismarck, "that the Emperor,
who had already exhausted all his ingenuity in
devising means of evincing his gratitude to his
Chancellor—who had lavished upon him all the
copious armory of his decorations, made him a
Count and a Prince, as well as dowered him with
extensive acres, and always loyally clung to him

through good and evil report—that the aged Emperor, at the head of all the princes of his House,
repaired to the residence of his septuagenarian
Chancellor and, affectionately embracing him, with
tears in his eyes, begged him to accept a reduced
and finely executed copy of Anton von Werner's
colossal painting of the 'Proclamation of the Empire at Versailles,' accompanied by an autograph
missive. . . . "To me and my House," said the
Emperor, "it is an especial pleasure to take part
in such a festival; and by the accompanying picture we wish to convey to you with what feelings
of grateful recollection we do this, seeing that it
calls to mind one of the greatest moments in the
history of the House of Hohenzollern—one which
can never be thought of without at the same time
recalling your merits. . . . Methinks that this painting will enable your latest descendants to realize
that your Kaiser and King, as well as his House,
were well conscious of what they had to thank you
for. With these sentiments and feelings, which
will last beyond the grave, I send these lines:
'Your grateful, faithful and devoted Kaiser and
King, Wilhelm.'"

A trait worthy of deepest respect in the Emper-
or's character has been his frankness in recognizing
the splendid services of the man who in history
will be given a place as a co-founder of German
unity and the German Empire.

CHAPTER XVI.

THE END.

In June 1886 the Emperor grieved deeply at the death by suicide in Lake Starnberg of King Ludwig II., of Bavaria, the young monarch who had readily cast the strength of his army in favor of Germany in 1870, and who had been the first among the German princes to call upon King William of Prussia to assume the imperial crown at Versailles in 1871. In the autumn he visited the Emperor Francis Joseph at Gastein, attended the military maneuvers in Alsace, and on March 22, 1887, he entered upon the ninetieth year of his momentous life with a vigor that promised to carry him through several more years to come. The anniversary was celebrated with great festivities at Berlin. During the year he made several important journeys, notably the one to Kiel, where, in June, he laid the foundation-stone of the Holtenau lock of the North Sea Canal. After Minister van Boettecher had read the address, the president of the Reichstag presented the Emperor with a trowel and hammer, whereupon his Majesty tapped the stone with the hammer, and in a clear voice pronounced the canal "a work of peace, honor, and progress—a defence in the event of war, and a blessing to the Empire." In July he celebrated the seventieth anniversary of the date on which he became chief of the regiment of the Royal Grenadiers, at Liegnitz. He paid visits to the watering-places during the summer, and in September celebrated at Baden-Baden the seventy-sixth anniversary of the birth of the Empress. He attended the autumn maneuvers as usual, but generally rode in a carriage, and not on horseback as in former years. To Stettin he was accompanied by Prince William and the Princess, Prince Frederick, Prince Leopold, and Count von Moltke. At the close of the review of the Second Army Corps, after great exertions in witnessing the evolutions, he drove slowly down the long, extended ranks of the societies of veterans, and sometimes alighted from his carriage during the review. A striking incident of the occasion was the appearance of Moltke at the head of a regiment, leading it before the Emperor. There was no trace of declining vigor displayed by the silent marshal when he galloped on horseback to the Emperor's carriage to make his report, when the Emperor warmly shook hands with him, amid the acclamations of the onlookers.

A paragraph from an account published in the London *Times* at the time may find space here. It is a picture of the Emperor as last seen among his troops :

" Favored by splendid autumn weather, the Emperor to-day passed in review the Second or Pomeranian Army Corps, which put into the field on a peace footing thirty-four battalions and a corresponding force of artillery, altogether a very fine body of troops, quite equal in drill and discipline to the Guards in Berlin. But it was not so much the military as the personal element in to-day's review which formed the chief object of attraction to all who witnessed it. The accident which prevented the Emperor from going to Königsberg had led the Pomeranians to fear that his visit to them might perhaps be marred by the effects of it ; but what was their joy and astonishment to behold their nonogenarian Kaiser, punctually, as usual, on the stroke of eleven, the appointed hour, drive up to the head of his waiting troops looking, as far as looks went, almost as hale and well as when he reviewed them in similar circumstances eight years ago, after returning from his meeting with the late Czar Alexander II. at Alexandrovo. After inspecting both lines of the troops, each of which seemed to stretch away over dale and down to the vanishing point, the Emperor drove up and took position with his large and brilliant suite, which included the Empress, with whom sat Princess William, Prince William, Prince Frederick Leopold (only son of the late Red Prince), looking all the manlier for his recent tour round the world, and Field Marshal Count von Moltke, fresh and straight still in spite of his eighty-seven years.

" The troops marched past twice in different for-
mations, and though this part of the show lasted
nearly two hours, the Emperor stood upright
most of the time in his carriage, which he occupied
alone, using no other support than what was afforded by a walking-stick. It was a proud moment for His Majesty when his grandson, Prince
William, led past his infantry regiment, but louder
still was the cheering when the twelve companies
of the Colberg Grenadiers came tramping past like
living walls, the proudest regiment on the field,
for their head is no less a personage than Count
von Moltke himself, and no one would think, to
see the Field Marshal pacing along so easy and
erect in the saddle, that he is only about three
years younger than the Emperor himself—physically almost a greater miracle still. The Emperor
beckons the great strategist to approach and ex-
tends his hand in silent gratitude and admiration
to him alone of all the commanders as to the man
who has done most to win all Germany's momentous battles. But the multitude of onlookers was
moved by another touching incident, and that was
when the Second Cuirassiers, in all their shining
panoply of mail, came moving on to the majestic
notes of the "Hohenfriedberg March," one of the
finest musical achievements of Frederick the
Great. For this was a king who not only could
win great and decisive battles. but also transmit
the memory of them to posterity in immortal
strains. The chief of the Second Cuirassiers is the
Empress, who had donned a white mantle edged
with magenta, in exact harmony with the tunics
of her magnificent troopers, and on their approach

Her Majesty rose up in her carriage, with the support of her staff, and thus remained until the five ponderous squadrons had defiled before her, evoking loud plaudits from the spectators. These cheers were partly out of compliment to the gallantry of the Emperor, who, seeing how his now rather infirm consort was engaged, had meanwhile left his carriage and stepped up to the side of the Empress, whose hand he kissed in recognition of the splendid efficiency of her regiment and her devotion to it."

After the Stettin visit, the Emperor had intended to go to Königsberg, but his physicians forbade him doing so, fearing the results of over-exertion. Nevertheless he was able afterwards to go on a hunting trip to the Count von Stolberg's castle, at Wernigerode, in the Harz Mountains. On the 26th of October he took a long drive through the mountains, and though this was followed by an hour's shooting in the cold, windy atmosphere, his Majesty had still strength enough to stand in the snow-storm viewing fourteen deer and twelve wild swine that had fallen to his gun. At night after a banquet he appeared at the castle windows, and viewed by torchlight the game laid out in the castle courtyard, and ended the day by playing a game of billiards, going to rest apparently as unwearied as the oldest huntsman present. On his return to Berlin he was apparently in excellent health, and when he stepped from his low victoria he was described by a correspondent who saw him as doing so, not as a man of over ninety, but as one twenty years younger might. His physicians thought him even more robust than he had been for five years past, and Dr. von Lauer himself is reported to have said that it was not only possible but probable that he would live five or six years longer.

After the visit of Czar Alexander to Berlin, the Emperor's condition grew worse. His mental faculties frequently failed him. However, he still kept to the daily routine that he had followed for years. He rose every day between six and seven and dressed himself with scarcely any assistance from servants up to a week or two before the end. Dr. von Lauer called every morning to see him and to give him a sort of certificate of health. The people of Berlin often grew anxious about him, and during the last winter of his life there were always little crowds of people standing near the statue of Frederick the Great before the Palace, waiting to see the Emperor appear at the famous window. Sometimes, at night, the people would watch to see a curious shadow-play which was thus described by a correspondent. "Soon after he entered the palace the crowd on Unter den Linden were treated to a series of unique shadow tableaux of an Emperor at supper. The imperial shadow, as outlined on the curtain of the palace window, ate a hearty, prolonged supper with such evident relish that the crowd outside lost all faith in the reports concerning the alleged serious illness. Afterward, while loitering over supper, the Imperial shadow unconsciously came near drawing applause from his subjects outside by holding within a few inches of the lamp a letter which apparently contained some puzzling word. The thought which occurred to the watching people was that the trouble was caused by some new request from his great-grandson, who is too anxious for fresh toys to pay much attention to the requirements of the old man's eyes. Finally the shadow rose and walked unassisted to the next room. The gorgeous shadow removed, the crowd dispersed."

The great affliction that had fallen upon the Crown Prince Frederick William had a depressing influence upon the aged Emperor. The Prince had been attacked by a disease of the throat that his physicians believed must eventually prove fatal. Under the care of Dr., later Sir, Morell Mackenzie, and German specialists, he had been taken to the Tyrol, and later to San Remo, where at last the operation of tracheotomy had to be performed to prevent death by suffocation. The Emperor was deeply affected by the news that was sent to him, and this, it is supposed, hastened on the end. Suddenly, without warning, the world was startled on the morning of Thursday, March 9, by the publication of despatches announcing that the Emperor was dead! The news proved to be premature, but there could be no doubt that the aged hero was dying. The report of the last day is touching. Shortly before noon Dr. von Lauer issued a bulletin in which he said: "The Emperor has passed a very restless night and is very weak this morning." Drs. Leuchthold and Tiernann had remained with him during the night. The Grand Duke and Grand Duchess of Baden and the Crown Prince of Sweden arrived during the morning in a special train. The official accounts said:

Noon.—Since nine o'clock this morning the Emporor has slightly improved. He suffers less pain, but is still greatly exhausted.

At twenty-five minutes past twelve Chaplain Kogel gave the last sacrament to the Emperor, who was occasionally delirious before noon.

At midday the Emperor was feverish, and his pulse was 108. It is stated that during an attack of delirium this morning the Emperor imagined that he was reviewing a battalion of the Guards.

Prince Bismarck visited the palace at noon, and had a long conference with Prince William. Shortly before two o'clock the Empress and the Grand Duchess of Baden were with the Emperor.

At two o'clock Prince Bismarck went to the bedside, and the Emperor spoke to him. His condition was then unchanged. Prince Bismarck left the palace at a quarter before four o'clock.

Four o'Clock.—The Emperor is not now able to recognize even the Empress, and is gradually sinking. An immense but silent crowd is standing near the palace, notwithstanding the fact that a cold rain is falling. The palace is guarded by a force of cavalry.

Twenty-five Minutes Past Nine o'Clock, P. M.—The Emperor fell into a swoon at five o'clock and remained unconscious until six o'clock. He afterward fell into a quiet sleep, which lasted till seven o'clock. Wine and other liquid nourishment are administered to him occasionally.

Midnight.—Between eight and ten the Emperor greatly improved. He repeatedly partook of soup, and drank one glass of champagne. He spoke to the doctors and expressed a desire to get up, but was not allowed to rise, except partially, so that the bed might be rearranged. Prince Bismarck and Prince William paid the Emperor a short visit at nine o'clock.

One o'Clock, A. M.—The improvement in the Emperor's condition continues. He is sleeping soundly, and his breathing is regular. He has taken substantial food, and appears to have a good appetite. He was given oysters and egg and a little champagne and sherry. His pulse has fallen from 116 to 96.

When he is awake he is fully conscious, showing an interest in what is passing around him. He asked the Grand Duchess of Baden, who sat by the bed, whether she had already dined, and with whom, and then asked why she had not dined with the Empress. He expressed regret that he was " causing so much trouble."

The scene in in the Kaiser's sick chamber between four and six o'clock in the afternoon, described by an English correspondent, was very impressive and affecting. At four o'clock the Emperor had been given up. When he rallied, some sixty persons were standing around his bed, among them being the Prince and Princess William, the Grand Duke and Grand Duchess of Baden, the Crown Prince and Crown Princess of Sweden, the Princess Frederick Charles and her son, Frederick Leopold, Prince von Bismarck, Count von Moltke, and the several Ministers of State. The old monarch was full of fortitude. He felt that his end was near, but he desired to utilize the last moments of his life. Court Chaplain Kögel offered up prayers, in which the Kaiser joined fervently, and then he took leave of everybody, speaking individually to many of those present. His mind was perfectly clear and his ideas were quite consecutive. For nearly half an hour he spoke with scarcely a pause, sitting up in the bed.

Then he lay down for a while, received some refreshment, and afterwards again conversed with those around him. When he was besought to husband his remaining strength, the Kaiser made the characteristic reply: "No; I feel I have not much more time to live. I prefer to say all I wish to say."

Addressing many of his remarks directly to Prince William, the Emperor went on to talk in minute detail of various civil and military affairs. He referred also to foreign matters and spoke of the relations of the empire to France. The effect of this marvelous recovery and no less marvelous discourse on his Majesty's hearers was indescribable. The doctors were astonished at the display of strength. Meanwhile the room was full—indeed much too crowded—and Prince von Bismarck demonstratively drew back in order to keep others from pressing too near to the Emperor's bedside. His Majesty did not exhibit the slightest fear of death, which he was prepared to meet with the indomitable courage he has exhibited on the field of battle.

But the end came at last, and at half-past eight, on the morning of Friday, the month of March, the Emperor passed away in death. The most striking figure of the nineteenth century was no more. He was the oldest sovereign in the world. When he was born Frederick William II. (nephew and successor of Frederick the Great) was King of Prussia ; George III. had reigned in England for thirty-seven years ; France was under the Directory ; in Russia Paul I. had succeeded to Catherine II., then dead only four months ; and George Washington was still President of the United States. He had lived so long that the world had almost given up the idea that he could be called away.

The record of his life is a part of modern German history. He had been hailed in life as the second Armin, as the modern Barbarossa. With him the dreams of the re-birth of the German empire were realized. Germans all over the world acknowledged the splendor of his efforts for German unity. Under his rule, and the inspiration of the Great Chancellor, Germany grew to be the ruling empire of the world. He himself became the bearer of the remarkable legendary idea connected with the Red Beard, who was said to lie in enchanted sleep underneath the Kyffhäuser, awaiting the time to come forth to re-establish the empire; and in 1870 he was acclaimed by the German poets and historians as the risen Emperor. He made the German name respected in all the world, and the Germans who remember the scorn with which it was once greeted will know how to appreciate the vast service that Kaiser Wilhelm rendered to his people. His death allows his son, the Crown Prince Frederick William (himself already under the shadow of death), to become Emperor, and the Crown Princess, the eldest daughter of Queen Victoria of England, to be Empress of Germany.

Forbes

ermany

	DATE DUE